EXPERT ADVISOR

Adobe Illustrator™

Diane Burns
S. Venit
David Smith

Addison-Wesley Publishing Company, Inc.
Reading, Massachusetts   Menlo Park, California   New York
Don Mills, Ontario   Wokingham, England   Amsterdam   Bonn
Sydney   Singapore   Tokyo   Madrid   San Juan

ISBN: 0-201-14397-6

Library of Congress Cataloging-in-Publication Data

Burns, Diane.
    Expert advisor: Adobe Illustrator 88 / Diane Burns, S. Venit, David Smith.
      p. cm. — (Expert advisor series)
    On t.p. the registered trademark symbol "TM" is superscript following "88" in the title.
    Includes index.
    ISBN 0–201–14397–6: $22.95
    1. Desktop publishing. 2. Adobe Illustrator (Computer program) 3. Printing, Practical—Layout—Data processing. 4. Computer graphics. I. Venit, Sharyn. II. Smith, David, 1948 June 26- III. Title. IV. Title: Adobe Illustrator 88. V. Series: Addison-Wesley expert advisor series.
Z286.D47864 1989   88-31831
686.2'2—dc19   CIP

Copyright © 1988 by Diane Burns, S. Venit, and David Smith

Sponsoring Editor: Carole Alden
Series Editor: Tanya Kucak
Technical Reviewer: David Healy
Cover design: Corey and Company
Text design: Joyce Weston
Set in 11-point Palatino by TechArt, San Francisco

ABCDEFGHIJ-AL-89
First printing, January 1989

Acknowledgments

First and foremost, thanks are due to the people at Adobe Systems who helped us gather some of the information, figures, and tips used in this book; they include John Warnock, John Kunze, Russell Brown, Luanne Cohen and Yvonne Perry. Thanks also to John Van Pelt (Detroit Free Press), and EarthSurface Graphics (Sherman Oaks, California) for contributing examples of their work for Part IV, and to Laurie Miller (Redondo Beach, California) for her careful editing of the manuscript.

Special thanks to Bruce Fraser (San Francisco) for his expertise and support in writing part of the manuscript and creating many of the figures used in this book and to David Healy and Jennette Fuschini for their careful readings of the manuscript.

Finally, thanks to the editors and staff at Addison-Wesley (Carole Alden, Rachel Guichard, Perry McIntosh, and Tanya Kucak) for their patience and flexibility in adapting the design of this book to meet the special needs of a graphics program.

This book was produced by TechArt, San Francisco, using Macintosh computers, a Microtek Scanner, Apple LaserWriter Plus, and a Linotronic 300 typesetter. Software used in production included Adobe Illustrator 88™, Microsoft Word 3.0, SuperPaint, and Page-Maker 3.0.

Contents

Introduction

Expert Advisor: Adobe Illustrator 88 is a complete reference designed to answer your questions about all Adobe Illustrator commands, tools, and techniques. The book includes expert advice about all Adobe Illustrator features, along with tips for increasing speed and productivity, and specific techniques used to create special effects.

The beginning user will quickly learn how to use a tool or command without reading volumes of text. The intermediate user will learn new and valuable techniques for customizing designs. The advanced user will receive expert tips on how to use Illustrator more effectively, and gain insight into how experienced artists create complex, layered art with Adobe Illustrator.

We have organized this book in four parts.

Part I: Tools is a reference to all of the tools in Adobe Illustrator. You will find an introduction to basic mouse operations and an overview of the toolbox, followed by detailed descriptions of all of the Illustrator tools listed as they appear on the palette of your Macintosh screen.

Part II: Commands is a reference to all of the commands in Adobe Illustrator. The introduction to this section provides a general description of how commands are selected and how to work with dialog box entries, as well as an overview of all the menus. Following the introduction, the Illustrator commands are organized alphabetically for easy reference.

Part III: Techniques contains an alphabetical listing of design effects available with Adobe Illustrator. In this section we give step-by-step descriptions of specific techniques that can be used to accomplish design tasks in the following areas:

- Alignment
- Fills and Patterns
- Layering
- Lines
- Shapes (Closed Paths)
- Three-Dimensional Effects

Part IV: Applications contains examples of complex finished art created with Adobe Illustrator. With each example you will find detailed descriptions of how the artist conceptualized and completed the final art.

The **Appendices** describe how to use two applications that come with Adobe Illustrator 88: DrawOver, to convert PICT files; and Adobe Separator, to print color separations. Included at the end of the book are a Glossary of special terms and a Quick Reference Guide to every tool, command, technique, and application that appears in this book.

Here are the subsections you will find in this book:

Overview

This section describes what the tool or command does. If you have forgotten a tool's or command's function, or if you want simply to learn how commands unfamiliar to you work, the overviews in Parts I and II will be helpful.

Procedure

This section gives step-by-step directions on how to use the tool or command most effectively, or how to execute a specific technique.

Warnings

This section offers guidelines on when not to use a particular tool, command, or technique, or describes some of the trade-offs that might be required (such as slower speed and larger file size in exchange for complex artwork).

Tips This section will make the most interesting reading for users who want to rapidly increase their expertise with Adobe Illustrator. Hints, tricks, and insights included in this section will enhance your productivity.

This book is much more than an encyclopedic reference to Adobe Illustrator. Beyond descriptions and examples of tools and commands, you will find a wealth of information gleaned from using and teaching Adobe Illustrator since it was first released. We hope you will find it a useful information source that serves you long and well.

Part I:
Tools

Introduction to Tools

Basic Mouse Operations

This part of the book presents all of the tools available in Adobe Illustrator as they appear on the menu. You can easily find each tool by referring to the icons at the top corner of each page.

In order to use these tools, you must become familiar with two mouse operations. First, position the mouse pointer on the screen, and then (1) click the mouse button once or twice, or (2) drag the mouse while holding down the mouse button. You will use each of these operations in working with Adobe Illustrator, sometimes combining these operations with holding the Shift key, Option key, Command key, or Spacebar. The terms used to define these actions are summarized below.

ACTION	DESCRIPTION
Click	First move the mouse without holding any keys or the mouse button in order to position the pointer over an object, then press the mouse button once and release it immediately.
Double-click	First move the mouse without holding any keys or the mouse button in order to position the pointer over an object, then press the mouse button twice, quickly.
Drag	First move the mouse without holding any keys or the mouse button in order to position the pointer over an object, then hold down the mouse button and move the mouse to a new position, then release the mouse button.
Shift-click	Click the mouse button while holding the Shift key down.
Option-click	Click the mouse button while holding the Option key down.
Shift-Option-click	Click the mouse button while holding both the Shift key and the Option key down.
Shift-drag	Drag the mouse button while holding the Shift key down.
Option-drag	Drag the mouse button while holding the Option key down.
Shift-Option-drag	Drag the mouse button while holding both the Shift key and the Option key down.

3

Illustrator Toolbox

Overview
Like other Macintosh graphics applications, the Illustrator toolbox is a palette, located vertically along the left side of the Illustrator screen, that contains icons for the various tools you use to create, select, and modify objects, and to adjust views of your files. The figure at left shows what the Illustrator toolbox looks like.

You will often find yourself accessing the tools in Adobe Illustrator using a two-handed approach—with one hand on the mouse and the other on the keyboard. Becoming familiar with this two-handed approach is the key to attaining fluency in Illustrator, because many of the activities you perform in Illustrator require a combination of keyboard strokes and mouse movements. Although the number of possibilities might at first seem intimidating, the various keys you will be using behave similarly with the different mouse tools, providing you with an economical and easy-to-learn set of powerful and flexible tools. Once you learn how to activate and use one of Illustrator's tools, you can readily apply the same or a similar technique to the other tools.

Procedure
To select any tool, click on the icon for that tool in the toolbox using the mouse. This will highlight the tool, indicating it has been selected. You can use shortcuts to activate several of the tools. For example, you can activate the Zoom tool from the keyboard using the Command key and the Spacebar (in combination with the mouse). When using the keyboard to change tools, hold down the key(s) *before* pressing the mouse button.

- Holding the Command key temporarily changes the current tool to the Selection tool for selecting or moving objects on the page.
- Holding the Spacebar temporarily changes the current tool to the Hand tool for moving the page view in the window.
- Holding the Command key and the Spacebar temporarily changes the current tool to the Zoom tool for enlarging.
- Holding the Option key, the Command key, and the Spacebar temporarily changes the current tool to the Zoom tool for reducing.

These keystrokes are considered shortcuts because many times you will be performing an action with one tool (for example, the Pen tool), and you will need to use another tool (for example, the Selection tool) to modify the action. In such cases, you do not have to divert your attention away from the drawing area of your screen, access the toolbox, select a new tool, and complete your activity. You simply hold down the appropriate key(s).

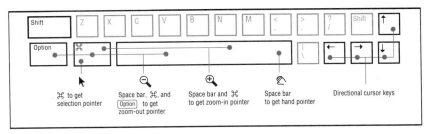

Keyboard shortcuts for the toolbox

The basic mouse operations used with the tools are *clicking* and *dragging*. The Spacebar, the Command key, the Shift key, and the Option key all work interactively with the mouse. The Shift and Option keys are used to modify or constrain the action of mouse clicks, mouse drags, and the action of the Command key and the Spacebar.

- Pressing the Shift key after pressing the mouse button constrains the action of tools. For example, when drawing with the Pen tool, straight lines are constrained to 45° angles. When drawing with the Rectangle or the Oval tool, rectangles are constrained to squares, and ovals are constrained to perfect circles. Similarly, movements are constrained to 45° angles when dragging an object with the Selection tool.
- When moving or transforming an object, Option-clicking on the Selection tool, or Option-clicking on the artwork after selecting the Rotate tool, Scale tool, Reflect tool, or Shear tool results in a dialog box that lets you enter numeric values for the action of the tool. This is a useful alternative to moving or transforming objects visually.
- When moving or transforming an object, Option-dragging produces a copy of the selected object. This is a useful alternative to the Copy and Paste commands.

5

Tools

The Selection Tool

Overview   You use the Selection tool, as its name implies, primarily to select objects for further manipulation or transformation. You also use the Selection tool to move objects, and to adjust curves by dragging curve segments, anchor points, or direction lines. It is the default tool; that is, the tool that is selected when Illustrator is first opened. It is also the most frequently used tool. In Illustrator, you must always first select an object before taking action on it. Thus, you will probably use the Selection tool more than any other tool.

Procedure   Choose the Selection tool by clicking the icon in the toolbox, or by holding down the Command key whenever any other tool is selected. When you release the Command key, the previously selected tool will once more be selected. When the Selection tool is active, the mouse pointer changes to an arrow.

Selecting Objects   Objects that you create and manipulate in Illustrator include text, anchor points, line segments, direction lines, paths, and grouped objects. The two basic methods of selecting objects are to click on the object, or to drag a selection marquee around the object.

 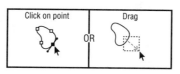

Two methods of selecting objects

Both of these methods are standard in many graphics applications and on the desktop of the Macintosh. The previous figure shows both methods of selecting objects. If two or more objects overlap, clicking will select the topmost one, and dragging the selection marquee around the objects selects both. (The selection marquee is a rectangle of dashed lines that appears when you drag the mouse onscreen without selecting any objects first.)

Objects that can be selected include anchor points, line segments, paths (anchor points and their connecting line segments), and text blocks. Selecting an anchor point also selects any segments that are connected to it, whereas selecting a segment does not select any anchor points. Holding down the Option key and dragging over part of a path selects the entire path.

 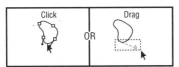

To select a line segment without selecting the anchor point, click anywhere on the segment or drag the selection marquee over the segment

 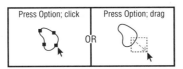

To select all of the anchor points and connecting line segments of an ungrouped path, Option-click anywhere on the path or Option-drag the selection marquee

To select type, simply click on the baseline of the text block, or drag the selection marquee around the baseline of text. If you have multiple lines of text, you may select the baseline of any of the lines of text.

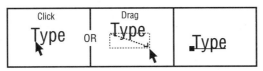

Two methods of selecting type

To extend a selection to include a second object (after one object is selected), Shift-click on the desired objects, or hold down the Shift key and drag a selection marquee around the desired objects. The same action applies for deselecting individual objects in a group selection: you can select any number of objects, then Shift-click to deselect one or more.

 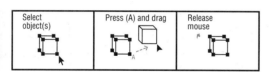

To select more than one object, hold down the Shift key before you select each object

Moving Objects   To move a selected object visually on the screen, drag it using the Selection tool. Shift-dragging constrains the movement to a multiple of 45° angles—that is, you will be able to move the object only along one of eight angles: 0°, 45°, 90°, 135°, 180°, 225°, 270°, and 315°. Option-dragging moves a copy of the selected object and leaves the original in place.

 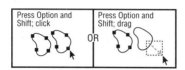

Moving objects

To move a selected object a specified distance, first select the object with the Selection tool, then Option-click the Selection tool icon in the toolbox. A Move dialog box appears, allowing you to specify: the distance and direction of the move; whether to move pattern tiles, and whether to move the selected object or a copy of it.

The Distance box is already selected when you call up the Move dialog box. To change this distance, simply type the new distance you wish to move the object, in the unit of measure shown (centimeters, inches, or points, as determined by the Preferences command).

Next, notice that the Direction defaults to the angle of the previous move. If you do not want the Direction to be the same as previously, click the button next to the direction you want—Horizontal, Vertical, or Angled. Directions of angled moves can be specified in degrees, with horizontal as 0° and angles measured counterclockwise for positive values, clockwise for negative values.

If you want to move pattern tiles, click in the Move pattern tiles box. A checkbox appears indicating this choice is selected. When you have specified all your choices for the move, click on either the OK button to move the selected object, or the Copy button to move a copy of the selected object.

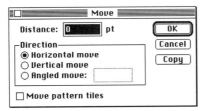

Option-click the Selection tool icon in the toolbox and enter in the Move dialog box the distance and angle you want selected objects to move in the Move dialog box

You can also move selected objects by pressing the arrow keys (available on most keyboards). The increment of movement per keystroke can be set in the Preferences dialog box. (See Preferences.)

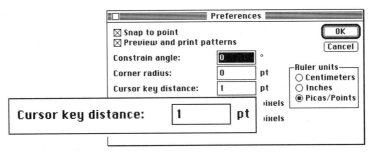

Set the increments for movement with the arrow keys in the Preferences dialog box

Using the Option key while dragging a selection marquee is not the same as Shift-dragging or Option-dragging. To use the Option key with the marquee, you must hold down the key *before* pressing the mouse button. To Shift-drag and/or Option-drag, you must hold down the key *after* pressing the mouse button to select the object you will be dragging.

Tips   Since the Selection tool is used so frequently, always use the Command key to access the Selection pointer temporarily while using another tool. For example, draw a curve with the Pen tool, then hold down the Command key and use the Selection pointer to adjust it. The only time you need to click on the Selection tool icon in the toolbox is when you want to move an object a specified distance.

You can see the distance and angle of a move by first moving an object visually on the screen, and then Option-clicking on the Selection tool to see the numeric values in the dialog box. This can be useful if you want to duplicate the same movement later.

(See also Select All.)

The Hand Tool

Overview   You can use the Hand tool as an alternative to the scroll bars. The Hand tool can move the image of your artwork in the active window vertically, horizontally, and diagonally. It moves the whole page, not the selected objects on the page. Think of the Hand tool as your own hand and the image in the active window as a piece of paper sitting on your desk. Just as you place your hand on top of the paper and move it across your desk, so does the Hand tool move the image across the screen. By using the Hand tool, you can scroll diagonally with one movement instead of having to click on two scroll bars to accomplish the same movement. You can also use the Hand tool to go quickly to the Actual Size or Fit In Window view, as described in the Procedure section that follows.

Procedure   Choose the Hand tool by clicking the icon in the toolbox, or hold down the Spacebar when a different tool is selected and temporarily activate the Hand tool. When you release the Spacebar, the previously selected tool will once again be active. When the Hand tool is active, the mouse pointer changes to a hand. To scroll with the Hand tool, position the hand on the active window, hold down the mouse button, and drag in the direction you wish to scroll. The figure below demonstrates using the Hand tool to scroll diagonally across the active window.

Dragging the Hand tool to scroll diagonally on the screen

To change to Fit In Window view, double-click on the Hand tool icon in the toolbox as an alternative to using the Fit In Window command (see Fit In Window). To change to Actual Size, Option-double-click on the Hand tool icon in the toolbox as an alternative to using the Actual Size command (see Actual Size). Note that this does not select the Hand tool, but leaves the currently selected tool still in effect.

The figure below summarizes the three ways of using the Hand tool to change views of your image in the active window.

Move view in window

Select tool (or press Spacebar), then drag

Fit In Window

Double-click on toolbox icon

Actual Size view

Option double-click on toolbox icon

Three uses of the Hand tool icon in the toolbox

Tips   Always use the Spacebar to quickly access the Hand tool while another tool is selected. The only time you need to click on the Hand tool icon in the toolbox is when you want to change to an Actual Size or Fit In Window view.

The Hand tool is one of the tools that remain active in Preview mode. The others are the Zoom tool, the Measure tool, and the Page tool.

The Zoom Tool

Overview   Use the Zoom tool to change the level of magnification at which you view your file. Illustrator provides nine levels of magnification, each increased or decreased by a factor of two. From actual size (100%), you can zoom in (magnify) to 200%, 400%, 800%, and 1600%, and zoom out (reduce) to 50%, 25%, 12.5%, and 6.25% of actual size.

Procedure   Choose the Zoom tool by clicking the icon in the toolbox, or hold down the Command key and the Spacebar to temporarily select the Zoom tool if you have another tool already selected. When you release the Command key and Spacebar, the previously selected tool will once again be selected.

The mouse pointer changes to a magnifying glass with a + in the center indicating that the tool is in zoom-in (magnify) mode. To change to zoom-out (reduce), hold down the Option key. The + in the mouse pointer changes to a –. When you click the Zoom tool on a particular point in the drawing, that area becomes the center of the window. The figure below shows the various pointer shapes for the Zoom tool: a plus sign enlarges the view, a minus sign reduces the view, and an empty Zoom icon indicates that you have enlarged or reduced to the limit.

The appearances of the Zoom tool: (1) A plus sign enlarges the view, (2) a minus sign reduces the view, (3) an empty Zoom icon indicates that you have enlarged (or reduced) to the limit.

To zoom in to the center of the active window, double-click the Zoom tool icon. To zoom out from the center of the active window, hold down the Option key and double-click the Zoom tool icon. Note that double-clicking does not select the Zoom tool, but leaves the currently selected tool in effect.

Tips   The Zoom tool is particularly useful when you need to magnify an area in order to see the anchor points for fine, detailed adjustment, or when you are working with several points or paths lying close together. The figure below illustrates the benefit of using the Zoom tool to magnify a section of your image for modification purposes.

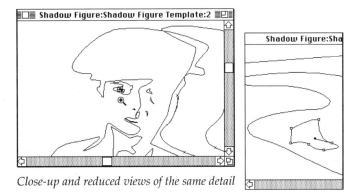

Close-up and reduced views of the same detail

Always use the Command key and Spacebar to magnify a detail of your drawing; this method is much faster than clicking the icon in the toolbox.

The Zoom tool is one of the tools that remain active in Preview mode. The others are the Page tool, the Measure tool, and the Hand tool.

The Type Tool T

Overview   Use the Type tool to set an alignment point for a new text block into which you will type new text.

Procedure   Choose the Type tool by clicking the icon in the toolbox. The mouse pointer changes to an I beam in the active window. Click the mouse to set an alignment point. As shown in the figure on the left, the crossbar on the I beam sets the baseline and anchor point for the text.

The Type dialog box appears. You can enter up to 255 characters of text here, in the large text box where you see the blinking cursor. You also use the Type dialog box to set the font, font size, leading, spacing, and alignment specifications. The figure below shows the Type dialog box.

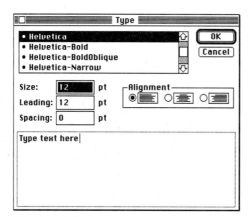

The Type dialog box

Typing Text   After you click on the Illustrator page on-screen with the Type tool, the Type dialog box appears. Use the mouse or the Tab key to position the insertion point inside the text area of the Type dialog box, then type the text you wish displayed on the screen. Create line breaks or carriage returns in the text by pressing the Return key after each line of text. (Line breaks shown in the dialog box do not necessarily reflect line breaks in the text block itself.)

Formatting Text   Select your font by clicking the font name in the scrolling window of the dialog box. You can scroll up and down to view the choices of fonts available to you. To scroll up or down, position the mouse pointer on the up or down arrows on the right side of the scrolling window.

To change the type size, select the text in the size box by tabbing into the box or double-clicking the existing point size. Then type in a new number to change the point size. The type size, leading, and spacing should all be given in points, using the same technique, including up to three decimal places for thousands of a point. Spacing is a measure of the space between letters. Enter a positive value to increase spacing between letters, or a negative value to decrease spacing. (Note that spacing in Illustrator is actually tracking. See the Glossary.) Clicking on the word Leading in the dialog box automatically sets leading to match the point size.

Click on the corresponding icon to set alignment to flush left, centered, or flush right text.

The effects of leading and spacing are shown in the figure below. The first column shows 9-point Helvetica with 9-point leading and 0 spacing. The second shows 9-point Helvetica with 11-point leading and 2 spacing. The third shows 9-point Helvetica with 8-point leading and –2 spacing.

```
HELVETICA      HELVETICA      HELVETICA
HELVETICA      HELVETICA      HELVETICA
HELVETICA      HELVETICA      HELVETICA
```

How size, leading, and kerning affect text: (1) 9-point Helvetica with 9-point leading, zero kerning. (2) 9-point Helvetica with 11-point leading and 2 kerning. (3) 9-point Helvetica with 8-point leading and –2 kerning

Editing Text   You edit existing text by selecting the text block on the screen using any of the techniques described under the Selection tool (see The Selection Tool). Selected text blocks are underlined on the screen. Once the text is selected, choose Type from the Style menu. The underlined text now appears in the text area of the Type dialog box. Select this text by dragging the I beam over it, or select a single word by double-clicking. The selected text will be deleted as

15

you begin typing. If the text block is longer than will fit in the dialog box display area, you can scroll through the text by pressing the mouse button and dragging the I beam up or down through the text.

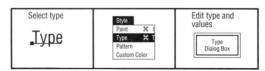

Method for editing type

Tips   To create blocks of text longer than 255 characters, type two or more text blocks. Then select all of the blocks and use the Group command to combine them into a single object (see Group).

You can change the type specifications and alignment of grouped blocks of text, but you cannot edit the text itself unless you ungroup the blocks and edit each one individually. (See Group and Ungroup for more details.)

(See also Aligning Text: Methods 1 and 2, Tabular Text, and Inline Type in Part III.)

The Freehand Tool

Overview   Use the Freehand tool to draw a continuous line of any shape freehand—that is, without clicking and dragging each anchor point (as required when using the Pen tool).

Procedure   Choose the Freehand tool by clicking the icon in the toolbox. The mouse pointer changes to an x in the active window. Hold down the mouse button and begin drawing your object by dragging the mouse along the path you wish to draw.

Dragging quickly results in less anchor points per any given distance than dragging slowly. You can also force more or fewer anchor points per distance by adjusting the tolerance level through the Preferences dialog box (see Preferences). A low tolerance value results in more anchor points per given distance than a high tolerance value. The figure below shows the effects of different tolerance settings.

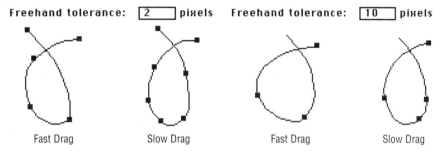

Freehand tolerance: [2] pixels   Freehand tolerance: [10] pixels

Fast Drag   Slow Drag   Fast Drag   Slow Drag

Set tolerance in the Preferences dialog box to control the number of anchor points created by the Freehand tool: (1) Line drawn with a tolerance value of 2 pixels; (2) Line drawn with a tolerance value of 10 pixels

After you have drawn a path with the Freehand tool, you can adjust the line segments and anchor points as described under the Pen tool, and set Stroke and Fill patterns as described in the Paint command in Part II. You can also erase anchor points while you are drawing by holding down the Command key and backing up along the line you have just traced with the Freehand tool.

 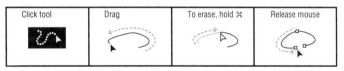

| Click tool | Drag | To erase, hold ⌘ | Release mouse |

Using the Freehand tool

Tips   Use a high tolerance setting (in the Preferences dialog box) and drag the Freehand tool quickly unless you *need* a lot of anchor points for fine adjustments, as anchor points add to the size of an illustration. You can always add anchor points with the Scissors tool if you need more (see The Scissors Tool).

You can change the Freehand tool to the Pen tool, without returning to the tool palette. Hold down the Control key (on SE or Mac II keyboards only), and the Freehand tool will change to the Pen tool.

The Autotrace Tool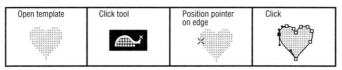

Overview You use the Autotrace tool to trace automatically the path around any solid object that is part of a template. This is faster and easier than tracing a template with the Freehand tool or the Pen tool, and works best if the template is composed of distinct areas of solid black or solid outlines with curved edges. The Autotrace tool always creates rounded joins, and is therefore not used to trace objects with pointed corners and straight lines.

Procedure Choose the Autotrace tool by clicking the icon in the toolbox. The mouse pointer changes to an x. Position the x pointer and click on the edge of a solid object in the template layer to trace a path around that object. You can adjust the sensitivity of the Autotrace tool in the Preferences dialog box (see Preferences). With Autotrace gap distance set at 0 in the Preferences dialog box, the Autotrace will read every pixel in the template. Set at 1, the Autotrace jumps across one-pixel gaps and connects them. Set at 2, it will jump across two-pixel gaps and connect them. This can be useful if your template is very sketchy.

Path drawn with the Autotrace tool

Once you have drawn a path with the Autotrace tool, you can adjust the line segments and anchor points as described under the Pen tool, and set Stroke and Fill patterns as described in the Paint command.

To trace only part of a shape, click on the Autotrace tool and position the x on the edge of the template at the point where you wish the tracing to begin. Instead of clicking, drag the cursor to the second point where you wish the tracing to end, then release the mouse button. Only the distance between those two points is traced.

Open template	Click tool	Position pointer on edge
Press on point A	Drag to point B	Release mouse

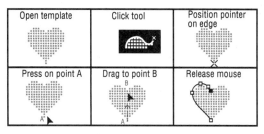

Tracing part of a shape

To trace hollow shapes, use Autotrace to trace the outer edge of the shape first. Then trace the inside edges. This way, the inside shape will always be on a layer above the outer shape, and you can set the hollow shape to have a White fill pattern. See also Three-Dimensional Effects in Part III.

Warning   Do not use the Autotrace tool to trace shapes made up of straight lines or rectangles, since the Autotrace tool may introduce curves. Use the Pen or Rectangle tools to draw straight lines or rectangular shapes.

Tips   As a rule, use the Autotrace tool on shapes with relatively smooth edges. Use the Freehand tool to trace edges that are extremely ragged or irregular (see The Freehand Tool).

The Pen Tool

Overview   You will use the Pen tool more than any other tool to create paths. A path is any line or shape drawn in Illustrator. Paths may be composed of both curved and straight line segments, and may be open (lines) or closed (shapes).

Procedure   Choose the Pen tool by clicking the icon in the toolbox. The mouse pointer changes to an x in the active window. To use the Pen tool, position the x pointer on the screen and click the mouse button. This positions an anchor point on the screen. Before releasing the mouse button, drag the x pointer to set a direction line for the anchor. As you drag the x pointer around the screen while holding down the mouse, the direction line for the anchor point changes. When you release the mouse button, the anchor point and direction lines are set and the pointer changes to a +, ready to position the second anchor point along the path.

The direction lines do not print. They are tangent to the line of the curve and determine which direction and how deep the curve will be drawn.

Drawing a Straight Line   Click the mouse button once to position the first anchor point. Do not drag the mouse yet. The mouse pointer changes to a +, indicating that the next point you click with the mouse will create another anchor point on the current path. Click again to set the anchor point for the other end of the straight line. A straight line automatically appears on the screen, connecting the two anchor points. Holding the Shift key before clicking on the second point constrains the line to 45° angles. The figure below shows how the steps combine to result in a straight line.

 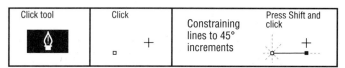

Drawing straight lines

Drawing a Curve   Hold down the mouse button to position the first anchor point, drag to create a direction line, then release the mouse button. The mouse pointer changes to a +, indicating that the next point you click or drag with the mouse will create another anchor point on the current path. If you click the second anchor point, you complete a curve (the curved line automatically appears on the screen). You then have the option of continuing the current path with either a straight line (by clicking the third point) or with another curve (by dragging the third point). If you drag the second anchor point, you can continue drawing a smooth curved line (by clicking or dragging the third point). Repeat the process to continue extending the path. The next figure illustrates the drawing of a curved line.

Click tool	Press and drag	Press and drag	Press and drag

Drawing curved lines

It will require practice with the Pen tool to learn where anchor points are best placed and how to drag direction lines, but a few suggestions are given here to help you understand the principles of drawing curves in Illustrator.

1. Direction lines are always tangent to the curves they create. In dragging a direction line after positioning an anchor point, drag in a direction that is tangent to the curve you intend to draw. Drag the direction line a distance that is about one third of the length of the curve between the current and the next anchor points.

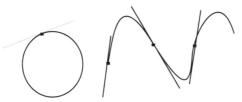

A tangent is a straight line that touches a curve at only one point

2. Anchor points along a curved path are best placed where the direction of the curve changes. Another way of saying this is that anchor points usually are not required in the middle of continuous curves, such as the peak of a hill or the bottom of a valley. You can think of the anchor points as the places along a winding mountain road where you would turn the wheels of the car from pointing right to pointing left, or vice

Anchor points placed where the direction of the wheels would change in driving around curves in a road

versa. Remember that when you are driving around the hump of a curve you are holding the wheels in one direction, and an anchor point is not required. By following this guide, you can create curves that are easy to control, and that can be edited with a minimum number of anchor points—two goals for efficiency and economy of disk space.

There should always be an element of the first method (that is, using visual clues as you draw) in applying the scientific approach, but the more efficiently you build your paths, the easier they will be to edit and the less likely you will need to edit them. (Editing techniques are described on the next page.)

The Option key lets you create corner points along a curve— points where the curve changes direction abruptly rather than at a rounded edge. To create a corner point, first click to set the anchor point and drag to set the direction line. Then hold down the Option key, click on the anchor point you have just set, and drag a new direction line.

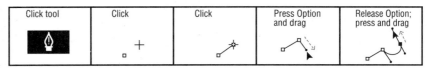

Creating corner points

Use combinations of the techniques that have been described to create paths composed of curved and straight line segments.

Drawing paths composed of curved lines and straight lines

Closing a Path To close a path and thereby create a solid shape, click the last anchor point position on top of the first anchor point of the path. The pointer changes from a + to an x, indicating that the Pen tool is available to start a new path.

Completing an Open Path To complete an open path (that is, end one path without closing it), click the Pen tool icon in the toolbox, or hold down the Command key to change the pointer to the Selection tool, then click anywhere on the page. The pointer changes from a + to an x, indicating that the Pen tool is available to start a new path.

Editing a Path To edit a path, use the Selection tool to move an anchor point, drag a curved line segment, or adjust direction lines. The figure below shows editing a path in each of these ways.

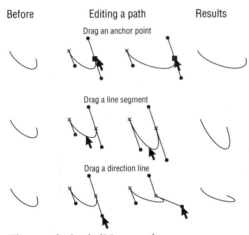

Three methods of editing a path

Warnings

If you forget to click the Pen tool icon in the toolbox to start a new path after completing an open path, you will end up with a line joining the last anchor point in the previous path to the first anchor point on your new path. If this happens, simply press Delete once to remove the new anchor point. Then click the Pen tool icon, or hold down the Command key to change the pointer to the Selection tool, and click anywhere on the page to start a new path.

Tips

You will find that using the Command key shortcut to switch to the Selection tool makes it easier to adjust curves while you draw. This way you don't need to end the path by going to the toolbox to select the Selection tool, and you can resume adding points to the same path after adjusting part of the path.

To draw a straight line of an exact length, create one anchor point, then Option-click on the Selection tool to get the Move dialog box. Enter the desired length of the line and click Copy to make a copy. Select both anchor points and use the Join command, which will draw a line connecting the two points.

Use the Scissors tool to open a closed path, to split an open path into two paths, or to add anchor points along a line segment. See The Scissors Tool.

The Rectangle Tool

Overview   You use the Rectangle tool to create rectangular objects or squares. The Rectangle tool produces an object composed of two grouped paths: a rectangular path consisting of four straight-line segments joined at the corners; and a single point in the center of the rectangle, which you can use to align the rectangle relative to other centered objects (text or graphics).

Procedure   You can draw a rectangle visually on the screen, or create one with dimensions and rounded corners as specified numerically in a Rectangle dialog box.

 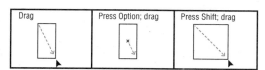

Three ways of using the Rectangle tool: (1) drag diagonally to draw a rectangle from corner to corner; (2) hold down the Option key and drag diagonally to create a rectangle from center to edge; (3) hold down the Shift key and drag diagonally to create a perfect square

Drawing a Rectangle Visually on the Screen   Choose the Rectangle tool by clicking the icon in the toolbox. The mouse pointer changes to a + in the active window. Press the mouse button to position a corner of the rectangle, then drag diagonally and release the mouse to complete the rectangle. To construct rectangles from center to edge (rather than corner to corner), press the Option key while you drag the mouse (Option-drag) diagonally. To constrain rectangles to a perfect square, press the Shift key while you drag the mouse (Shift-drag) diagonally.

Drawing a Rectangle with Numerically Specified Dimensions
Click on the Rectangle tool icon in the toolbox, then click once in the active window. The Rectangle dialog box appears. You use the dialog box to enter specific dimensions for a rectangle, including width, height, and corner radius. The center point of the rectangle is defined by where you clicked on-screen.

The Rectangle dialog box

The default corner radius, zero points, creates rectangles with square corners. As you increment the points (from 0 to 1008 points), the corner radius becomes more curved, approaching an oval shape, as shown in the figure below. The corner radius cannot exceed half the length of the short sides of the rectangle. If you enter a larger value, Illustrator will draw the largest oval that can fit into the rectangle. You can set a corner radius for all rectangles in your drawing by using the Preferences command from the Edit menu. (See Preferences for more details.)

	Width:	36 pt		Width:	36 pt
	Height:	36 pt		Height:	36 pt
	Corner Radius:	0 pt		Corner Radius:	12 pt
	Width:	36 pt		Width:	36 pt
	Height:	36 pt		Height:	36 pt
	Corner Radius:	6 pt		Corner Radius:	15 pt
	Width:	36 pt		Width:	36 pt
	Height:	36 pt		Height:	36 pt
	Corner Radius:	9 pt		Corner Radius:	18 pt

Examples of rounded corners

Tips　　Rectangles are grouped as one object when they are first drawn. You can modify the grouped rectangle using the Scale, Rotate, Reflect, and Shear tools, but to move individual anchor points you must first ungroup the rectangle (see Group and Ungroup).

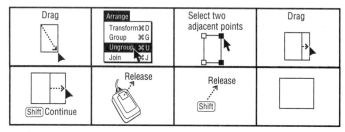

Drag	Arrange	Select two adjacent points	Drag
	Transform ⌘D Group ⌘G Ungroup ⌘U Join ⌘J		
(Shift) Continue	Release	Release (Shift)	

Ungroup to modify a rectangle

The Oval Tool

Overview　　You use the Oval tool to create elliptical objects or circles. The Oval tool produces an object composed of two grouped paths: an elliptical path consisting of four curved segments joined by anchor points every 90°; and a single point in the center of the ellipse, which you can use to align the object with respect to other centered objects (text or graphics).

Procedure　　With the Oval tool, you can draw ellipses visually on the screen, or create an ellipse with dimensions and rounded corners as specified numerically in the Oval dialog box (see next page).

Drawing an Oval on the Screen　　Choose the Oval tool by clicking the icon in the toolbox. The mouse pointer changes to a + in the active window. Press the mouse button to position one edge of the ellipse, then drag diagonally and release the mouse to complete the ellipse. To construct ellipses from the center of the oval to the edge (rather than corner to corner), press the Option key, then drag the mouse (Option-drag) diagonally in the desired direction. To constrain ellipses to perfect circles, press Shift while you drag the mouse

(Shift-drag) in the desired direction. In both cases, the farther you drag from the starting point, the larger the object becomes. These techniques are shown in the figure below.

Three ways of using the Oval tool: (1) drag diagonally to draw an ellipse from edge to edge; (2) hold down the Option key and drag diagonally to create an ellipse from center to edge; (3) hold down the Shift key and drag diagonally to create a perfect circle

Drawing an Ellipse with Numerically Specified Dimensions
Click on the Oval tool icon in the toolbox, then click once in the active window. The Oval dialog box appears, which you use to enter specific dimensions (width and height) in points. (You can change the unit of measure shown in the dialog box with the Preferences command; see Preferences). The oval width and height must be between 0 and 1008 points. As with the Rectangle tool, the center point of the oval appears where you clicked the tool on the screen.

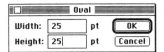

The Oval dialog box

Tips

Ovals are grouped objects when they are first drawn. You can modify the grouped oval using the Scale, Rotate, Reflect, and Shear tools, but to move individual anchor points you must first ungroup the oval (see Group and Ungroup).

The Blend Tool

Overview   Use the Blend tool to transform one object into another object in a series of steps. You create the starting object and the resulting object using Illustrator's tools. The intermediate objects are created automatically during the transformation process.

Procedure   Create two objects. One object represents the beginning of the transformation series, and the second object represents the resulting object after the transformation series is completed. Be sure both objects are ungrouped (see Group and Ungroup). Select one or more anchor points on each object. These will serve as corresponding reference points during the transformation. Next, click the Blend tool in the toolbox. This changes the mouse pointer to a cross hair pointer. Click the cross hair pointer on one point of each of the two objects: these points will be the primary points of correspondence throughout the transformation. When you click a point on the second object, the Blend dialog box appears as shown in the figure below. You can enter a number from 1 to 1008 to determine how many intermediate objects will be created by the blending process.

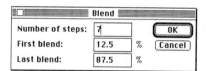

The Blend dialog box

The first object you click *after* you select the Blend tool will fall on the bottom layer of the blended series of objects; the second object will fall on the top layer.

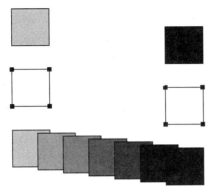

Sequence of layers: (1) leftmost rectangle was clicked first, (2) rightmost rectangle was clicked second

You can use the Blend tool for a variety of effects: to create a series of gradual changes of color or pattern; to create a series of gradual changes from one shape to another; or to create different views of the same shape using the Scale, Rotate, Reflect, or Shear tools.

Objects must be ungrouped (see Ungroup) for the Blend tool to work correctly. Objects created with the Rectangle tool or the Oval tool must be ungrouped before they can be transformed with the Blend tool. Both the starting object and the resulting object must be either closed or open paths; you cannot blend a closed path with an open path. (See The Pen Tool for definitions of open and closed paths.) The following figures illustrate three examples of blending.

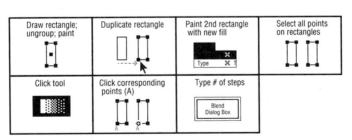

Blending to create gradual changes in color or shading

Draw an apple and a highlight	Paint highlight 100% white fill	Select points on objects
	Style Paint ⌘ I Type ⌘ T	
Click tool	Click corresponding points (A)	Type # of steps
		Blend Dialog Box

Example of blending to create a three-dimensional appearance

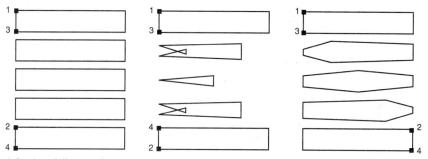

Example of blending to change shapes

Before using the Blend tool, select the points of the two objects in pairs; that is, hold down the Shift key, then click the Selection tool on a point on the first object, then click the Selection tool on the corresponding point on the second object. You can select more than one pair of points. Generally speaking, you select only one pair if the two objects and all blended results have the same shape. Select more than one pair of points if the two objects have very different shapes, or if you want the blended results to assume new shapes. Different sequences of pairs produce different results.

Selecting different pairs of anchor points produces different effects

Tips When printing to a 300 dpi laser printer, 25 blends are usually adequate for creating a gradual transition from white to black. On a 600 dpi printer, 45 blends is usually adequate. On a 1270 dpi phototypesetter, you need approximately 200 blends; on a 2540 dpi phototypesetter, use at least 448 blends. Using too few blends may create "banding"; that is, the colors may not transition smoothly.

The Scale Tool

Overview You use the Scale tool to change the size of selected objects. Scaling an object stretches or compresses it horizontally, vertically, or both, relative to some fixed point you choose. The Scale tool is one of four transformation tools, the others being the Rotate, Reflect, and Shear tools. The Option key works consistently with each: Option-clicking to set the origin of transformation always brings up a dialog box, allowing you to set transformation parameters numerically.

Procedure First select the object(s) to be scaled. Then choose the Scale tool by clicking the icon in the toolbox. The mouse pointer changes to a + in the active window. You can scale objects visually on the screen or by an amount specified in the Scale dialog box.

Scaling Objects Visually on the Screen Click to set a point of origin for the scaling transformation. The pointer changes to an arrowhead. Position the pointer away from the point of origin and drag away from the origin to enlarge the object, or towards the origin to reduce the object.

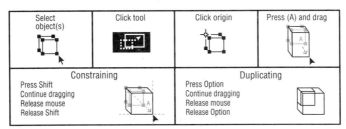

Scaling objects visually on the screen: (1) click to establish an origin point, then (2) drag to scale the object relative to the origin. Use the Shift key to constrain scaling; use the Option key to produce a duplicate.

31

Shift-dragging the arrowhead constrains the scaling to only horizontal, only vertical, or proportional scaling. Option-dragging the arrowhead leaves the original object unchanged and produces an enlarged or reduced scaled duplicate.

Scaling Objects by a Specified Percentage To scale by a specified amount, hold down the Option key when you click to set a point of origin for the scaling transformation. The Scale dialog box appears as shown in the figure below, allowing you to specify scale parameters. The Scale parameters you can change include Uniform scale, Non-uniform scale, and Scale pattern tiles (see Paint and also Pattern in Part II). The Scale dialog box also allows you to make a copy of the scaled object by clicking on Copy. If you select uniform scaling (that is, scaling equally in the x and y directions), you can also scale line weights.

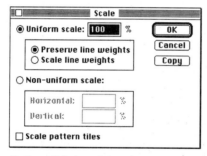

Option-click the origin point to enter scaling amounts through the Scale dialog box

You can create a set of concentric shapes by selecting a path, then using the Scale tool. Click at the center of the shape to set the origin of the transformation, then Option-drag to produce a transformed copy. Press Command-D (to select Transform Again from the Arrange menu) to produce a series of objects scaled to the same proportion. Draw the outer edge first, and produce progressively smaller duplicates layered *on top* of the first object (see Transform Again in Part II).

Tips

See also: The Blend Tool, which can be used to create a series of concentric shapes, and Print, which can be used to scale whole illustrations during printing.

The Rotate Tool

Overview Use the Rotate tool to rotate selected objects, relative to a fixed point.

Procedure First select the object(s) to be rotated, then choose the Rotate tool by clicking the icon in the toolbox. The mouse pointer changes to a + in the active window. You can rotate objects visually on the screen, or by an amount specified in the Rotate dialog box.

Rotating Visually on the Screen Click to set a point of origin for the rotation. This point functions like an anchor when you rotate the object. When you click the mouse, the pointer changes to an arrowhead. To make the object rotate, position the pointer away from the point of origin, hold down the mouse button, and drag in the direction of the desired rotation. Release the mouse button when you have rotated as much as you want.

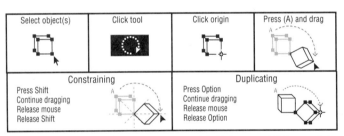

Rotating objects visually on the screen: (1) click to establish an origin point, then (2) drag to rotate the object relative to the origin. Use the Shift key to constrain rotation; use the Option key to produce a duplicate

Shift-dragging the arrowhead (pressing the Shift key as you drag the mouse) constrains the rotation to multiples of 45° angles. Option-dragging the arrowhead (pressing Option when releasing the mouse) leaves the original object unchanged and produces a rotated duplicate.

Rotating by a Specified Amount Hold down the Option key when you click to set a point of origin for the rotation. The Rotate dialog box appears, allowing you to specify the angle of rotation (in degrees), and whether or not to rotate pattern tiles (if the object is filled with a custom pattern; (see Paint and also Pattern in Part II). You can also make a copy of the rotated object by clicking Copy before clicking OK. When parameters are set as you wish, click on OK. Angles are measured *counterclockwise*, with zero at twelve o'clock. You can rotate objects in a *clockwise* direction by entering a negative number.

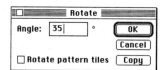

Option-click the origin point to enter the angle of rotation through the Rotate dialog box

Tips

To create a radially symmetrical object, such as a flower, draw a single petal, then use the Rotate tool and the Transform Again command from the Arrange menu to produce rotated copies. This reproduces the original petal, and is complete when the rotated copies form a flower. For best results, Option-click the origin point to get the Rotate dialog box, and enter the number of degrees yielded by the following formula:

(number of degrees) = 360° / (number of symmetrical elements)

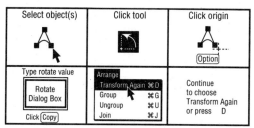

Creating symmetrical objects with the Rotate tool and the Transform Again command

See Radial Symmetry: Methods 1 and 2 for other examples using the Rotate tool.

The Reflect Tool

Overview   You use the Reflect tool to transform an object into a mirror image of itself.

Procedure   First select the object(s) to be transformed, then choose the Reflect tool by clicking the icon in the toolbox. The mouse pointer changes to a + in the active window. You can reflect objects across an axis that you set visually on the screen, or at an angle specified in the Reflect dialog box.

Reflecting a Mirror Image Visually on the Screen   Select the object, choose the Reflect tool, and click the + pointer at some point on the object to set a point on the axis of reflection. The pointer changes to an arrowhead. Position the pointer away from the point of origin and click to define a second point on the axis of reflection, or drag to pivot the axis if needed.

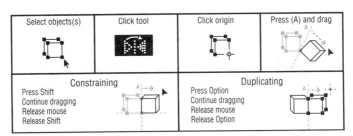

Reflecting objects visually on the screen: (1) click to establish point on the axis of reflection; (2) click to establish a second point and thereby establish the axis of reflection; (3) drag to pivot the object around the axis. Use the Shift key to constain the reflection axis; use the Option key to produce a duplicate

Shift-dragging the arrowhead (pressing Shift and dragging the mouse) constrains the reflection to multiples of 45° angles. Option-dragging the arrowhead (pressing Option before releasing the mouse) leaves the original object unchanged and produces a reflected copy.

35

Reflecting by a Specified Amount   With the Reflect tool selected, Option-click to set a point of origin for the reflection transformation. The Reflect dialog box appears, allowing you to specify which axis to reflect across: horizontal, vertical, or angled. You can make a copy of the object, reflected, by clicking on Copy prior to clicking on OK.

The angles for reflection are measured *counterclockwise*, with zero at twelve o'clock. You can reflect over an axis in a *clockwise* direction from twelve o'clock by entering a negative number.

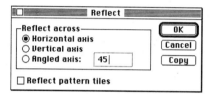

Option-click the origin point to enter the angle of reflection through the Reflect dialog box

Warning   The Reflect tool is one of the most difficult tools to control at first. The further you move away from the origin point to drag, the more incremental, and therefore, slower, the reflection will occur.

Tips   To avoid unwanted effects, always group the object, then make a copy by holding down the Option key as you use the Reflect tool. If the copy is correct, delete the original. Or, if the effect is not correct, delete the copy and repeat.

The Shear Tool

Overview   You can use the Shear tool to change the angle between the axes of selected objects. (Normally the x and y axes are set at 90° angles.) Shearing is easy to picture if you think of the term as describing the action of the blades of scissors, as shown in the figure that follows. (The Shear tool is unrelated to the Scissors tool, however.)

In shearing, the change of the angle between the axes is similar to the movement of the blades on scissors

Procedure

First select the object(s) to be sheared, then choose the Shear tool by clicking the icon in the toolbox. The mouse pointer changes to a + in the active window. You can shear objects visually on the screen, or at an angle specified in the Shear dialog box.

Shearing Visually on the Screen   Select the object to shear, select the Shear tool, and click on the object to set a point of origin for the shear axis. When you release the mouse, the pointer changes to an arrowhead. Position the pointer away from the point of origin and drag. The direction in which you drag defines the axis of shear: if you drag left or right you change the angle of the vertical axis; if you drag up or down you change the angle of the horizontal axis. The distance you drag defines the angle of shear.

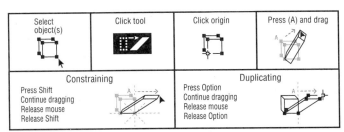

Shearing objects visually on the screen: (1) click to establish an origin point, then (2) drag horizontally to change the angle of the x axis, or vertically to change the angle of the y axis. Use the Shift key to constrain shearing to 45° increments; use the Option key to create sheared copy

Shift-dragging the arrowhead constrains the axis of shear to multiples of 45° angles. Option-dragging the arrowhead leaves the original object unchanged and produces a sheared copy.

Shearing by a Specified Amount Select the object, choose the Shear tool, and Option-click in the active window to set a point of origin for the shear transformation. The Shear dialog box appears, allowing you to specify the angle of shear, the axis to shear along, and whether or not to shear pattern tiles (see Paint and also Pattern in Part II). You can also specify that a copy of the sheared object be made by clicking on Copy before clicking on OK.

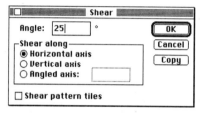

Option-click the origin point to enter the angle of shear through the Shear dialog box

The Scissors Tool ✂

Overview You use the Scissors tool to add anchor points to a path, open a closed path, or break a path into two or more separate objects. You can also use the Scissors tool to add anchor points to a path for finer control. It operates only on ungrouped paths (see Group and Ungroup). Splitting a closed path produces one open path. Splitting an open path produces two open paths. (See The Pen Tool for definitions of open and closed paths.)

Procedure First click anywhere on the ungrouped path you wish to split or add anchor points to, then choose the Scissors tool by clicking the icon in the toolbox. The mouse pointer changes to a + in the active window.

You can split an ungrouped path anywhere except the endpoints of an open path. Wherever you click on the ungrouped path the Scissors tool splits the path, producing two new end points, as shown in the top part of the figure that follows.

To add an additional anchor point to a path, Option-click with the Scissors tool on a segment of the path. This results in a single new anchor point along the path, rather than two new endpoints.

 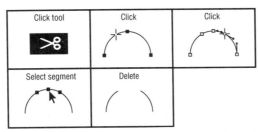

First click anywhere on an ungrouped path, then select the Scissors tool and click on a line segment to cut the line (and create two endpoints)

 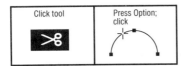

Option-click to create a new anchor point

Tips
After splitting a path, you can use the Selection tool to separate the new endpoints of the two paths. Click the Selection tool in any open space in the drawing window to deselect all objects. Click on the location of the two new endpoints. This selects one of the endpoints, which you can then drag to separate the ends of the path(s).

The Scissors tool cannot delete anchor points, but you can remove unwanted anchor points following the procedures shown in the figure below. (See also Shared Borders in Part III for an example of using the Scissors tool.)

Removing an anchor point

The Measure Tool

Overview   You can use the Measure tool to measure the distance and angle between any two locations on the page.

Procedure   Select the Measure tool, then click on two points. The points do not have to be anchor points. The Measure dialog box, shown in the figure below, displays the distance and angle between the two points you have clicked.

Measure		
Distance:	125.6328	pt
Angle:	-2.96	°
Horizontal:	125.4656	pt
Vertical:	-6.478	pt

OK

The Measure dialog box

Tips   The Measure tool is one of the tools that remain active in Preview mode. The others are the Zoom tool, the Page tool, and the Hand tool.

The Page Tool

Overview   You use the Page tool to control the tiling of an Illustrator file onto printed pages. The Illustrator drawing area is a square measuring 18 by 18 inches. When you print a file, Illustrator tiles, or subdivides, it into pages that match the paper size used in your printer. In other words, the Page tool lets you specify where the pages break. Normally, artwork is drawn on page 5 and pages 1–4 are not printed.

Procedure   Choose the Page tool by clicking the icon in the toolbox. The mouse pointer changes to a + in the active window.

   Hold down the mouse button and a dotted rectangle appears, marking the area that can be printed on a single page. The mouse is positioned at the lower left corner of the page. Use the mouse to drag the rectangle to define where you wish the pages to break.

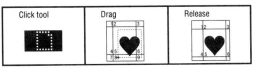

Drag the dotted rectangle to set the page breaks

Tips

The Page tool is one of the tools that remain active in Preview mode. The others are the Zoom tool, the Measure tool, and the Hand tool.

The Page tool is easiest to use in the Fit In Window view (see Fit In Window). Illustrator displays page numbers at the lower left corner of each page boundary on the screen (see Fit In Window in Part II).

Part II: Commands

Introduction to Commands

Choosing a Command

In this part, you will find a description of how to choose commands and make dialog box entries, and an overview of the menu titles, followed by an alphabetical listing of all the commands in Adobe Illustrator. Adobe Illustrator, like all applications that run on a Macintosh, displays a menu bar at the top of the screen, listing the names of the menus of available commands. Commands are displayed below each menu title. To select a command, position the mouse pointer over the menu title, hold down the mouse button, drag down the menu until the desired item is highlighted, then release the mouse button.

Some commands can be selected using keyboard shortcuts instead of the mouse. The shortcuts are listed on the menus next to the commands that have shortcuts.

Some of the command names displayed on the menus are followed by ellipses (. . .). A dialog box will be displayed whenever you use one of these commands, offering the opportunity to select from various options, enter information required by the command, or cancel the command. Note that commands that are not followed by ellipses have an immediate result that cannot be canceled unless the Undo command is available.

Dialog Box Entries

Some of Illustrator's commands result in the display of a dialog box on the screen. A dialog box is a window on the screen, and most dialog boxes can be moved around on the screen by dragging the title bar, just as any other window can be moved. A dialog box may contain any or all of the following:

- Warnings or messages.
- Boxes for typing text or numbers.
- Scrolling lists of fonts or file names.
- Check boxes that let you choose one or more options from a list.
- Radio buttons, small circular buttons that are used to select one option from a list of several mutually exclusive choices.
- Larger rectangular buttons that close the dialog box, offering options such as OK and Cancel, or that open additional dialog boxes.

Choose a command that is followed by an ellipsis on the menu list. When the dialog box appears, make selections or text entries as appropriate, then click on one of the rectangular buttons that close the dialog box. Some of the general procedures that apply to all dialog boxes are described here. Specific dialog box entries are described in detail under the specific commands that display dialog boxes, in the alphabetical listings that follow this section.

Warnings or Messages If the dialog box displays only the text of a warning or message, you have the option of clicking OK (to indicate that you have read the message) or Cancel (to indicate that you have read the warning and you wish to cancel the current command).

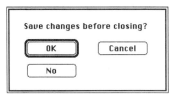

Dialog box with a message or warning

Reduce or Enlarge: 100 %

Text Boxes If there are any text boxes for typing text or numbers in the dialog box, the cursor will normally be positioned in the first such box when the dialog box opens. You can move the cursor from one text box to another by clicking on the text label that describes the entry, using the mouse to position the pointer inside the text box and clicking to postion the cursor, or by pressing the Tab key. You can select text inside a text box by clicking on the text label that describes the entry to select all of the text, using the mouse to drag the cursor over the text, double-clicking to select a word, or tabbing into the text box to select all of the text.

Scrolling Lists Lists of fonts or file names are often displayed in a small window within the dialog box, with scroll bars on the right for moving up or down the list. You select from a scrolling list by using the scroll bar (if necessary) to find the name you wish to select, then clicking on the name to highlight it. In some cases, you can jump ahead in a long alphabetical list by typing the first letter of the name you wish to choose.

Scrolling list of files from the New, Open, or Place dialog box

Check Boxes   You can choose one or more options from a list that displays check boxes. Options that are selected show an x inside the box. Otherwise, an empty check box indicates that the option is not selected. Check boxes are toggles: clicking on an empty box selects the option, clicking on a box with an x deselects the option. You can also select or deselect these options by clicking on the text label that describes the entry.

Printer Effects:
☒ Font Substitution?
☒ Smoothing?
☒ Faster Bitmap Printing?

Check boxes from the Print dialog box

Radio Buttons   Small circular buttons are used to select one option from a list of several mutually exclusive choices. The current selection is indicated by a dark circle inside the button. You can change the selection by clicking on another button in the list, or by clicking anywhere on the text label that describes that option.

Paper: ⦿ US Letter   ○ A4 Letter
           ○ US Legal   ○ B5 Letter

Radio buttons from the Print dialog box

Eject

Drive

Open

Cancel

Rectangular Buttons   Larger rectangular buttons are used to close the dialog box, offering options such as OK and Cancel, or to open additional dialog boxes. Often, one rectangular button is framed in a double-rule border, indicating that pressing the Return key will have the same effect as clicking on that button.

Menus

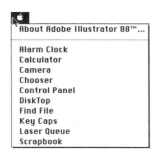

Apple Menu

As in other Macintosh applications, the Apple menu contains all of the Macintosh desk accessories that you have installed in your system folder, along with a command specific to Illustrator called About Adobe Illustrator 88™.... The figure above shows the pull-down Apple menu.

Other sections in this part of the book describe the About Adobe Illustrator 88™ command and other Apple menu desk accessories that are especially useful with Illustrator, including the Control Panel (for setting up color display on a Mac II), Chooser, and MultiFinder, the Macintosh system software that allows you to switch between several active applications. (See About Adobe Illustrator, Chooser, Control Panel, and Application Titles Running under MultiFinder.)

You can add desk accessories to the Apple menu using the Font/DA Mover application program that is supplied by Apple on the Macintosh system disk, or the desk accessory's installation program. You can also add fonts to the System using the Font/DA Mover application. Refer to your Macintosh user manual for more information on how to do this.

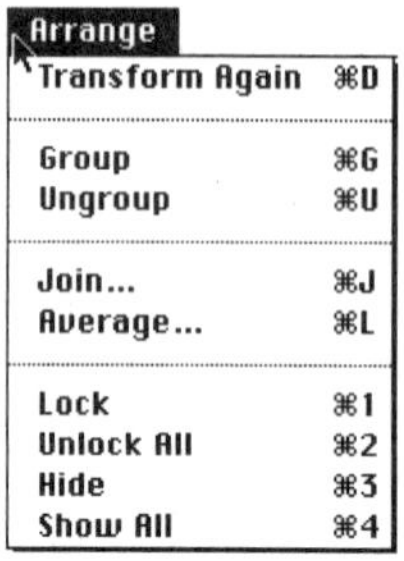

```
Arrange
Transform Again    ⌘D

Group              ⌘G
Ungroup            ⌘U

Join...            ⌘J
Average...         ⌘L

Lock               ⌘1
Unlock All         ⌘2
Hide               ⌘3
Show All           ⌘4
```

Arrange Menu

The Arrange menu, shown in the figure above, has commands that affect the arrangement of an object or objects. Commands in the Arrange menu enable you to repeat a transformation, group and ungroup objects, join endpoints, average anchor points, and lock, unlock, hide, and show objects.

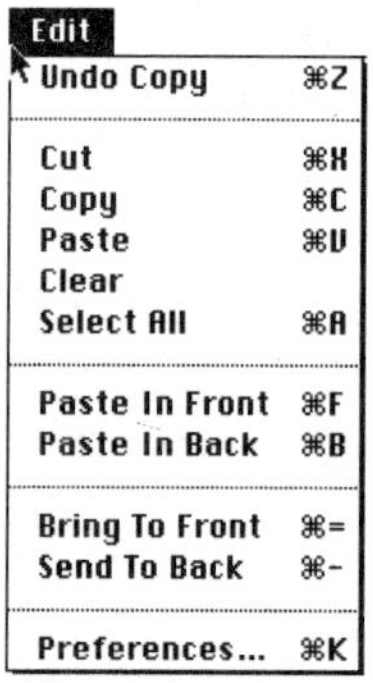

```
Edit
Undo Copy          ⌘Z

Cut                ⌘H
Copy               ⌘C
Paste              ⌘U
Clear
Select All         ⌘A

Paste In Front     ⌘F
Paste In Back      ⌘B

Bring To Front     ⌘=
Send To Back       ⌘-

Preferences...     ⌘K
```

Edit Menu

The Edit menu, shown above, contains commands for generally editing your Illustrator work, including undoing or redoing your last operation; managing the Macintosh Clipboard by cutting, or copying to it, and pasting from it; selecting all the objects in a file; deleting selected objects; pasting objects in front or in back of other objects; and assigning preferences.

Although different applications have different menu commands, and hence different keyboard shortcuts, the Command-key equivalents for Undo, Cut, Copy, and Paste are constant throughout all Macintosh applications. Knowledge and use of these keyboard shortcuts is basic to Macintosh literacy—if you learn only four Command-key menu equivalents, they should be Undo, Cut, Copy, and Paste. These Command-key menu equivalents use the four keys located closest to the left-hand Command key: Command-Z is Undo, Command-X is Cut, Command-C is Copy, and Command-V is Paste.

File Menu

The File menu has commands that apply to entire Illustrator files. When you start an Illustrator session, the File menu will likely be the first menu you access. You use File menu commands to open new or existing Illustrator files; to close and save Illustrator files you are working on; to prepare files for printing and to print Illustrator artwork; and to quit an Illustrator session.

Style Menu

The Style menu, shown above, affects the style of your illustration. This menu has commands to set paint attributes when filling paths or stroking paths, and to set type attributes. The Style menu also provides commands for defining custom colors and patterns.

View Menu

The View menu, shown in the figure above, affects the way your artwork is displayed on the screen. This menu contains commands to create multiple views of your file and to control what is displayed in the active window. You can preview the image as it will appear when printed, view the artwork and view the template together, view only the artwork, or view only the template. The View menu also contains commands to fit an entire file into a window or to display the file in its actual size, and to allow you to show or hide the rulers. See also The Zoom Tool for methods of changing magnifications of artwork.

Window Menu

As you can open more than one Illustrator file at a time, or open more than one window on a single file, the Window menu, shown in the figure above, provides commands that open new windows or change the active window from one open window to another. The window that is active will have a check mark next to its name in the Window menu.

If your drawing is complex, you can open several windows containing different views of the same document. The Window menu provides an easy way to switch from one view to another.

See New Window later in Part II.

Commands

About Adobe Illustrator 88™...

Overview   Choosing About Adobe Illustrator 88™... from the Apple menu displays a dialog box that shows the version of Illustrator you're using, the authors of Illustrator, a copyright notice, and the amount of free memory available (in bytes and as a percentage of total memory). As your artwork becomes larger, the free memory will decrease.

The About Adobe Illustrator dialog box

Procedure   Choose About Adobe Illustrator... from the Apple menu after starting Adobe Illustrator by double-clicking the program icon on the desktop.

Warning   Illustrator will open on a machine with 1 Mb of memory, but you will not be able to produce complex artwork because of memory limitations. Illustrator prefers 2 Mb of RAM to function efficiently.

Actual Size

Overview   The Actual Size command displays the file in its "actual size" in the active window. The file is centered in the active window and scaled so that one screen pixel represents one point (approximately 1/72 of an inch). The keyboard shortcut is Command-H.

Procedure   To view the illustration in actual size, choose Actual Size from the View menu, press Command-H, or Option-double-click on the Hand tool icon in the toolbox. Actual size is shown in the first view of the figure below.

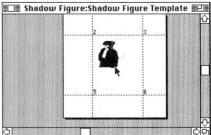

Artwork in Actual Size and Fit In Window views

Tips   To go to Actual Size, you can Option-double-click on the Hand tool icon in the toolbox. Note that this does not select the Hand tool, but leaves the currently selected tool in effect.
              Use the Zoom tool to magnify artwork larger than actual size when working on fine details in your drawing.

Application Titles Running under MultiFinder

Overview   MultiFinder allows you to use multiple software applications simultaneously. When you are running Multifinder, a list of all open applications appears below the list of desk accessories under the Apple menu. Choosing an application from the Apple menu makes it the active application, displays that application's menu bar, and makes its most recently active window visible.

Procedure   Choose an application that has already been started under Multi-Finder and that is displayed under the Apple menu.

You can run Adobe Illustrator with other applications. For example, you can concurrently run MacPaint to create or edit bitmaps (see Glossary) as templates for Illustrator artwork; you can use MacDraw to create or edit PICT files (see Glossary) as templates for Illustrator artwork; and you can run a page composition application (such as PageMaker or QuarkXPress) to place Illustrator artwork with text and graphics from other sources on a final page layout. Under MultiFinder, you need not quit one application to start another.

Warning   For maximum efficiency, you should have at least 1 Mb of memory for each application open under MultiFinder. Otherwise you may not be able to open more than one application at a time.

Artwork & Template

Overview   The Artwork & Template command displays both the Illustrator artwork and your template in the active window. You can use a template to trace over objects, and you can use bitmap or PICT files as templates. The template appears on-screen when you use this command, but it will not print. The keyboard shortcut is Command-E.

Procedure   Choose Artwork & Template from the View menu or press Command-E. The template is displayed if you are linked to this Illustrator file. (See also Open and New for methods of loading or changing templates.)

Artwork Only

Overview   The Artwork Only command displays only the Illustrator artwork in the active window. The keyboard shortcut is Command-W.

55

An illustration shown in Artwork Only view

Procedure Choose Artwork Only from the View menu, or press Command-W when you wish to see your artwork without the template.

Average...

Overview The Average command moves two or more selected anchor points to the average position of the selected points along the axis you specify: the horizontal axis, vertical axis, or both axes. You can average points and text objects. The keyboard shortcut is Command-L.

Procedure Select two or more anchor points or objects with the Selection tool, then choose Average... from the Arrange menu or press Command-L. If you don't properly select two anchor points, you will get an alert message asking you to "please select two or more points to average." (See The Selection Tool for methods of selecting points and objects.) The Average dialog box, shown in the next figure, appears, offering the options of averaging along the horizontal axis, the vertical axis, or both (the default setting). If you average points along both axes, they move to the same location—that is, halfway between their original positions. If you average along one axis only, each point moves to the halfway point along that axis.

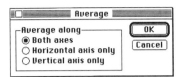

The Average dialog box

The figure below shows the effect of averaging two anchor points along both the horizontal and vertical axes.

Two anchor points, before and after using the Average command

Tips

Averaging two or more anchor points enables you to maintain a curved path while bringing two points together before using the Join command (see Join). Otherwise the Join command creates a straight line between the two points. Remember that averaging does not join anchor points. If you wish to join the points, you must use the Join command after averaging. First, select the endpoints you wish to average with the Selection tool. Choose Average… from the Arrange menu, or press Command-L. Then choose Join… from the Arrange menu, or press Command-J. The figure below illustrates how this is done.

 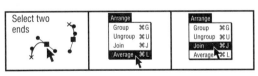

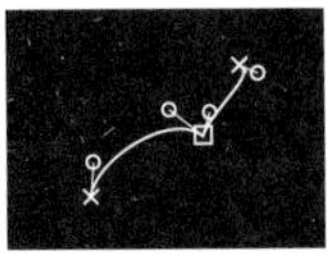

Connecting endpoints

The Average command is also useful for aligning blocks of text along a horizontal or vertical axis, as shown in the figure that follows.

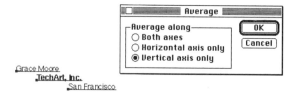

Text blocks before and after averaging along a vertical axis

Bring To Front

Overview   The Bring To Front command moves selected objects to the top layer in the artwork. The keyboard shortcut is Command-= (equal sign).

Procedure   Select the object(s) you wish to move to the front layer and choose Bring To Front from the Edit menu or press Command-=. If a selection itself is composed of more than one layer, the layers retain their relative positions.

   If you want to resequence the layering of an object, start by selecting the layer you want to become the bottom layer. Choose Bring To Front from the Edit menu, then select each layer in the order you want it to appear, from the bottom up, and use Bring To Front until the desired layer is on top.

Warning   Illustrator is normally very reliable in maintaining the order of layers when rearranging objects or groups of objects. However, if you have a complex illustration and use these commands frequently on groups of objects, you might find that you have inadvertently sequenced some objects improperly. Always check your artwork carefully by using the Preview command or by printing the illustration after rearranging layers.

Chooser

Overview   Since the AppleTalk network lets you connect up to thirty devices on a single network, you can have more than one printer available to any Macintosh. The AppleShare network also allows more than one file server to be accessed. The Chooser lets you select which printer you will use to print your artwork, or which file server you wish to access.

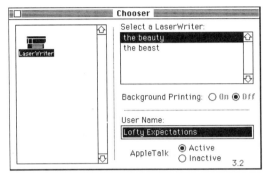

The Chooser dialog box

Procedure   Select the Chooser from the Apple menu. Click on a printer driver icon or the AppleShare icon. A list of all available devices will appear. Then click on the appropriate device name. Click the close box when you are done.

Warnings   The dialog box displays only those devices for which the power switch is on. If the full list of printers on your network is not displayed, it may be due to a loose cable connection between your machine and the printer.

Clear

Overview   The Clear command deletes all selected objects from the artwork. This command is the equivalent of pressing the Delete (or Backspace) key. Cleared objects are not stored in the Clipboard (a "storage area" in the computer's memory).

Procedure   Select the object or objects to be cleared using any of the techniques described under The Selection Tool in Part I. Then choose Clear from the Edit menu or press the Delete (or Backspace) key.

Warnings   Since objects deleted with the Clear command or the Delete (or Backspace) key are *not* copied to the Clipboard, you must use the Undo command immediately if you wish to reverse the command and retrieve the objects (see Undo).

Tip   The Delete (or Backspace) key is the most efficient method of clearing objects.

Close

Overview   The Close command closes the active Illustrator window. You can also close the active window by clicking the window's close box.

Procedure   Choose Close from the File menu, or click the close box in the upper left corner of the active window. If you have more than one window open on the same file, this action simply closes the active window. If you have only one window open on the file, this action closes the window and closes the file.

    If you made any changes to the Illustrator file since last saving it, Illustrator displays a dialog box asking whether you want to save your changes whenever you use the Close command. If you click OK, and the current window is named Untitled art, Illustrator displays the Save As dialog box so you can assign the file a name (see Save As).

Control Panel

Overview   Choosing Control Panel from the Apple menu displays the Control Panel, which is standard with Macintosh System software version 4.1 or later. Icons in the main portion of the General Control Panel provide access to different system functions. Using the Control Panel, you can change some of the configuration settings of your Macintosh, including the desktop pattern, the blinking rate of the text insertion point, the blinking rate of pull-down menus, the system time, the system date, the date format (a 12-hour or 24-hour clock), the speaker volume, the amount of RAM cache in use, and whether the RAM cache is on or off.

The icons in the left column represent different parts of your Macintosh System configuration. Two of these are of particular interest to Illustrator users: the General Control Panel and the Monitors Control Panel (for setting color display on the Macintosh II).

Procedure   Choose Control Panel from the Apple menu. The Control Panel dialog box appears, as shown in the next figure. When you have made the desired adjustments, click the close box to close the window.

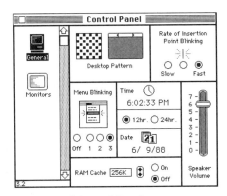

The General Control Panel

Click the General icon in the Control Panel to gain access to the RAM cache controls. If you are running Illustrator on a Macintosh equipped with 1Mb of RAM, you should turn the RAM cache off. If you have larger amounts of RAM available, and are running under MultiFinder, you may wish to use the RAM cache; although Illustrator will not benefit from it, other applications may.

If you are using a Macintosh II equipped with a color monitor and you wish to use Illustrator's color preview features, you can set the monitor to either 16 or 256 colors, depending on how much memory you have installed on your video card. To do this, click the Monitors icon in the left column of the Control Panel and make the appropriate selections by scrolling through the Colors scroll box and then clicking on the desired number of colors, as shown in the next figure.

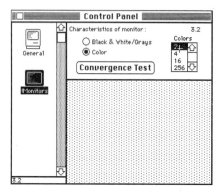

The Monitors Control Panel

Tip   If you do not need color to display, you can have quicker screen response and save memory by selecting two colors and changing to black-and-white mode.

Copy

Overview   The Copy command copies the selected objects to the Clipboard (a "storage area" in the computer's memory), leaving the objects in place as artwork, and replacing whatever was previously in the Clipboard. The keyboard shortcut is Command-C.

Procedure   Select the object or objects to be copied, then choose Copy from the Edit menu, or press Command-C.

You can copy an Illustrator file into a PICT format which can then be pasted into Microsoft Word, PowerPoint, and some other (but not all) Macintosh applications that cannot handle PostScript formats. To do this, hold down the Option key and choose Copy from the Edit menu, or press Option-Command-C. This action copies not only the PostScript information in the Illustrator file, but the screen bitmap as well, making it possible to paste the artwork into the other applications that support bitmapped or PICT formats. (See *bitmap* in the Glossary.)

Warning The Copy command in conjunction with the Option key will work as described above only if adequate memory is available.

Tips The Copy command is most useful when you want to store selected objects in the Clipboard for repeated use (over a short period), when you need to paste the copies between layers (not onto the top layer), and when you need to copy selected elements from one document to another.

Otherwise, copy objects by holding the Option key as you move an object with the Selection tool, or when you use any of the transformation tools (the Scale, Rotate, Reflect, and Shear tools). This is a more efficient method of copying objects when you want to align the copies, or when you want to combine the copy procedure with a movement or a transformation before using the Transform Again command (from the Arrange menu) to repeat the procedures. See The Selection Tool, The Scale Tool, The Rotate Tool, The Reflect Tool, and The Shear Tool in Part I for methods of copying selections without storing them in the Clipboard.

The Copy command does not delete objects from the artwork; to delete objects use the Cut or Clear command or the Delete (or Backspace) key (See Cut and Clear).

As with the Cut command, the Copy command replaces the contents of the Clipboard.

Custom Color...

Overview The Custom Color command displays the Custom Color dialog box and lists the custom colors you have created and stored, or the Pantone colors included on the Illustrator disks (if you have opened that document). It also lets you create new custom colors or change existing custom colors.

Procedure   Choose Custom Color… from the Style menu. You do not have to
                select any object(s) to customize a color. The Custom Color dialog
                box appears, as shown in the next figure, allowing you either to
                create your own custom colors by naming a new color and then
                entering the percentages of cyan, magenta, yellow, and black, or to
                select an existing color and adjust the percentage mix of colors.

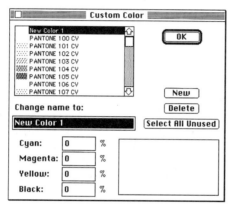

The Custom Color dialog box

To create a new custom color, click New and type a name in the
text box below *Change name to*: (or you can use Illustrator's default
naming convention, New Color 1). Type percentage values for Cyan,
Magenta, Yellow, and Black. You can see the resulting color mix in
the lower right corner of the dialog box if you have a color monitor,
but the best way to ensure a precise color match is to use a process
color swatchbook (available in art supply stores). By clicking New,
you can continue to add more custom colors.

To edit an existing color, click on the name of the color in the list
at the top left of the dialog box, then change the percentage values
and/or the name of the color. Changes made to an existing color will
be reflected in the artwork wherever that color has been used.

To create a new color based on an existing color, first click on the
existing color name and make a note of the percentage values. Then
click New, type a name for the new color, and enter percentage
values that vary from those you noted for the existing color.

Click Delete to remove the selected name (and color) from the list. Objects that were filled with that color will revert to the default fill pattern (100 percent black).

Click Select All Unused to select the names of all colors that are not currently used in the artwork. You can delete these colors to save memory and storage space.

The names of newly created colors appear in the Paint dialog box when you select its Custom Color button.

You can print custom colors for spot color (see Appendix A).

You can use one of the Pantone color files as a basis for creating custom colors by opening the file along with your artwork. However, you should avoid modifying the Pantone color file itself. Always close the Pantone color file without saving any changes.

Warning   If you select an existing color and change the name and percentage values, the effect is to delete the previous color from the list and replace it with the new entry. To avoid this problem, follow the procedure outlined above for creating a new color based on an existing color.

Tips   If you want to create your own library of custom colors, save them all in a file created for this purpose. You can make any color available for use in a new file by simply opening the file that contains the desired color.

Cut

Overview   The Cut command deletes the selected object(s) from the Illustrator artwork and stores it in the Clipboard (a "storage area" in the computer's memory), replacing whatever was previously in the Clipboard. The cut object can be pasted back into the current file or another Illustrator file using the Paste command. The keyboard shortcut is Command-X.

Procedure   Select the object or objects you wish to cut, then choose Cut from the Edit menu or press Command-X. To view the contents of the Clipboard, select Show Clipboard from the Window menu. (See also Show/Hide Clipboard and Window Menu.)

Tips   Use the Cut command whenever you wish to remove selected
                objects from the artwork and temporarily store them in the Clip-
                board. If you want to remove objects from the artwork but do not
                want to lose the contents of the Clipboard, select one of these alter-
                natives to the Cut command:

                - Press the Delete (or Backspace) key, or choose the Clear
                  command from the Edit menu. This action removes the
                  selected objects from the artwork but it does not store them
                  in the Clipboard. (See also Clear.)
                - Before using the Cut command, move the contents of the
                  Clipboard back to the artwork by choosing Paste (see Paste).
                - Drag the selected objects off to the side of the illustration for
                  storage as part of the artwork until you delete them.

Fit In Window

Overview   The Fit In Window command displays the entire 18-by-18-inch
                working area, centered, in the active window. The keyboard short-
                cut is Command-M.

Procedure   Choose Fit In Window from the View menu, or press Command-M,
                or double-click on the Hand tool icon in the toolbox, to fit the entire
                illustration into the active window. The effect of this command is
                shown in the figure below.

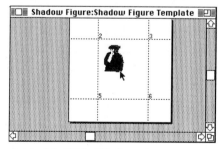

Artwork in Fit In Window view

Tips   Use this command to preview your artwork periodically to find stray objects and to ensure that the artwork falls squarely within the page boundaries (indicated on the screen by dotted lines).

To go to Fit In Window, you can double-click on the Hand tool icon in the toolbox. Note that this does not select the Hand tool, but leaves the currently selected tool in effect.

Group

Overview   The Group command combines selected objects into a group. Objects which are grouped can be selected with a single click of the Selection tool, making this command especially useful in maintaining control of multiple layers and selections in a complex drawing. The keyboard shortcut is Command-G.

Procedure   Select an ungrouped path, or any group of objects, using any of the techniques described in The Selection Tool, and choose Group from the Arrange Menu or press Command-G. If you select some but not all of the anchor points in a path, this command adds the entire path to the group.

A group itself can be composed of subgroups. Select a set of elements and group them, then select additional elements, including the grouped set, and group again. You need to invoke the Ungroup command twice to ungroup both sets in this instance (see Ungroup).

You can modify grouped paths using any of the transformation tools (including Scale, Rotate, Reflect, and Shear) or the Paint or Type command. But you cannot change parts of the grouped paths by editing text or moving the lines, anchor points, or direction lines (see The Selection Tool). Rectangles and ovals drawn with the Rectangle or Oval tool are automatically grouped when you draw them.

Tips   Clicking on objects with the Selection tool tells you whether objects are grouped or ungrouped. If all anchor points are selected (that is, they all display as black rather than white squares), the elements are grouped. When you click on an ungrouped object, only the line or anchor points touched by the Selection tool are selected.

You can transform and move grouped objects as a whole, but grouped objects retain their individual paint and type attributes as set or determined via the Paint and Type commands, respectively, in the Style menu (see Style Menu). If you choose the Paint command and a group of objects with different paint attributes is selected, the Paint dialog box (invoked by the Paint command) will display only those selections that are common to all elements in the group. If you make no entries in the Paint dialog box, all elements of the group retain their different attributes. If you change the paint or type attributes for a group, all the objects in the group will be changed to the new attributes.

(See Tips under Select All for grouping objects that share the same attributes. See also Paint and Type.)

Hide

Overview   The Hide command hides all selected objects from view in both Artwork and Preview modes and in the printed artwork. The keyboard shortcut is Command-3.

Procedure   Select an object or objects with the Selection tool, and choose Hide from the Arrange menu or press Command-3. Hidden objects do not display in Preview mode, nor do they appear on printed versions. You can redisplay all hidden objects by choosing the Show All command (Command-4).

Holding down the Option key while choosing Hide from the Arrange menu hides all unselected objects.

Warning   You lose the Hide attribute when you quit or save the document.

Tips   This command is extremely useful for complex drawings. You can hide parts of the illustration, thus making the artwork less complex and reducing the time it takes Illustrator to refresh the screen in Preview mode. You can also hide parts of drawings as you complete them, thus leaving only incomplete objects visible on the screen.

See also Lock. See other Hide commands listed under Show/Hide in this alphabetical sequence.

Join...

Overview   The Join command connects two endpoints with a straight line segment, or, if the two points you wish to join are on top of one another, replaces them with one point. In the latter case, the Join dialog box, shown in the figure below, allows you to choose a smooth point or a corner point. The keyboard shortcut is Command-J.

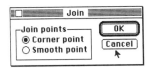

The Join dialog box

Procedure   Select two ungrouped endpoints with the Selection tool, and choose Join... from the Arrange menu or press Command-J. You must have only two endpoints selected when you use this command, and the endpoints must not belong to a grouped object.

If you select two points that are not already touching, the Join command creates a straight line that connects the two points. When the endpoints are joined, both endpoints and the straight line segment between them become selected.

Two endpoints, before and after using the Join command

If you select two points that are already within two pixels of each other (or the Snap to point setting in the Preferences dialog box is two pixels), using the Join command results in the Join dialog box, which allows you to determine whether the joined point will be a corner or smooth.

To join two points that have been averaged, use the Join command immediately after using the Average command (see Average).

To join two points that result when the Scissors tool is used on a line segment, use the Join command immediately after the Scissors tool (see The Scissors Tool in Part I).

Tips   Some paths may appear closed until you try to use a command that requires that the path be closed. If you make this mistake, you will get an alert box with a message that the path is open. To find the endpoints along what looks like a closed path, scroll along the path in maximum magnification (see The Zoom Tool). Anchor points that fall along the closed path display as white boxes when you select any part of the path, or as black boxes when you select the anchor points themselves. Endpoints, on the other hand, display as small x's rather than boxes. (See also The Pen Tool for descriptions of how to create open or closed paths.)

Lock

Overview   The Lock command locks selected objects so you cannot select, move, or modify them until you unlock them. This command protects parts of your illustration from accidental changes. The keyboard shortcut is Command-1.

Procedure   Select an object or objects with the Selection tool, and choose Lock from the Arrange menu or press Command-1. Locked objects remain locked until you use the Unlock command. The locked attribute is stored with the document when you close it, and remains with the document when it is reopened, until the Unlock command is used.

Tips   Use this command when you create complex artwork. Locked objects can be seen but not selected, thus enabling you to work easily with adjacent objects without affecting the locked objects. See Tip under the Select All command for locking all elements except the group you are currently working on. See also Osaka Railway Map in Part IV.

The Lock command is especially useful when working with grid systems. (See also Grid: Methods 1–4 in Part III.)

New...

Overview   The New command creates a new Illustrator artwork file. The keyboard shortcut is Command-N.

Procedure   Choose New... from the File menu or press Command-N. Illustrator displays a dialog box, shown in the figure, listing all of the bit-mapped and PICT files available on the disk (see *bitmap* and *PICT format* in the Glossary).

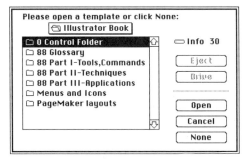

The New dialog box

You can select one of these PICT files as a template file and use it as the background from which to trace new artwork. If you do not want to use a template, click the None button. If you click the None button, Illustrator presents you with an untitled, blank page. You can cancel the entire command by clicking the Cancel button or by using the keyboard shortcut, Command-(period).

Tips   As with other Macintosh applications, Illustrator opens a file and assigns it the name Untitled art in the title bar. You can change the name of the file by choosing Save or Save As... from the File menu. You can also name the file when you close it by clicking the file's close box or by choosing Close from the File menu. If you close the file using either of these methods, and you have unsaved work on the screen, Illustrator displays an alert box asking if you want to save changes. If you click the Yes button, Illustrator displays the Save As dialog box (see Save As).

71

New Window

Overview   The New Window command creates a duplicate window of the active file. The original window and its duplicate are linked, so that changes to artwork in one window are duplicated in the second window. You can view one window in Preview mode and the other in Artwork mode, and zoom in one window independently of the other.

Procedure   Choose New Window from the Window menu. The duplicate window appears slightly offset from the original window. The newly created view becomes the active window, which you can move, resize, or close just like any Macintosh window.

When two or more views of the same file are on the desktop, Illustrator assigns each a number that appears in the window's title bar: Untitled art:1, Untitled art:2, and so on. When you close a window from a set of multiple views, Illustrator renumbers the remaining windows accordingly.

You can work in full views or overlapping views, and you can change the active window by choosing from the Window menu.

Artwork and Preview   Work in two views of the same illustration, one in Artwork Only (or Artwork & Template) view and one in Preview. This way, you can see the results of changes in real time as you work in the Artwork view on the wireframe image. Working in this way is especially good for making the final touches on artwork.

Preview and Artwork views

Actual Size and Close-up   Work in two different magnifications: an actual size (or smaller) view of the entire artwork, and an enlarged view of the detail on which you are working. This allows you to see extended sections of long paths in the smaller view, and to pinpoint anchor points easily in the enlarged view.

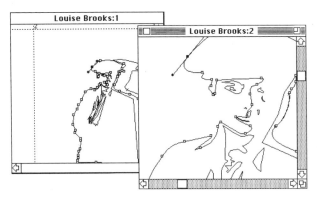

Two magnifications of wireframe artwork

The reduced view can be in either Artwork or Preview mode.

Artwork and Paint Palette   View the artwork of the illustration in one window, and a palette of Paint settings in another window.

Artwork and Control Area   View the artwork of the illustration in one window, and a control area of group selection icons or repeatedly used elements in another window. See Osaka Railway Map in Part IV for a specific application of this methodology.

Multiple Illustrations   You can view two or more illustrations at once. This is useful when you want to compare images, overlay images, or copy elements from one document to another.

Warning   Working with windows open in the Preview mode may slow down the system if the illustration is complex, because the Preview mode constantly refreshes the screen. It may not be practical to work this way for long periods on complex drawings.

Tips   You can have several windows open on your screen at once (depend-
               ing on the size of the files and the amount of memory available). You
               compound the possibilities by having three or more windows open
               at once.

Open...

Overview   The Open command opens an existing Illustrator file or a template
               file. The keyboard shortcut is Command-O. The number of files you
               can have open simultaneously is limited by available RAM. You can
               switch between windows by selecting one of the open windows
               listed under the Window menu.

Procedure   Choose Open… from the File menu or press Command-O. Illustra-
               tor displays the Open dialog box, as shown in the figure, listing all
               Illustrator files and template files on the selected disk.

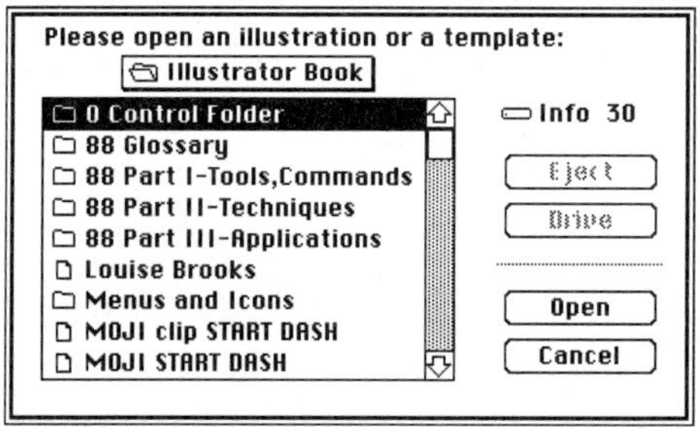

The Open dialog box

               To select a file, scroll through the file list to locate your desired file,
               click its name, and then click the Open button, or double-click on the
               file name. Click the Drive button to view the list of files from another
               disk. Click the Eject button to change disks. To work on an existing
               Illustrator file, select the file. Illustrator opens a new window dis-
               playing both the artwork and its template, if any. The window's title
               bar has a name in the form *artwork:template*, where *artwork* is the
               name of the Illustrator file and *template* is the name of the template
               file.

To create a new Illustrator file based on an existing template file, select the template file from the Open dialog box. Illustrator opens a new window with the name *Untitled art:template* in the title bar, where *template* is the template file name. You can change the Illustrator file name from *Untitled art* to something more meaningful when you save the Illustrator file.

Tips

From the desktop, double-click the icon of an Illustrator document to bring up the file immediately at startup time.

You can force Illustrator to prompt you for a template file whenever you open an existing Illustrator artwork file by holding down the Option key when you choose Open... from the File menu. By using the Option key in this way, you can work on existing artwork without being forced to continue using the template that you may have traced originally. In addition, you can open a different template and add a second traced drawing to existing artwork.

Page Setup...

Overview

The Page Setup command controls the page settings that determine how an artwork file will be printed. The Page Setup command lets you select the paper size, the reduction or enlargement percentage, the page orientation (tall or wide), and special printer effects, such as font substitution, smoothing, and faster bitmap printing. This command affects the printing of each page for the file in the active window.

Procedure

Choose Page Setup... from the File menu. Illustrator displays the Page Setup dialog box, which is specific to the printer you select with the Chooser from the Apple menu (see Chooser). The next figure shows the Page Setup dialog box for an Apple LaserWriter Plus printer.

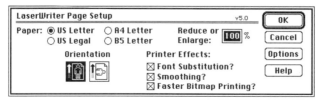

The Page Setup dialog box for the Apple LaserWriter Plus, a PostScript laser printer

Set the Paper setting to match the paper tray loaded in the printer. Select this setting by clicking on the desired option. The Orientation setting lets you choose whether your artwork will be printed vertically (tall) or horizontally (wide) on the page. The Reduce or Enlarge setting lets you specify a percentage reduction or enlargement. You can print enlarged drawings in pieces on several pages. The Printer Effects options—Font Substitution, Smoothing, and Faster Bitmap Printing—have no effect on Illustrator files. You can leave them all checked, which are their default settings.

The Options button, when clicked, displays a second dialog box, the Options dialog box, shown in the figure below. This dialog box lets you flip the image vertically or horizontally, invert (reverse) the image, align bitmap printing more precisely by way of a 4 percent reduction, or use a larger print area than normal (which will reduce the allowable number of downloadable fonts). The print area option has no effect on Illustrator files.

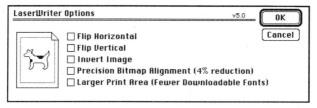

The Options dialog box

These Option dialog box options are specific to the LaserWriter Plus. Other PostScript printers may have different options.

You can also choose Help from the Page Setup dialog box. Click on the Help button to get details on how Page Setup options affect printing.

Paint...

Overview   The Paint command displays the Paint dialog box, which lets you set attributes for existing objects or for new objects you create, including settings for how paths or text characters are filled and stroked. Fills can be None (transparent), White, Black, Process Color, Custom Color, or Pattern. Strokes can be dashed or solid lines, with a line weight of 0 to 1008 points, in None (transparent), White, Black, Process Color, Custom Color, or Pattern. The keyboard shortcut is Command-I.

Procedure   Select an object or objects with the Selection tool, then choose Paint... from the Style menu or press Command-I to display the Paint dialog box, shown in the figure below.

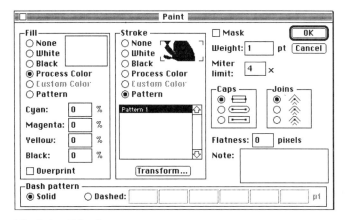

The Paint dialog box

   The Paint dialog box allows you to change the following attributes by clicking on the appropriate option, or by typing in the desired values.

Fill

- None designates no fill, or a transparent fill.
- White designates a white, or opaque, fill.

- Black designates a black fill, which can be set to percentages (shades of gray), by entering a value in the text box next to *Black*. The figure below shows examples of fill percentages, from 100 percent to 10 percent in increments of 10 percent.

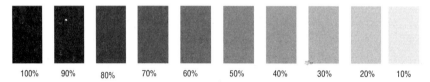

100%   90%   80%   70%   60%   50%   40%   30%   20%   10%

Examples of percentage fills

- Process Color yields virtually any color when you enter percentages for Cyan, Magenta, Yellow, and Black. Percentages can include one decimal place. As you define each color, it appears in a rectangle to the right of the list on your color monitor. Representations of colors show as shades of gray on a black-and-white monitor.
- Custom Color shows a list of all custom colors you created using the Custom Color… command in the Style menu, or shows a list of all Pantone colors. The file *Pantone Colors* (which comes with Illustrator 88) must be open to show the Pantone color list. You can screen Custom Colors, including Pantone colors, by various percentages.

- Pattern shows the list of patterns that have been defined with Pattern… under the Style menu. As you click on each item in the list, a miniature view of the pattern appears to the right of the list. You can have access to patterns created in another file simply by opening the other file. As long as the other file is open, you will have access to all its patterns in the current file.
- When you click on Transform…, the Transform Pattern Style dialog box appears. Transformations include moving, scaling, rotating, reflecting, and shearing the pattern. The pattern swatch in the Paint dialog box does not change, but the objects filled with the transformed pattern will show when you preview them. You can use the Transform Pattern Style

as a style sheet, in that if you make a change in the Transform Pattern Style dialog box, all objects painted with that pattern change.

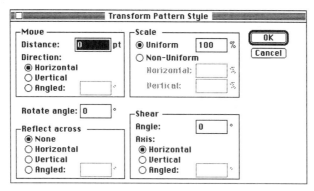

Transform Pattern Style dialog box

- Overprint results in the selected object overprinting colors and percentages of black on the objects below the selected object. The default is for a knockout, a term for an overlay that "knocks out" part of an image from another image. For example, in printing white type on a black background, the white type is knocked out of the background.

Stroke   A stroke (border) of an object can have any of the attributes described under Fill, as well as a weight (thickness), miter limit, end cap, join style, and dashed pattern. These features are described below.

Mask   When you turn this option on by clicking in the checkbox in the Paint dialog box, the selected objects become a *mask* for viewing parts of the object(s) in your drawing. In PostScript programming this is called "clipping." You can view your drawing through any shape you draw.

Mt. Placid

Example of a letter shape masking a mountain scene

The object assigned as the mask must be in the backmost layer. See Masking in Part III for further explanations of how to create masks. The figure below outlines the procedure for masking.

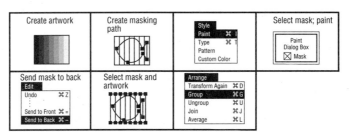

Procedure for masking

Weight   You can set the line weight of the stroke in points or decimal fractions of a point, from 0 to 1008 points in quarter-point increments, when Stroke is set to something other than None. This option is not available when Stroke is set to None. Lines are stroked from the center of the line that is displayed in Artwork view, outward in both directions.

Miter Limit   The miter limit determines the point at which, when two lines meet at a sharp angle, Illustrator switches from a miter (pointed) to a bevel (squared-off) join. You can set the miter limit only if you have specified a miter join, otherwise the option is disabled. The miter limit default value is 4, which means that when the length of the spike formed by the miter join reaches 4 times the line weight, Illustrator switches from a miter (pointed) to a bevel (squared-off) join. You can set the miter limit from 1 to 10. A value of 1 always creates a bevel join. See the next figure for examples of miter settings.

Caps   You have a choice of three end caps for lines. This refers to the shape of the end of the line. Butt caps (the default) are squared off perpendicular to the path; the cap does not extend beyond the path. Round caps end the line in a semicircular cap with a diameter equal to the line weight. Projecting caps have square ends that project half the line weight beyond the end of the path.

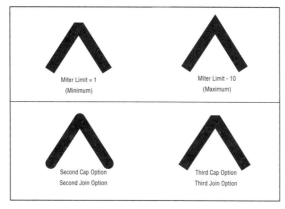

Examples of miter limit, end cap, and joins settings

Joins   You have a choice of three joins for corners. Miter joins (the default) extend the edges of two converging strokes until they meet. See *Miter Limit* above. Round joins connect corners with a circular arc whose diameter is equal to the line weight. Bevel joins finish the converging lines with butt caps and fill the resulting notch with a triangle, giving the corner a squared-off appearance. See the figure above.

Flatness   This feature determines the precision with which Illustrator calculates curves. Illustrator constructs curves by linking anchor points with a series of very short straight line segments (though the resulting curves appear smooth to the naked eye). A low flatness value causes Illustrator to use a greater number of short line segments to create a more accurate curve. The default value is zero. Normally you do not need to adjust this value. But if you draw a very long curve, you may get a PostScript language *limitcheck* error, or your artwork may not print due to the large number of anchor points. Increasing the flatness value can prevent this error.

Note that flatness settings are device-dependent. A flatness setting that works with a laser printer may not work with a Linotronic typesetter. With the flatness at the default value of zero, the screen uses a flatness setting of one and the printer uses its own preset value. You can also use a high flatness value while working to speed up screen redrawing, then change it back to a low value for final printing.

Note   You can type descriptive notes about a particular set of Paint settings as shown in the Note area of the dialog box. These notes do not print out, but you can use them as production aids or descriptions of when the specified Paint attributes are to be used. They appear as comments in the generated PostScript code, so you can also use the Note area for comments that will help you find specific portions of code if you will be modifying the PostScript code directly.

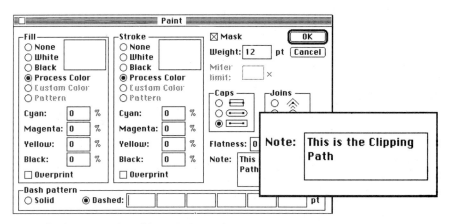

Example of Note text describing a Paint setting

Dash Pattern   This is enabled when Stroke is set to any weight (that is, not set to None). Otherwise the Dash pattern option is disabled.

You can set up custom dashed lines by clicking on Dashed. If you want an evenly dashed line with black dashes the same length as the white gaps, as shown in the first illustration below, enter one value (in points) for the interval in the first box provided. If you want two different measurements for the black and white portions of a line with a black stroke, which produces variations of dashed and/or dotted lines, enter the length of the black intervals in the first box and the length of the white interval in the second box. You can create complex dashed lines by entering up to six values for intervals. The fourth part of the figure below shows three values for intervals, and the last part shows values entered in all six interval boxes.

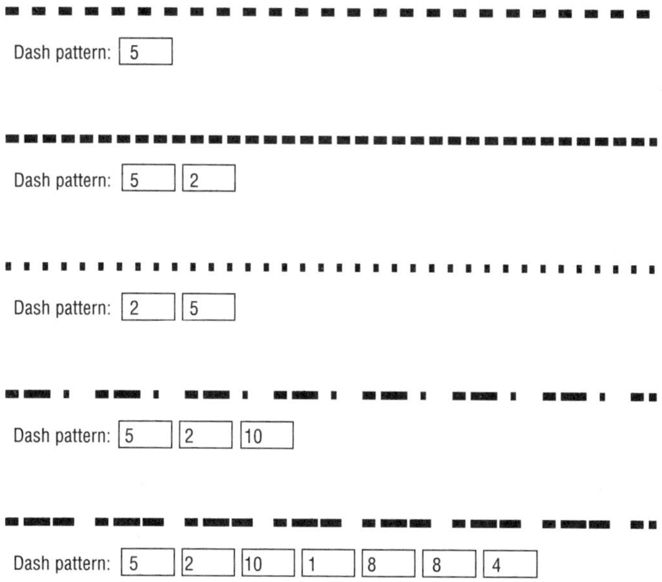

Dash pattern: 5

Dash pattern: 5 2

Dash pattern: 2 5

Dash pattern: 5 2 10

Dash pattern: 5 2 10 1 8 8 4

Examples of dashed line settings

Paste

Overview   The Paste command pastes the contents of the Clipboard to the center of the active window, on top of all the other objects. The keyboard shortcut is Command-V.

Procedure   After storing the desired objects in the Clipboard using the Copy or Cut command, choose Paste from the Edit menu or press Command-V. The pasted objects appear in the center of the screen and become the currently selected objects. All other objects are deselected.

Warning   All pasted objects are selected when they appear on the screen. It's a good idea to use the Undo, Cut, Send To Back, Bring To Front, or Group command immediately, or move the pasted selections into position immediately, before clicking elsewhere and deselecting an ungrouped selection of pasted objects.

Tip   Pasting objects from the Clipboard does not remove them from the Clipboard. (See also Paste In Front and Paste In Back.)

Paste In Back

Overview   The Paste In Back command pastes artwork from the Clipboard in back of all currently selected objects. The keyboard shortcut is Command-B.

Procedure   Select an object or objects with the Selection tool. Use the Cut or Copy command to store the object(s) you select in the Clipboard. Then select the objects in back of which you wish to paste the Clipboard object(s), and choose Paste In Back from the Edit menu or press Command-B. If you have not selected any objects, the pasted objects become the backmost objects in the artwork, at the same location on the page from which they were cut or copied. The pasted objects become the currently selected objects and all other objects are deselected.

Warning   You cannot paste text or graphics from other applications into Illustrator.

Tips   This command is especially useful for pasting objects between other objects, as an alternative to the Paste In Front command (see Paste In Front).

If you simply want to move selected objects to the bottom layer, which is frequently required for masking or for patterning, it is more efficient to use the Send To Back command than the Cut and Paste In Back commands.

Paste In Front

Overview The Paste In Front command pastes artwork objects from the Clipboard in front of all currently selected objects. The keyboard shortcut is Command-F.

Procedure Select an object or objects with the Selection tool. Use the Cut or Copy command to store the object(s) you select in the Clipboard. Then select the objects in front of which you wish to paste the Clipboard objects(s), and choose Paste In Front from the Edit menu or press Command-F. If you have not selected any objects, the pasted objects become the frontmost objects in the artwork, at the same location on the page from which they were cut or copied. The pasted objects become the currently selected objects and all other objects are deselected.

Warning You cannot paste text or graphics from other applications into Illustrator.

Tips This command is especially useful for pasting objects between other objects. If you want to paste in front of all objects in your artwork—not in front of selected objects only—you can use the Paste command. Another difference between Paste and Paste In Front is that Paste brings the objects to the center of the window, whereas Paste In Front positions the objects over their last location.

If you want simply to move selected objects to the top of the artwork, it is more efficient to use the Bring To Front command than the Cut and Paste In Front commands.

Pattern...

Overview   The Pattern command displays the Pattern dialog box, which allows you to create a new pattern or delete, paste, or change the name of an existing pattern. The scrolling list displays all existing patterns.

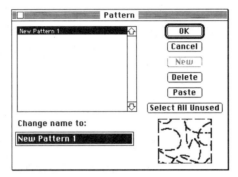

The Pattern dialog box

Procedure   Draw a pattern shape or design and color it. Using the Rectangle tool, draw a rectangle around your art defining the "tiling element." The rectangle need not completely surround the design. Select the rectangle and use the Send To Back command to position it behind the design. Select both the design and the rectangle. Then choose Pattern... from the Style menu. The Pattern dialog box appears, as shown in the figure above. Click New to display the selected pattern in the bottom right area of the dialog box, and name the pattern by entering the name in the text box. When you close this dialog box, the pattern will then be available in the Paint dialog box.

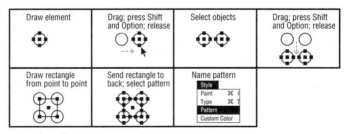

Procedure for creating a pattern

Click Paste to paste a copy of the original tiling element artwork on the page if you want to edit the pattern, then close the dialog box, edit the pattern artwork, select it, and choose Pattern... again to store the changed pattern under the same name or a new name.

Click Delete to remove the selected name (and pattern) from the list. Objects that were filled with that pattern will revert to the default fill pattern (100 percent black).

Click Select All Unused to select the names of all patterns that are not currently used in the artwork. You can delete these patterns to save memory and storage space.

Click OK to close the dialog box and record the changes, or click Cancel to close the dialog box without recording any changes.

You can apply patterns listed in this dialog box to selected objects by clicking the Pattern button in the Paint dialog box (see Paint).

Tips
If you frequently use custom patterns, save them in a file created for this purpose. Opening the file will make your previously created patterns available, allowing you to use them in other Illustrator files. You can make any pattern available for use in a new file by simply opening the file which contains the desired pattern.

See Patterns: Methods 1–3 in Part III. See Japan Fan and Kimono in Part IV for use of patterns.

Place...

Overview
The Place command imports an EPS (encapsulated PostScript) file. Scans, as well as files from Freehand, Cricket Draw, PageMaker, Pixel Paint, and other applications, may be saved in EPS format.

Procedure
Choose Place... from the File menu. Illustrator displays the Place dialog box, which lists all EPS files on the selected disk, as shown in the figure that follows.

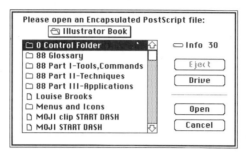

The Place dialog box

To select a file, scroll through the file list to locate the desired filename, click on the name, and then click the Open button, or double-click on the file name. The Drive button and Eject button operate as described earlier under Open . You can manipulate EPS files imported using the Place command as single objects with any of Illustrator's transformation tools (the Scale tool, Rotate tool, Reflect tool, or Shear tool), but you cannot change the strokes of lines or of fill patterns, or otherwise make detailed edits to the EPS graphic.

EPS files display only as a box with an *x* in the center in Artwork mode but display correctly in Preview mode.

Warning   Illustrator may need to refer to the original EPS files whenever you open or print the document, so be sure to keep a copy of the original EPS file in the same folder with your artwork.

Tip   Files imported by the Place command can be masked, but they cannot be made into patterns.

Preferences...

Overview   The Preferences command lets you change settings that affect how various commands and tools in Illustrator work. The keyboard shortcut is Command-K.

```
┌─────────────────────────────────────────────────────────┐
│ ▣▦▦▦▦▦▦▦▦▦▦  Preferences  ▦▦▦▦▦▦▦▦▦▦▦                     │
│ ☐ Snap to point                          ┌──────────┐    │
│ ☒ Preview and print patterns             │    OK    │    │
│ ☐ Transform pattern tiles                └──────────┘    │
│                                           ┌──────────┐    │
│ Constrain angle:        [0       ]  °     │  Cancel  │    │
│                                           └──────────┘    │
│ Corner radius:          [0    ]  pt   ┌─Ruler units──────┐│
│                                       │ ○ Centimeters    ││
│ Cursor key distance:    [1    ]  pt   │ ○ Inches         ││
│                                       │ ● Picas/Points   ││
│ Freehand tolerance:     [5    ]  pixels└──────────────────┘│
│                                                           │
│ Auto trace gap distance: [0   ]  pixels                   │
│ ┌─────────────────────────────┐                          │
│ │ Change Progressive Colors...│                          │
│ └─────────────────────────────┘                          │
└─────────────────────────────────────────────────────────┘
```

The Preferences dialog box

Procedure Choose Preferences… from the Edit menu or press Command-K. Illustrator displays the Preferences dialog box, shown in the figure above, which lets you set the following preferences by either clicking the appropriate checkbox or button, or typing in desired values:

Snap to Point   This turns the Snap to point feature on or off. The normal default setting of Snap to point is on. Snap to point causes two points to snap together when they are within two pixels of each other, and moves objects in two-pixel increments. With Snap to point off, you can move objects one pixel at a time. Snap to point is very useful for aligning objects, but you can turn this feature off when you are positioning objects very close to each other but do not want them to touch.

Preview and Print Patterns   This setting controls how patterns are viewed and printed. The default setting for Preview and print patterns is on, which allows you to view and print patterns fully. When Preview and print patterns is set off, the screen refreshes faster because you have instructed Illustrator not to preview the patterns, which take more time to draw. Also, when the setting is off, the illustrations print drafts without patterns, which will print faster than if printing with patterns.

Transform Pattern Tiles   When turned on, this will cause patterns within objects to be changed along with the path of the object when any transformation tool is used. (Transformation tools include the Scale, Rotate, Reflect, and Shear tools.) Otherwise, with Transform pattern tiles off (the default setting), only the path is transformed, not the pattern. (See description of Transform option in Paint dialog box.)

Constrain Angle   When set to zero degrees (default setting), this constrains all objects to the normal horizontal and vertical positioning. However, by changing this value, you can change the normal positioning so that objects will draw at the angle specified.

Corner Radius   When set to zero points (the default), this results in rectangles with square corners. Adding points to this setting changes the square corners to curved corners. Corner radius values must be between 0 and 1008 points, but cannot exceed half the length of the short sides of the rectangle. If you enter a larger value, Illustrator will draw the largest oval that can fit into the rectangle. See The Rectangle Tool for examples of different corner radius settings.

Cursor Key Distance   This determines the distance a selected object or group of objects will move when you press one of the arrow keys. You can enter a value from 1 to 1008 points (or decimal equivalents in other units of measure).

Freehand Tolerance   This sensitizes the mouse movement and determines the number of anchor points that will be created when you use the Freehand tool to draw an object. When you enter a higher number, fewer anchor points occur along a path and the mouse becomes less sensitive. When the tolerance is set higher, using the Autotrace tool also yields fewer anchor points (see The Autotrace Tool). When you enter a lower value, more anchor points occur along a path because the mouse becomes more sensitive to movement. You can set the tolerance from one to ten pixels. If you set tolerance beyond this range, an alert box appears. See The Freehand Tool for examples of different tolerance settings.

Autotrace Gap Distance   This determines the number of pixels Illustrator reads when the Autotrace tool is in use. With Autotrace gap distance set at zero (the default setting), the Autotrace tool will read every pixel in the template. With the setting at two, Autotrace will jump across two-pixel gaps and connect the pixels on either side of the gap, which is useful if your template is very sketchy. With the Setting at one, Autotrace connects across one-pixel gaps.

Ruler Units   These options, displayed in a box in the right portion of the dialog box, determine the units of measure displayed on the ruler. You can select Centimeters, Inches, or Picas/Points (the default).

Change Progressive Colors   When selected, this brings up the Progressive Colors selection box, shown in the next figure. When you use this option with a sample progressive color bar provided by Adobe or your printer, you can adjust your monitor and screen colors for current lighting situations. This allows you to customize your monitor without mechanically altering internal settings. Double-clicking on a color swatch in the Progressive Colors box yields the Apple Color Picker, which allows you to choose from a palette of more than sixteen million colors.

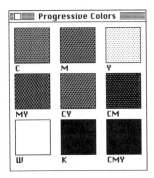

The Progressive Colors selection box

Warning   Preference settings cannot be reversed with the Undo command. They are stored as part of the Illustrator application settings and are *not* stored differently for each document. Before changing these values, make a note of the original settings in case you wish to revert.

Preview Illustration

Overview   The Preview Illustration command displays a preview image of the artwork in the active window. The keyboard shortcut is Command-Y. A preview image is an approximation on the screen of how the artwork will look when it is printed.

An illustration shown in two different views: Artwork Only and Preview

Procedure   Choose Preview Illustration from the View menu or press Command-Y to check the printed appearance of your artwork. The second view in the figure above shows a previewed illustration.

You cannot make changes to the artwork in Preview mode, but you can have multiple windows open with different views of a file. One window can show the image in Artwork Only mode, and the other window can show the image in Preview mode. The window containing the preview image is updated whenever you make changes to the artwork (see also New Window).

You can use the Hand tool, Zoom tool, Measure tool, and Page tool in the Preview mode.

Warning   Working with a Preview window open may slow down processing as you work.

Tips   You will use this command so frequently that you should learn to use the keyboard shortcut, Command-Y.

If you wish to stop the page from previewing after you have invoked the Preview Illustration command, but before the screen has finished redrawing in Preview, press Command-(period).

92

Print...

Overview　　　The Print command prints the artwork in the active window to the printer that has been designated with the Chooser (see Chooser). The keyboard shortcut is Command-P.

Procedure　　　Choose Print... from the File menu, or press Command-P. Illustrator displays the Print dialog box, which is specific to the printer you select with the Chooser. The following figure shows the Print dialog box for an Apple LaserWriter Plus printer.

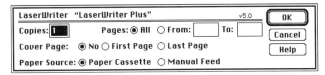

The Print dialog box for an Apple LaserWriter Plus printer

　　　The Copies setting lets you specify the number of copies you wish to print. The Pages settings let you print all pages (by selecting All), or a range of pages (by selecting From and To and specifying the range, for example, from 1 to 3). The page numbers are shown at the corners of pages bordered with dotted lines on the screen display of the artwork, as shown in the following figure.

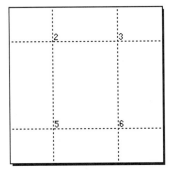

Page numbers shown on screen display

You can choose to print, as either first or last page, a Cover Page. The Cover Page will contain the user name (that you have entered in the Chooser), the application you used to print the document, the document name, the date and time of printing, and the printer name. You will find this feature useful in identifying your printouts when several computers share the same printer over an AppleTalk network. The Paper Source settings let you choose paper cassette or manual feed. By clicking on the Paper Cassette option, you choose to use the paper source in the printer's paper tray. If you click on the Manual Feed option, the system will prompt you to feed paper to the printer one page at a time. You can also choose Help from the Print dialog box. Click on the Help button to get more information on printer settings and options that affect your printed output. Help will display only if the Help files are loaded on your system.

Quit

Overview   The Quit command quits Adobe Illustrator and returns you to the desktop. The keyboard shortcut is Command-Q.

Procedure   Choose Quit from the File menu or press Command-Q. If you choose to quit Illustrator and have made changes since you last saved any file that is open, Illustrator asks you if you want to save that file, as shown in the figure below. If you click Yes, Illustrator saves the file using the artwork name in the title bar or, if the window is named Untitled art, Illustrator displays the Save As dialog box, prompting you to enter a new name for the file. Once you do this, Illustrator completes the Quit command, returning you to the desktop.

The Quit dialog box, asking if you want to save the file

Save

Overview   The Save command saves the latest version of the active Illustrator file. The keyboard shortcut is Command-S.

Procedure   Choose Save from the File menu or press Command-S. Illustrator saves the file that is in the active window using the same name as shown in the artwork portion of the title bar. If the Illustrator file name is Untitled art, Illustrator displays the Save As dialog box, prompting you to provide a new artwork file name. (See Save As).

   Illustrator saves the file on the current disk and leaves the active file window on the screen. If there is not enough room on the disk, Illustrator notifies you that you do not have enough room with an alert dialog box, and you can then choose Save As... from the File menu and save the file on another disk.

Warnings   The Save command always saves the artwork in Illustrator's default format. To save the artwork in a format that will preview as a graphic when you import it to a page composition application, you must always use the Save As command.

Tips   You should save frequently to prevent losing the work you have completed. At the very least, always save your work before you print. This is recommended because, when printing, the application accesses the AppleTalk network, thus becoming slightly more vulnerable to failure than when working locally on your Macintosh. And although system crashes may be rare, you can bet that the one system crash you experience per year will happen when you did not save your file and you have a critical deadline to meet. It is much easier to press Command-S frequently than to redraw your work.

Save As...

Overview   The Save As command saves the file in the active window under a new name or on a different disk or in a format that will display the artwork when it is imported into a page layout application. There is no keyboard shortcut for the Save As command.

Procedure   Choose Save As... from the File menu. Illustrator displays a dialog box, shown in the next figure, into which you enter the name for the file you wish to save and from which you specify the disk and file folder in which you wish the file to be saved. Illustrator saves the file and leaves the active file window on the screen so that you can continue working on it.

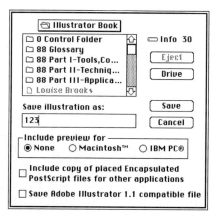

The Save As dialog box

There are five file formats that you can specify through the Save As dialog box. The three modes of Preview are mutually exclusive; that is, to save under more than one of these formats, you must save the file under a different name for each format. The last two options can be selected for any Preview format.

1. *Include preview for None* saves the file as a PostScript-only file, with minimum space requirements. This is the default file format in which the artwork is always saved when you use the Save

command. You can place files saved in this format in other Macintosh applications, such as PageMaker or Quark XPress. If you do this, the illustrations will be displayed on the screen as gray boxes, and you will not be able to see the artwork until you print on a PostScript printer. Artwork that displays as a gray box on the screen will also print as a gray box on dot-matrix printers, such as the ImageWriter.

2. *Include preview for Macintosh* saves the file in a format that you can still edit in Adobe Illustrator, and that will be displayed on the screen as artwork when placed in other Macintosh applications, such as PageMaker or Quark XPress. This format takes up more disk space than the Include preview for None (that is, PostScript-only) format. You select this format by clicking the Macintosh button.

3. *Include preview for IBM PC* saves the file in a format that you can still edit in Adobe Illustrator, but that you can also transfer to an MS-DOS system and place in MS-DOS applications, such as PageMaker and Ventura Publisher. To select this file format, click the IBM PC button. The artwork will be displayed on the screen as either artwork or a place-holding box, depending on the application. Both PageMaker for the PC and Ventura Publisher display the actual artwork. To transfer the Macintosh Illustrator file to the IBM PC, use a file transfer program such as MacLink (binary format), transfer the file over a network such as TOPS or Appleshare, or telecommunicate the file in binary format through modems.

4. *Include copy of placed Encapsulated PostScript files for other applications* includes in the File menu a copy of the EPS files you placed in your artwork using the Place command. To select this option, click in the box or anywhere on the label. A check mark appears indicating it is selected

5. *Save Adobe Illustrator 1.1 compatible file* saves the file in a format that can be opened by Illustrator 1.1. Effects that are not supported by version 1.1 will not preview (that is, display on the screen), but they will print out. To select this option, click in the checkbox or anywhere on the label.

Warnings   Whenever you use the Save command after saving a file the first time by selecting it from the File menu or pressing Command-S, Illustrator reverts to PostScript-only format. To save a file in any other format, you must use the Save As command every time you save, and specify the preferred format.

Tips   You can give an Illustrator file a name up to thirty characters long (including spaces), but the list of files displayed in the Open dialog box will display only the first twenty characters. It is a good idea to name related files with the same initial characters (so they will be grouped together in an alphabetical list), but be sure to differentiate between the names within the first twenty characters.

Select All

Overview   The Select All command selects all objects that are not locked or hidden. The keyboard shortcut is Command-A.

Procedure   Choose Select All from the Edit menu or press Command-A. All objects, except those hidden or locked, will be selected. You may then perform any action on them which will affect the objects as a group.

   The most obvious use of the Select All command is to select all of the elements of the artwork at once, especially if the artwork extends past the boundaries of the active window and you cannot select all by dragging the Selection tool.

Tip   When you wish to select most but not all of the objects in a file, it often saves time to use Select All, then deselect those objects you do not wish to be selected by holding down the Shift key and clicking on them.

Send To Back

Overview   The Send To Back command moves selected objects to the backmost
layer in the artwork. The keyboard shortcut is Command-(hyphen).

Procedure   Select the object(s) you wish to move to the back layer using any of
the techniques described under The Selection Tool, and choose Send
To Back from the Edit menu or press Command-(hyphen). If the
selection itself is composed of more than one layer, the selected
objects retain their relative positions in layers.
   (See Procedure and Warning in Bring To Front.)

Tips   Use this command to send an object that you wish to use as a mask
to the back, since the mask will not occur unless the path is the
backmost object. See the Mask option in the Paint description, and
see Masking a Mask in Part III.
   Also, use this command on the rectangle that defines a pattern,
since that rectangle must be the backmost object. (See Pattern. See
also Patterns: Methods 1–3 in Part III.)

Show All

Overview   The Show All command shows all parts of the artwork and deacti-
vates the Hide command for all hidden objects. The keyboard
shortcut is Command-4.

Procedure   Choose Show All from the Arrange menu or press Command-4 to
show hidden objects. When you choose this command, all hidden
objects display and are automatically selected. Previously selected
objects are deselected. If you have not hidden any objects, choosing
Show All has no effect.

Tips   To "glimpse" all hidden elements and then hide them again, choose
Show All (or press Command-4), then choose Hide (Command-3)
while the previously hidden objects are still selected, before clicking
any other selections. To add a group of elements to a hidden set, first

group the new elements, then choose Show All, Shift-click on the new group to add it to the selection, then choose Hide (see also Hide).

Show/Hide Clipboard

Overview   The Show/Hide Clipboard command opens (or closes) the Clipboard window and displays its contents.

Procedure   Choose Show Clipboard from the Window menu to make the contents of the Clipboard become the active window. This command becomes Hide Clipboard if the Clipboard is already the active window. Choose Hide Clipboard to hide the contents of the Clipboard, close the Clipboard window, and show the previously active window. You can also close the Clipboard window, or any active window, by clicking in the close box in the upper left corner of the window.

The phrase *<n> artwork objects* appears in the Clipboard window when you choose the Show Clipboard command, where *<n>* is the number of objects in the Clipboard. If you cut or copy any text into the Clipboard while editing text, the text itself appears in the Clipboard window. If you hold the Option key down while you use the Copy command, the Clipboard window displays a bitmapped version of the objects (see Copy for more details; see *bitmap* in the Glossary). You cannot edit the contents of the Clipboard window.

Illustrator uses the Clipboard as temporary storage for artwork or text that you cut, copy, or paste. Illustrator artwork objects from the Clipboard can be pasted only into an Illustrator file window. Text can be pasted only into the text area of a dialog box. The following figure shows how the Clipboard works as a temporary storage in memory for objects that you cut, copy, or paste.

Use the Copy command while holding down the Option key to place a bitmapped image of your Illustrator artwork into the Clipboard

To close the Clipboard, click the close box of the Clipboard window, choose Close from the File menu, or choose Hide Clipboard from the Window menu.

Tip   You can resize the Clipboard window and move it around the screen just like any other Mac window. This can be helpful if you want the Clipboard window always open but out of the way of your artwork.

Show/Hide Rulers

Overview   The Show/Hide Rulers command displays (or hides) rulers along the inside of the scroll bars in the active window. The keyboard shortcut is Command-R.

Procedure   When you choose Show Rulers from the View menu, two rulers appear, one along the bottom edge and one along the right edge of the window.

As you move the pointer, dotted lines in the rulers track your movements to indicate the current position. To remove rulers, choose Hide Rulers from the View menu or press Command-R.

Tips   Set the type of measurement system desired using Preferences... on the Edit menu (Inches, Centimeters, or Picas/Points). When the unit of measure is points (the default), the rulers display either picas or picas and points, depending on the zoom scale.

Show/Hide Toolbox

Overview   The Show/Hide Toolbox command shows (or hides) the Toolbox palette, which normally appears along the left side of the Illustrator screen.

Procedure   Hide the toolbox by choosing Hide Toolbox from the Window menu or by clicking the toolbox's close box. Display the toolbox by choosing Show Toolbox from the Window menu.

Tips   Hiding the toolbox lets you use the full screen for your drawing area. You can also move the toolbox around the screen by clicking on the top border of the toolbox window and dragging it with the mouse. (Note that you can choose the Selection tool, the Hand tool, and the Zoom tool from the keyboard as well as from the toolbox. See descriptions of those tools for details.)

Template Only

Overview   The Template Only command displays only the template in the active window.

Procedure   Choose Template Only from the View menu when you wish to examine a template without seeing your artwork.

Transform Again

Overview   The Transform Again command repeats the most recent transformation. The keyboard shortcut is Command-D. Transformations that can be repeated are those created using the Scale, Rotate, Reflect, and

Shear tools. Moving of objects can also be repeated using Transform Again. Blending cannot be transformed again. If the last transformation also made a copy of the object, Transform Again will transform and make another copy.

Procedure　　After transforming an object, choose Transform Again from the Arrange menu or press Command-D to repeat the transformation.

There are numerous applications for Transform Again. For example, you can draw a single object, use the Rotate tool to rotate a copy around a central point, then press Command-D as many times as needed to make a radially symmetrical object. (See also The Rotate Tool and Radial Symmetry: Methods 1 and 2 in Part III for examples of objects created this way.)

In another common application, you can draw a single object, use the Scale tool to scale a slightly smaller copy inside the first object's closed path, then use Paint… from the Style menu to set a lighter fill for the second object. Press Command-D as many times as you need to make a series of progressively smaller objects of the same shape, each time following Command-D with Command-I (for the Paint command). You can intersperse other commands with Command-D in this way, as long as only one of the commands is a transformation, such as Scale, Rotate, Reflect, Shear, or Move. (See also The Scale Tool for examples of objects shaded in this way, The Blend Tool, and Highlights in Part III.)

Tip　　Each newly transformed copy will appear on the top layer of the artwork. When creating a series of objects, always start with the one that will end up on the bottom layer.

Type

Overview　　The Type command displays the Type dialog box, shown in the next figure, which is the same dialog box that Illustrator displays when you add new type with the Type tool. The Type dialog box lets you specify the font style, size, leading, spacing, and alignment of selected type, and type text in the bottom box. The keyboard shortcut is Command-T.

Procedure   Choose the Type tool and click on the page to type a new text block; the Type dialog box appears automatically. To edit existing text, select a text block or blocks using any of the techniques described under The Selection Tool, then choose Type... from the Style menu or press Command-T to display the Type dialog box.

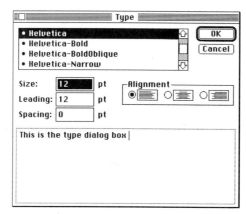

The Type dialog box

   If you choose Type... from the Style menu when only one type block is selected, you can also edit the text in the text box at the bottom of the Type dialog box. If you choose Type... when more than one type block is selected, you can globally change the font, style, size, leading, spacing, or alignment for all selected blocks, but you cannot edit the text in any of the type blocks.
   Refer to The Type Tool in Part I for details on the various options of the Type dialog box.

Undo/Redo

Overview   The Undo/Redo command reverses the last operation you performed. The keyboard shortcut is Command-Z.

Procedure   Choose Undo or Redo from the Edit menu or press Command-Z. The text of the command that is displayed in the menu varies depending on the last operation. If the operation can be undone, the Undo command becomes *Undo*, followed by the name of the action—for example, *Undo Clear*. If the action cannot be undone, Undo appears dimmed, indicating that the Undo command is disabled.

Examples of the Undo command

After you undo an action, the Undo command becomes *Redo*, followed by the name of the action—for example, *Redo Clear*. This way, you can redo undone actions. The specific Undo/Redo command remains on the Edit menu until you choose another command.

Ungroup

Overview   The Ungroup command breaks a group into independent objects, ungrouped paths, or subgroups (if a group has grouped objects within it). The keyboard shortcut is Command-U.

Procedure   Select a grouped path or a group of objects with the Selection tool, and choose Ungroup from the Arrange menu or press Command-U. If a group consists of other grouped objects, you must ungroup the subgroups repeatedly to reduce them into individual objects.

Tip   If you draw objects with the Rectangle tool or Oval tool, you must ungroup them in order to move individual anchor points. You do this by selecting Ungroup from the Arrange menu or by pressing Command-U.

Unlock All

Overview   The Unlock All command unlocks all locked objects so they can be selected and modified. The keyboard shortcut is Command-2.

Procedure   Choose Unlock All from the Arrange menu or press Command-2. This action unlocks all locked objects and automatically selects them. You do not need to select objects before unlocking them. Previously selected objects are deselected. If you have not locked any objects, Unlock All has no effect.

Tips   If you inadvertently select the Unlock All command, immediately select Lock again (see also Lock). Since invoking Unlock All results in all locked objects being selected, this quick recovery makes it easy to restore the locked status of the selected objects.

Window Titles

Overview   The last section of the Window menu contains a list of all currently open windows. Selecting a window name from the menu places a check mark beside its name in the Window menu, and makes that window the active window.

Procedure   Using the usual techniques of selecting from a menu, choose the name of the window you wish to make active from the Window menu.

Tip   If you can see part of a window behind the active window, you can activate it by clicking on it on the screen; you need not use the Window menu.

Part III:
Techniques

Introduction to Techniques

This part of the book presents over fifty different techniques for achieving specific effects that can be applied to a wide range of applications. Variations of these techniques can be used to create the particular effects you wish to apply in your own artwork.

The techniques are divided into six basic categories:

CATEGORY	DESCRIPTION
Alignment	Techniques for aligning objects, measuring objects, and creating grids as backgrounds for artwork that requires careful alignment.
Fills and Patterns	Techniques for creating custom fill patterns, blending colors, and using a custom paint palette for quickly selecting the fill and stroke settings you want to use repeatedly in developing complex or multiple pages of artwork.
Layering	Techniques for working in layers, including creating compound lines, hiding parts of artwork, masking, and creating overlays.
Lines	Techniques for creating dotted lines, lines with a hand-drawn look, and parallel curves.
Shapes	Techniques for creating arrows, bar charts, organization charts, pie charts, polygons, symmetrical designs, objects that share irregular borders, star shapes, and solid objects with "see-through" holes cut out of the center.
Three-Dimensional Effects	Techniques for drawing cubes, coils, drop shadows, flowers, and highlights.

Within each of these categories, you will find each technique listed alphabetically. The results of each technique are shown at the top outside corner of each page for easy reference, and you can use the Quick Reference Guide at the back of the book to look up a specific technique by name.

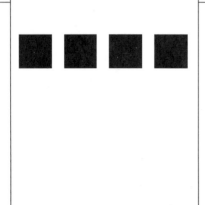

Alignment

Aligning Objects: Method 1

There are two approaches to aligning objects: (1) aligning them as you create them (described here), and (2) aligning them after you create them (described in the next technique).

Any illustration that is composed of more than one object, such as the series of squares illustrated in the accompanying figure, probably calls for careful alignment procedures.

There are two strategies you can use to align objects. The first strategy is to drag the first object while holding both the Shift key (to force alignment along the horizontal or vertical axis) and the Option key (to create a copy of the object). You may then edit the copied object if you desire.

1

Create the first object using whatever tool is appropriate (Freehand tool, Autotrace tool, Pen tool, Text tool, Rectangle tool, or Oval tool). For example, use the Rectangle tool to create a rectangular object, as shown in the figure on the left.

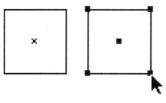

2

If subsequent objects are to be identical, drag the first object to the new position, and hold the Shift and Option keys to align and copy the object as you release the mouse button.

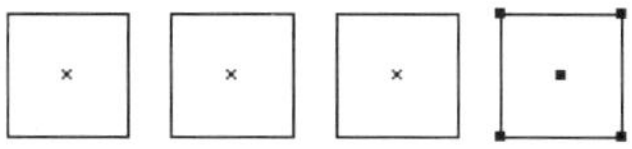

3

Select Transform Again from the Arrange menu (Command-D) to align another copy of the object the same relative distance apart. Press Command-D for each additional copy you wish to make.

4

Modify the copied objects as appropriate *after* you have used the Transform Again command.

5

Once you have positioned all of the objects, you can select them all and use the Group command under the Arrange menu (Command-G) to group them and thereby keep them in alignment when you want to move them as a unit.

See also Aligning Objects: Method 2, Aligning Text: Methods 1 and 2, and Tabular Text.

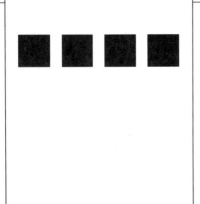

Aligning Objects: Method 2

The second strategy for aligning objects, to align objects after you create them, is to draw nonprinting guidelines on the page. You can also use this technique to align scissor cuts when cutting an object in half.

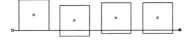

1

Create the objects using whatever tools are appropriate, positioning them roughly where you wish them to be on the screen.

The figure on the left shows four squares created with the Rectangle tool. Notice that they are not exactly aligned.

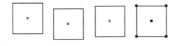

2

Use the Pen tool with the Shift key to draw a straight line along the axis of alignment you want the objects to be on. Choose Paint... from the Style menu (Command-I), and set the Fill and Stroke options to None. Click the OK button.

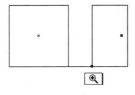

3

Select the Zoom tool (or hold down the Command key and Spacebar) and click on the objects you wish to align, to invoke a magnified view. Press the Command key to get the Selection tool, and drag each object to touch the alignment axis.

4

Once you have positioned all of the objects, you can select them all and use the Group command under the Arrange menu (Command-G) to group them and thereby keep them in alignment when you want to move them as a unit.

See also Grid: Methods 1–4.

Text

Text

Text

Aligning Text: Method 1

There are two issues involved in aligning text: (1) alignment along the same vertical grid line, and (2) alignment of two successive text blocks that are part of the same paragraph (that is, making sure there is the same spacing between blocks as between lines). This technique covers both cases.

This technique is especially useful when you need to create blocks of text that are longer than 255 characters, which is the limit imposed by Adobe Illustrator.

The basic strategy in aligning text along a vertical grid is to drag the first block while holding both the Shift key (forcing alignment) and the Option key (creating a copy of the block). You can then edit the copied block. The trick to line spacing (leading) alignment between successive text blocks is to leave a blank line at the end of each block.

Text block with extra carriage return on last line

Text block with extra carriage return on last line

1

Select the Text tool and click on the screen where you wish the text to start. The Type dialog box appears. Type the first block of text in the text area at the bottom of the dialog box, leaving a blank line (an extra carriage return) at the end.

To create even line lengths in the final, printed text, press Return at about the same relative position of the Type dialog box after each block of text.

Click the OK button. Notice that the blank line at the end of the block is displayed as a small dot on the screen when the text block is selected.

By leaving more than one blank line at the end of a block, you can create additional spacing guides for positioning blocks that will appear two or more lines below the first block, or for positioning blocks of text that use larger type than the first block.

›Text block with
extra carriage
return on last
line
›Text block with
extra carriage
return on last
line
•

2

Hold down the Command key to get the Selection tool, and drag the text block down, positioning the text anchor point on the small dot that represents the blank line at the end of the first block. Hold the Shift and Option keys to align and copy the text as you release the mouse button.

›Text block with
extra carriage
return on last
line
›Changed second
block with extra
carriage return
on last line
•

3

Choose Type… from the Style menu (Command-T) to edit the new block of text and change the text content. Leave the blank line at the end of the text if you will be aligning more text blocks below this one.

4

Continue creating new blocks by copying and aligning the most recently changed block with the Option and Shift keys.

Warnings: Be sure to choose the correct type specifications (font size, style, and so on) before you perform this procedure. If you change the specifications of the blocks *after* you align them, you may have to realign each one.

115

Text

Text

Text

Aligning Text: Method 2

A second strategy for aligning text blocks after you create them is to use the Average command. This technique can be used to align a series of text blocks vertically or horizontally. The technique cannot be used to adjust the spacing between text blocks.

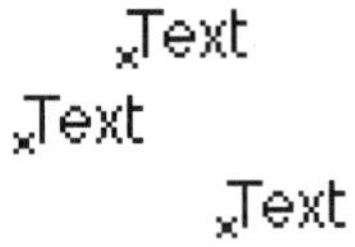

Text
Text
Text

1

Create the text blocks using the Type tool, roughly positioning them where you wish them to be on the screen.

The figure on the left shows three separate text blocks. Notice that they are not exactly aligned.

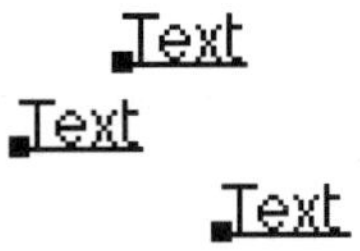

Text
Text
Text

2

Select all of the text blocks using the Selection tool or the Select All command under the Edit menu (Command-A), or by dragging the selection marquee around the baselines of the type (see The Selection Tool).

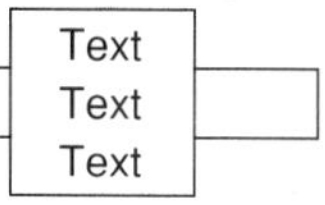

Text
Text
Text

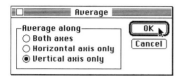

Text

Text

Text

3

With all of the text blocks selected, choose Average… from the Arrange menu (Command-L). In the Average dialog box, click Horizontal axis only if the text blocks are already arranged beside each other; or click Vertical axis only if the text blocks are already arranged one above the other; then click OK or press Return to close the dialog box and align the text blocks.

See also Average in Part II, and Aligning Objects: Methods 1 and 2 and Grid: Methods 1–4 in Part III.

117

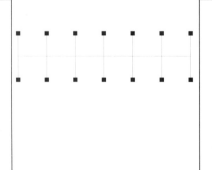

Dividing Equally

You may find that it is necessary to divide a shape or a line into a specific number of segments. Even dividing something in half can be difficult if you rely on the rulers or the Measure tool as your only aids. With the following technique, you do not need to actually calculate the divisions; Illustrator 88 does it for you.

Common applications for this technique include dividing lines and shapes for illustrating statistical data or creating grids and guidelines for templates and artwork. This is also an easy way to create tick marks (as in the example shown here) for charts or forms.

1

For this demonstration, first use the Pen tool with the Shift key to draw a horizontal line of any length. This is the line you will divide into equal segments.

2

Select the Pen tool and draw a short vertical line. With the Snap to point option turned on, snap this vertical line to one endpoint of the horizontal line. Hold down the Command key to get the Selection tool and drag this vertical line to the opposite endpoint of the horizontal line and snap once again, holding down both the Shift key (to align the second tick relative to the first tick along the horizontal axis) and the Option key (to create a copy) as you release the mouse button.

3

Using the Selection tool, Option-Shift-click both vertical lines to select both lines and their anchor points.

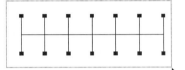

4

Choose the Blend tool and click once on the top point of each of the vertical lines. When the Blend dialog box appears, type in a number that is one less than the number of parts you would like. For example, if you would like to divide the line into six equal parts, type in 5 for number of steps. Click OK. In this example, five tick marks are added at six equal intervals between the two endpoint tick marks.

This procedure adds tick marks but does not actually break the horizontal line into segments. If you want to break up the horizontal line into separate parts, you can use the Scissors tool.

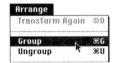

5

If the divisions look correct, drag the marquee over all of the lines and choose Group from the Arrange menu (Command-G). This way the tick marks will retain their relative positions if you move them later.

See also The Measure Tool, Measuring with a Point, and Grid: Methods 1–4.

119

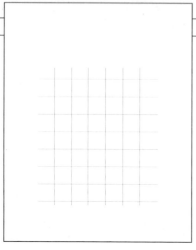

Grid: Method 1
Quadrille Rules

Often you will need to have an accurate grid or guidelines to follow in an illustration. For instance, some artists like to create custom perspective guidelines and use them as templates. Or maybe you have a custom grid for your newsletter.

If you have a drawing of the grid or guidelines and you have a scanner, you can scan the printed grid and use the scanned template as a background while you work. But you may find the lines on a scanned template are too coarse for your needs. Using the grid as the template also precludes using other images as the template.

This grid technique shows you how to create a grid of squared rules at a scale you choose. You can use this type of grid as a template for any illustrations that require a squared grid for alignment.

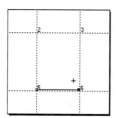

1

Select the Pen tool and hold down the Shift key as you click the mouse on two endpoints to draw a straight horizontal line across the bottom of the page, as shown in the figure on the left.

Note that in steps 1 and 3, the page area can be the entire 18-inch Illustrator page, or the smaller paper size (8 1/2-by-11). For large pages, perform steps 1 and 3 in the Fit In Window view, which you select from the View menu or by pressing Command-M.

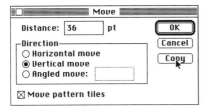

2

Hold down the Command key to get the Selection tool, and Option-click on the line to select the entire path. Option-click the Selection tool in the toolbox to get the Move dialog box. Select Vertical move by clicking this option, and enter a value in the Distance box (in points) that matches your desired grid size—for example, 36 points (one-half inch). Click Copy to close the box and make a copy of the first line.

Use Tranform Again (Command-D) as many times as you need to fill the image area with grid lines.

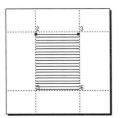

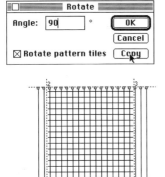

3

Choose Select All from the Edit menu (Command-A), then select the Rotate tool and Option-click on the center of the grid to get the Rotate dialog box. Type 90 (degrees) in the Angle box, and click Copy to close the box and rotate a copy of the horizontal lines, to create a vertical grid.

121

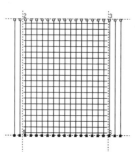

4

While the vertical grid lines are still selected, move them if necessary to center over the horizontal grid lines.

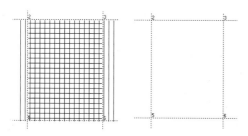

5

Choose Select All from the Edit menu (Command-A), then choose the Group command from the Arrange menu (Command-G) to make the grid a single object. Use Paint... from the Style menu (Command-I) to set the Stroke and Fill options to None. The lines will display in Artwork views, but will not display in Preview or on printed versions.

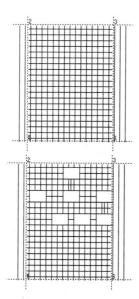

6

Use the Lock command in the Arrange menu (Command-1) to lock the grid in place so it will not be selected or moved as you work. Save the grid as a boilerplate document that you can use repeatedly.

When you open the master to start a new document, use the Save As command (from the File menu) to give it a new name so the original grid boilerplate document will remain unchanged.

Tips: Keep the grouped grid lines locked in place while you are working, so they will not be selected or moved. As you finish other elements of the illustration, you can use Unlock All (Command-2) to unlock the grid, then select the grid and the finished elements, use Lock (Command-1) to lock the selections, and continue working.

Using the grid as part of the artwork will give you the possibility of more precision in positioning objects relative to the grid, but it will also increase the overall size of files. You can reduce file size by deleting the grid when the artwork is finished.

See also Grid: Method 4.

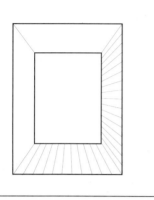

Grid: Method 2
Perspective

Grid: Method 1 showed you how to create a simple squared grid. This technique enables you to create a grid that shows perspective, like the one shown in the accompanying figure.

You can use this grid as a template for any illustrations that show three-dimensional perspective of single objects, or for several objects that will appear to be standing beside each other.

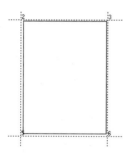

1

Use the Rectangle tool to draw a rectangle the size of the finished illustration. In the figure on the left, the size of the rectangle is the size of the page. Use the Ungroup command (Command-U) to ungroup the rectangle, and delete the center point by selecting it and pressing the Delete or Backspace key.

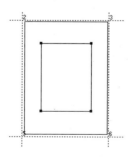

2

Use the Scale tool to make one smaller copy of the rectangle (see The Scale Tool in Part I). Position the smaller rectangle inside the first rectangle.

The smaller the copy, the deeper the perspective will seem. Also, the positioning of the smaller rectangle will determine the viewer's perspective.

124

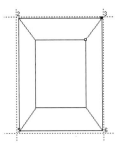

3

Use the Pen tool with the Shift key to connect corresponding corners of each rectangle with straight lines, as shown in the figure on the left.

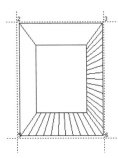

4

Use the Blend tool to add more grid lines for depth (see The Blend Tool in Part I). To keep the grid as simple as possible, add grid lines only to two sides, such as the bottom and right sides of the field, as shown in the figure on the left.

Select All (Command-A), use the Paint command (Command-I) to set Fill and Stroke to None, and use the Lock command (Command-l) to hold the grid in place as you work.

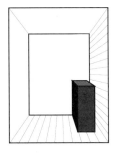

5

In drawing three-dimensional objects, use the diagonal depth lines as guides in drawing the side walls of the object, but maintain horizontal and vertical lines for the front face of the object. For example, in the figure on the left, the front and back faces are normal rectangles, but the side walls follow diagonal grid lines.

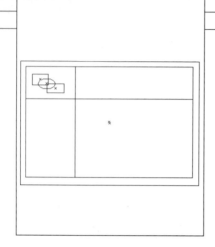

Grid: Method 3
Page Layout

You can use the grid shown in the accompanying figure in creating a series of illustrations that must all conform to the same page layout specifications. Then use this grid as a template for creating each document.

You can use this technique to create any template system for consistent page layout, such as a series of ads, a series of overheads or slides, or a series of charts.

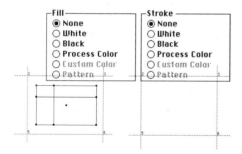

1

Determine the basic "grid" of the page layout and sketch it with the Pen tool and/or the Rectangle tool.

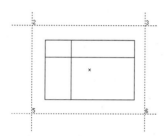

2

Use the Select All command and the Group command from the Arrange menu to make the grid a single object. Use the Paint command to set the Stroke and Fill options of the Paint dialog box to None. The lines will display in Artwork views but not in Preview or on printed versions.

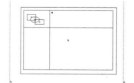

3

Add ruled lines and standing text that are intended to print on every page. Use Select All (Command-A) and Lock (Command-1) to lock the grid in place so it will not be selected or moved as you work.

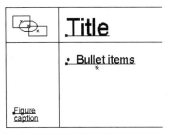

4

Add dummy text blocks that will change on each page, and move them into their fixed positions. The figure on the left shows dummy text blocks. Grid lines show in Artwork view, but do not print or display in Preview.

The content of the dummy text blocks will be altered for each page, but their positioning will not.

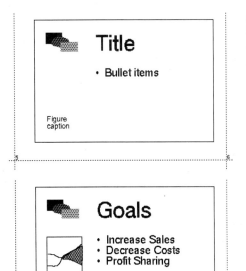

5

Save the grid as a boilerplate document that you can use repeatedly.

Tip: When you open the boilerplate to start a new document, immediately use Save As… from the File menu to give it a new name so the original grid boilerplate document will remain unchanged.

See also Spacing Guides.

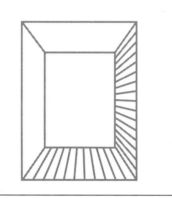

Grid: Method 4
Grid Templates

A template document is a bitmap image or PICT format image that you can trace over in Adobe Illustrator. The bitmap or PICT image can be displayed on the screen, with or without the artwork, but it will not display or print out with the finished artwork.

The most common use of a template is as an image that will be traced or used as a basis for creating an illustration. A template can also be used as a grid—to be used as a guide for positioning objects rather than to be traced.

Sources of bitmap images include: scanned images, images created in a paint program, screen shots (created by pressing Command-Shift-3), and Illustrator artwork copied to the Clipboard in bitmap format (and then pasted into a drawing application that supports bitmap or PICT format, to be saved as a template).

The technique described here can be used to convert Adobe Illustrator artwork into a bitmap format that can serve as a grid template.

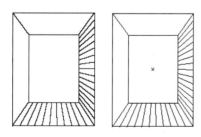

1

Create a grid using one of the techniques described in the previous three sections, but instead of setting Fill and Stroke to None in the Paint dialog box (Command-I), set Stroke to Black and Fill to None. The lines in this case will display in Preview and will print out.

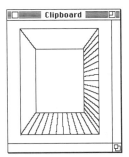

2

Use Select All (Command-A) and Option-Copy to create a bitmap version of the document in the Clipboard. (In other words, hold down the Option key and choose the Copy command.)

3

Then quit Adobe Illustrator, and open a drawing application that supports bitmap or PICT format (such as MacDraw or SuperPaint). Next, using the Paste command (Command-V), paste the bitmap version of the grid from the Clipboard into the drawing application, and save it as Grid Template.

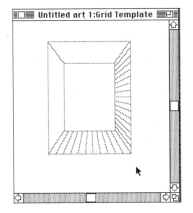

4

Whenever you want to use this grid as a background for artwork, open a new Illustrator document and select Grid Template as the template.

Tips: Using the grid as a template, rather than as part of the Illustrator artwork (as described in the previous three techniques), will keep the file size small, but you will not be able to trace other templates while the grid template is in use.

A template can be a bitmap or PICT document that will in fact eventually be merged with the Illustrator artwork (through a page composition application, for instance). This can be useful if the two images must overlap or share the same scale in the final printing.

129

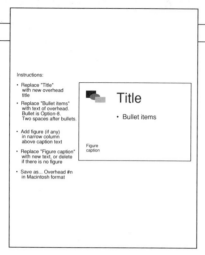

"Hidden" Notes

In working with complex illustrations that involve many grouped objects and layers, you can type notes about how the file is organized for your own reference or for others who might need to edit the artwork later.

This technique is especially useful if you are working in a group where work on a single illustration is shared among several people, or when you are working on many different, complex illustrations that you must modify over a period of time. Hidden notes can also be helpful on a boilerplate document that will be "cloned" to create many illustrations in a series, as in this example.

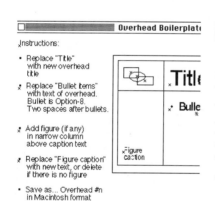

1

Use the Type tool to type notes (such as instructions about alignment or how the artwork is organized) as text, directly on the artwork. These can be typed in one area on a page of the document that is not used by the artwork, or they can be scattered around on the artwork, with each note close to the object(s) it addresses.

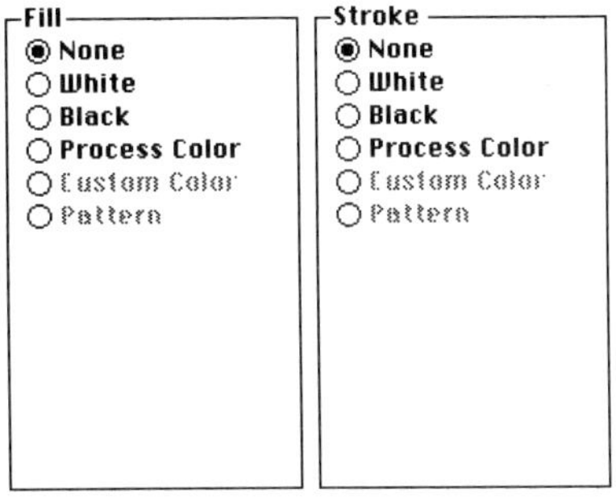

Instructions:
• Replace "Title" with new overhead title
• Replace "Bullet Items" with text of overhead.

Fill
- ◉ None
- ○ White
- ○ Black
- ○ Process Color
- ○ Custom Color
- ○ Pattern

Stroke
- ◉ None
- ○ White
- ○ Black
- ○ Process Color
- ○ Custom Color
- ○ Pattern

2

Select all notes, group them (Command-G), and use the Paint command (Command-I) to give them a Fill and Stroke of None so they do not print out as part of the artwork.

If the notes are grouped, you can easily change the paint specifications from Fill Black (for drafts on which the notes will print out) to Fill None (so the notes will not print out).

Tip: Use a small font that is easy to read on the screen. To fit many notes in a small space, you can make the font as small as 1 point so the notes will be readable on the screen only at the highest magnification.

■ 1 inch ■

Measuring with a Point

Here is a quick and effective way to measure distance and angle. It is the only way to measure in Illustrator 1.1, and it is a great supplement to Illustrator's Measure tool.

You can use this technique on any artwork. By keeping your measuring point handy, you will not need to select the Measure tool.

1

Create a single anchor point by clicking the Pen tool once on the page, as the figure on the left shows. This point will be your measuring point.

2

Using the Selection tool, click on and move the point to a starting place for measuring, as shown in the figure on the left. You can measure an actual object you have drawn or measure empty space in the drawing window.

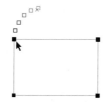

3

Select the point again and move it across the page the distance you would like to measure. If you are measuring a horizontal or vertical distance, hold down the Shift key to constrain your movement and measurement along 45° angles.

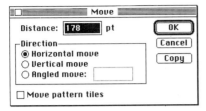

4

Option-click on the Selection tool to view the Move dialog box. The distance and angle that you moved the point will be shown here.

See also The Measure Tool in Part I and Grid: Methods 1–4.

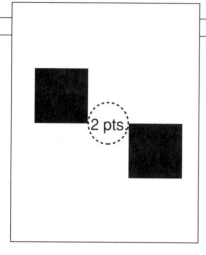

Spacing Guides

It is a good idea to apply consistent standards for spacing between objects in an illustration. Here is one technique that supplements the Measure tool by storing the spacing information, as part of the artwork, in the form of a graphic object with Fill and Stroke of None.

This technique is especially useful when you need to create a series of illustrations that meet consistent standards for spacing between objects or between graphic elements and text elements.

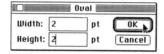

1

Select the Oval tool and click once in the active window to get the Oval dialog box. Enter the same value for the Height and Width of the oval, to draw a perfect circle. The value should match the space that you wish to make consistent between objects.

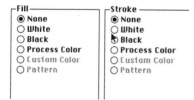

2

Choose Paint... from the Style menu (Command-I). Set the Stroke and Fill options of the circle to None. This way you can keep the circle as part of the artwork but it will not display in Preview or print out. Click OK to close the dialog box.

134

3

Whenever you need to position two objects next to each other, drag the circle to meet one edge of one object, then bring the second object to meet the opposite edge of the circle.

4

If you need more than one spacing guide to measure different distances, type a text label for each guide using the Text tool, group the label with the circle by selecting the guide object and the text and choosing Group from the Arrange menu (Command-G), and set the Stroke and Fill of the text to None using Paint… from the Style menu (Command-I).

Tips: By using a circle instead of a line or a rectangle as a measuring guide, you can measure distances consistently at any angle—not only vertical and horizontal distances.

See also Grid: Methods 1–4, Measuring with a Point, The Measure Tool, "Hidden" Notes.

Year	Sales	%	Goals Met
1986	15,356	16%	NO
1987	21,872	19%	YES
1988	29,845	23%	YES

Tabular Text

Adobe Illustrator does not have tab settings as word processors do, but the technique described here can be used to create the appearance of tabular material. The different columns of text need not be set in the same font.

This technique is useful whenever you need to create columns and rows of text that are aligned horizontally as well as vertically.

The basic strategy in setting up columns of text is to create the column that will use the largest font first, and then copy that column and change the type specifications (if necessary) to create all other columns.

1986
1987
1988

1

Select the Type tool and click on the screen where you wish the text to start. The Type dialog box appears. Type the first column of text in the text area at the bottom of the dialog box. Set the alignment to left, centered, or right, as appropriate for this column, then click OK to close the dialog box and see the text displayed on the screen.

See Aligning Text: Method 1 for a description of setting up columns that call for more than 255 characters.

1986   1986
1987   1987
1988   1988

2

Hold down the Command key to get the Selection tool, and drag the text block to the right to form the second column. Hold the Shift and Option keys to align and copy the text as you release the mouse button.

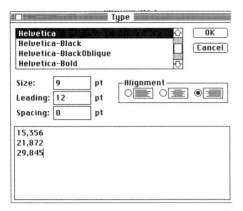

Year	Sales
1986	15,356
1987	21,872
1988	29,845

3

Choose Type… from the Style menu (Command-T) to edit the new block of text and change the text content. You can change alignment (left, centered, right) and the font and the point size of the type, but do not change the leading between lines if you wish to maintain horizontal alignment between columns of text.

1986	15,356	16%	NO
1987	21,872	19%	YES
1988	29,845	23%	YES

4

Continue creating new columns by copying and aligning the last changed block with the Option and Shift keys, respectively.

Year	Sales	%	Goals Met
1986	15,356	16%	NO
1987	21,872	19%	YES
1988	29,845	23%	YES

5

After you have typed all columns, adjust the space between columns using the Selection tool with the Shift key depressed to drag each column left or right to refine the overall layout of the columns.

Tips: Be sure to set up the column with the largest font size before you go through this procedure. Otherwise, the lines of text might run into each other when you set up columns that call for larger type, and you will have to change the leading for all of the columns.

Once you have typed and aligned all of the text blocks, select them all and use the Group command under the Arrange menu (Command-G) to group them to keep them in alignment when you move them. You will need to ungroup the blocks to edit the text.

137

Text on a Curved Path

This technique uses the Rotate tool and the Transform Again command (Command-D) to set text along a curved path. In this section you will learn to set text along the boundary of a circle, as shown in the figure. But you can apply the technique to a path of any shape.

This technique is especially useful for logos, labels, maps, and other applications that require text to follow an arbitrary path.

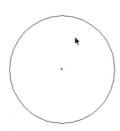

1

Use the Oval tool from the toolbox with the Shift key to draw a perfect circle. (Recall that the Shift key constrains the Oval tool to creating perfect circles.) The curvature of the circle should match that of the text you wish to create.

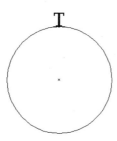

2

Choose the Type tool from the toolbox. Then click the text block pointer in the active window, so that the Type dialog box appears, with the blinking insertion point inside the text block. Type only one character and set it in the font you wish to use for the text. Then click on the center icon in the Alignment box to center the text block. Click OK, and center the text block by positioning it at the twelve o'clock position on the circle.

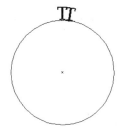

3

Select the text, then select the Rotate tool, Option-click the center of the circle, and the Rotate dialog box will appear. Click Copy. This action rotates the copy to the position for the next character.

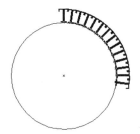

4

Use the Transform Again command from the Arrange menu (Command-D) to create as many text blocks as there are characters (including spaces) in the text string you wish to set. In this example, there are fourteen characters on the path, and the figure shows the character T rotated fourteen times.

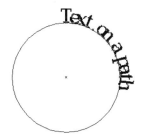

5

One by one, select each letter of the text, then choose Type... from the Style menu (Command-T). This brings up the Type dialog box. Edit each text block until you have the text string you want.

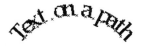

6

Using the Selection tool, select all the text blocks. Use the Rotate tool to rotate them about the center of the circle until the text is oriented the way you want it. Select the circle and ungroup it using the Ungroup command (Command-U), but leave the center point as a guide in case you have to make further adjustments.

Fills and Patterns

Blending Colors or Grays

You may want a color that is exactly halfway between two PMS colors, two process colors, or two gray fills. This technique uses the Blend tool to generate the color automatically. The result of the example you create here appears as shades of gray in the accompanying figure.

This is a good alternative to defining a new color numerically or visually through the Pattern dialog box (from the Style menu), especially if you do not have a color screen.

1

Draw two objects (closed paths) and use Paint... from the Style menu (Command-I) to assign them the two Fill colors (or grays) you wish to blend. In the figure on the left, the two rectangles are assigned different percentages of black fill. If you are using color, you must already know the cyan, magenta, yellow, and black percentages of the two starting colors, or use custom colors that have already been created (either your own custom colors or the PMS colors provided by Adobe).

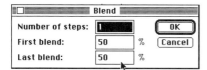

2

Select two corresponding points on each of the objects, and use the Blend tool to specify 1 (one) step of blending between your two colors. (See The Blend Tool in Part I. Remember that objects must be ungrouped in order to be blended.) By leaving the defaults, the first blend to 50 percent and the last blend to 50 percent, you will produce a new color that is exactly halfway along the spectrum between the two starting colors. This same procedure can be used to create automatically colors that are 1/3, 1/4, 1/5, or even 1/400 of each other simply by increasing the number of steps or by adjusting the percentages entered in the Blend dialog box.

Click OK in the Blend dialog box. The Blend tool will produce the midway color and fill a new object with that color automatically in the active window.

3

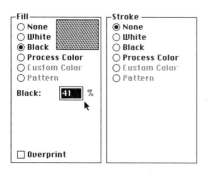

Select the new object created by the Blend tool using the Selection tool, then choose Paint… from the Style menu (Command-I) to view the cyan, magenta, yellow, and black percentage attributes of the new color fill.

See also Paint Palettes.

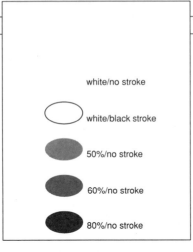

white/no stroke

white/black stroke

50%/no stroke

60%/no stroke

80%/no stroke

Paint Palettes

If you know that you will be using certain attributes—such as colors, fills, or stroke combinations—repeatedly in a drawing, it is useful to create a paint palette of your choices as part of the working artwork in your file. Before you draw a new object, you can set the paint attributes with a click and three keys: click, Command-I, Return.

This is a useful productivity aid when creating artwork that uses different paint attributes.

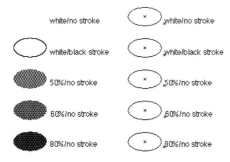

white/no stroke

white/black stroke

50%/no stroke

60%/no stroke

80%/no stroke

white/no stroke

white/black stroke

50%/no stroke

60%/no stroke

80%/no stroke

1

Draw a series of ovals with the Oval tool, and line them up off to the side of your drawing. Paint each oval with the paint attributes you want using Paint... from the Style menu (Command-I), and label each oval using the Text tool. In this example, five ovals are set up as the palette, each with different fill and stroke attributes: (1) white fill, no stroke; (2) white fill, black stroke; (3) 50 percent black fill, no stroke; (4) 60 percent black fill, no stroke; and (5) 80 percent black fill, no stroke.

2

Once this palette is set up, simply click on a palette oval to select it, choose Paint... from the Style menu (Command-I), and press Return. In other words, click, Command-I, Return. The next object you draw will have the attributes of the chosen palette oval.

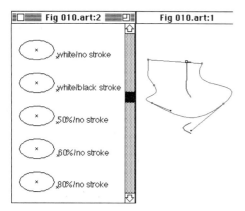

3

When working in close-up views of the artwork, you can keep the palette visible in a second open window. To do this, choose New Window from the Window menu. Size the windows so they do not overlap. The palette window can be small and show a reduced view of the palette artwork.

143

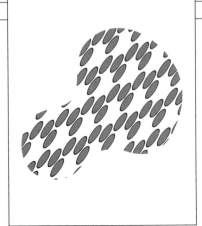

Patterns: Method 1
Discrete Objects

Pattern repeat and all its nuances can be a difficult concept. Until you can see the result of a simple graphic repeat, you are not sure it is what you want. With traditional pen-and-ink methods, creating a pattern repeat could be a costly and time-consuming exercise, often producing unexpected results. Adobe Illustrator 88 automatically generates repeating *tiles* of a pattern for you to see. The program does the tough work and all you have to do is decide whether you like the results.

Here is one example of how to build a simple pattern of geometric shapes. Besides creating your own custom fill patterns for charts or graphs or any shape, you can use Illustrator's pattern feature in designing fabrics or wallpapers.

1

Build a basic shape with one of the drawing tools. The figure on the left shows a circle shape customized in a particular color and stroke. This is the shape that will be repeated in a pattern.

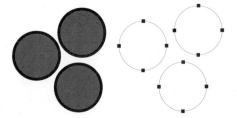

2

Repeat the shape by Option-dragging to make copies. The goal is to arrange a small area as the basic tile that will be repeated as a fill pattern later.

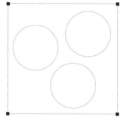

3

Using the Rectangle tool, draw a nonfilled, nonstroked rectangle over the area you would like to serve as a pattern fill. To have the repeat line up well, position your rectangle (called the *tiling rectangle*) to surround all of the graphics, without letting any graphic cross the border of the rectangle, and with the space between the rectangle and the graphics roughly half the space you intend between graphics when the pattern is used to fill a shape. (See Patterns: Method 2 for a description of how to create tiles with cross-over patterns.)

4

Send the tiling rectangle to the back by selecting it and choosing Send To Back from the Edit menu (Command-hyphen).

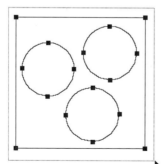

5

Select all the geometric shapes and the tiling rectangle by dragging the selection marquee over them (see The Selection Tool in Part I).

145

6

Choose Pattern… from the Style menu and click New to define the new pattern in the Pattern dialog box. You can use Illustrator's default pattern name (New Pattern 1), or type a name that you will recognize as describing this particular design. Click OK to close the dialog box and save the pattern.

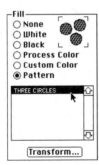

7

Now that you have created the pattern, you can fill any new shape with it by choosing Paint… from the Style menu (Command-I) and clicking Pattern under the Fill or Stroke option. The new pattern name should appear in the scrolling window that lists any patterns you have created in the current window or in any other artwork that is open in other windows.

8

In order to preview the pattern, you need to be sure that the Preview and print patterns option is checked in the Preferences dialog box. The default setting is *not* to Preview and print patterns (because patterns will slow screen processing time and printing time considerably), and when this option is off the Preview and printed versions will represent any pattern simply as a gray fill.

As a rule, you will want to work with the Preview and print patterns option on when you are creating a new pattern, but then turn it off while you work to build a complex illustration that uses the pattern.

9

You can edit the pattern by changing the artwork that you used originally to create the first pattern tile, then choosing Pattern… from the Style menu, selecting New, and giving the revised pattern a new name. You will have to use the Paint command (Command-I) to apply the revised pattern to the artwork. You cannot edit a pattern and change the artwork simultaneously (as you can with custom colors).

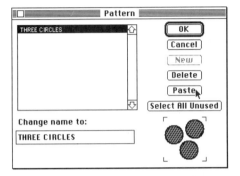

10

When you are satisfied with the pattern design, you can delete the tile artwork; the pattern will remain stored with the current file. If you want to edit the tile later, you can retrieve it by choosing Pattern... from the Style menu, selecting the pattern name from the list, and clicking Paste. This creates a copy of the original tile artwork, which you can edit to create a new pattern.

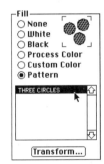

11

You can change many aspects of your fill without redrawing a tiling element. To do so, return to the Paint dialog box from the Style menu. Click Transform... at the bottom of the Fill box. After the Transform Pattern Style dialog box appears, as shown in the figure at the lower left, make any changes you would like to the pattern (such as changing the size of the geometrics or the angle of the pattern).

Warning: The Transform... button appears in the Paint dialog box only if a pattern has already been defined and the Pattern option is selected.

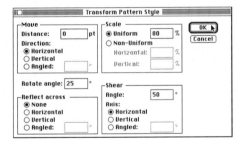

✓ Transform...

12

Click in the Transform Pattern Style dialog box. When you return to the Paint dialog box you will notice a check mark next to the Transform... button, indicating the pattern has been altered. Click in the active window and choose Preview Illustration from the View menu (Command-Y) to see the transformed pattern.

Tip: In this example we did not fill or stroke the tiling rectangle; this left our background transparent. To produce an opaque background, you can assign a color or fill to the tiling rectangle.

See also Patterns: Method 2.

Patterns: Method 2
Continuous Symmetry

The previous technique described how to create a simple pattern that is not continuous. In other words, the graphics of the pattern did not overlap the edges of the tiling rectangle. The process is a bit more complicated if you want to create continuous patterns, requiring that the graphics flow in a continuous connection from one tile to another. The technique described here can be used to create tiles that form a continuous, symmetrical pattern.

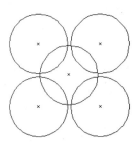

1

Create a symmetrical design with one of the drawing tools. A symmetrical design is one in which the top half is a mirror image of the bottom half, and the left half is a mirror image of the right half. The figure on the left shows a symmetrical design composed of five interlocking circles.

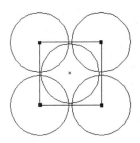

2

Using the Rectangle tool, draw a nonfilled, nonstroked rectangle over the area you would like to create as a pattern fill. To have the design cross over from one tile to another and line up well, position your rectangle so that its center point precisely matches the center of the symmetrical design. Send the tiling rectangle to the back by selecting it and choosing Send To Back from the Edit menu (Command-hyphen).

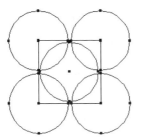

3

Select all the geometric shapes and the tiling rectangle by dragging the marquee over them or choosing Select All from the Edit menu (Command-A).

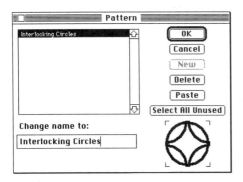

4

Choose Pattern... from the Style menu and click New to define the new pattern in the Pattern dialog box. You can use Illustrator's default pattern name (New Pattern 1), or type a name that you will recognize as describing this particular design. Click OK to close the dialog box and save the pattern.

5

Now that you have created the pattern, you can fill any new shape with the pattern by choosing Paint... from the Style menu (Command-I) and clicking Pattern under the Fill or Stroke option. The new pattern name appears in the window that lists patterns you have created in this or any other artwork that is open in other windows.

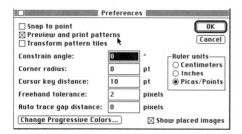

6

In order to preview the pattern, you need to be sure that the Preview and print patterns option is checked in the Preferences dialog box (Command-K).

Tip: As a general rule, you will want to work with the Preview and print patterns option on when you are creating a new pattern, but then turn it off while you work to build a complex illustration that uses the pattern.

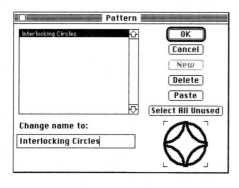

7

When you are satisfied with the pattern design, you can delete the tile artwork; the pattern will remain stored with the current file. If you want to edit the tile later, you can retrieve it by choosing Pattern… from the Style menu, selecting the pattern name from the list, and clicking Paste. This creates a copy of the original tile artwork, which you can edit to create a new variation.

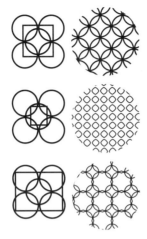

8

Edit the pattern by clicking Paste in the Pattern dialog box to copy the artwork that you used originally to create the first pattern tile, changing it, then choosing Pattern… from the Style menu and selecting New, giving the revised pattern a new name. Use the Paint command (Command-I) to apply the new pattern to the artwork. You cannot edit a pattern and change the artwork simultaneously (as you can with custom colors).

Notice that you can achieve different results in the overall pattern by changing the size of the rectangle. The figure at left shows three variations in the size of the rectangle and the resulting patterns.

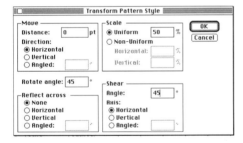

9

You can change many aspects of your fill without redrawing a tiling element. To do so, return to the Paint dialog box from the Style menu (Command-I). Click Transform… at the bottom of the Fill box. After the Transform Pattern Style dialog box appears, make any changes you would like to the pattern (such as the size of the geometrics or the angle of the pattern).

Click in the Transform Pattern Style dialog box. When you return to the Paint dialog box you will see a check mark next to the Transform button, indicating the pattern has been altered. Choose Preview Illustration from the View menu to see the transformed pattern.

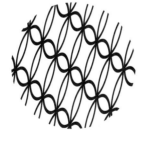

Tip: Create more intricate symmetrical designs by drawing one quadrant of the design and using the Reflect tool to create the other four quadrants.

153

Patterns: Method 3
Continuous Asymmetry

The previous technique described how to create a continuous, symmetrical pattern. The technique described here can be used to create a continuous pattern from an asymmetrical or amorphous design.

1

Create a design with one of the drawing tools. The figure at left shows a design composed of an amorphous shape.

2

Using the Rectangle tool, draw a nonfilled, nonstroked rectangle over the area you would like to serve as a pattern fill. Send the tiling rectangle to the back by selecting it and choosing Send To Back from the Edit menu (Command-hyphen).

The trick in this step is to make sure that the same number of lines cross the top of the tiling rectangle as cross the bottom, and that the same number of line segments cross the left edge of the tiling rectangle as cross the right edge. In other words, if the design crosses the top edge at three points, you want the bottom of the rectangle to be crossed at three points also.

Additional precautions are required if all the design elements do not share the same stroke and fill. For example, if three lines cross the top border and use three different strokes, then the three lines that cross the bottom border must have the same sequence of strokes.

If any fill patterns will be used, then the edges of any filled shape must cross over a border an even number of times and cross the same number of times on the opposing sides of the tiling rectangle.

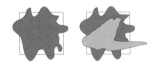

3

Next, make the lines that cross from one tile to the next meet. That is, you want lines that cross the left edge of the rectangle to match the vertical position of lines that cross the right edge, and lines that cross the top edge of the rectangle to match the horizontal position of lines that cross the bottom edge. You can move points visually on the screen.

Or, you can draw straight lines across the tile as guides for adjusting corresponding points, then delete the guidelines before going on to the next step.

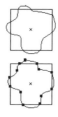

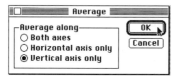

Or, you can adjust the design so that an anchor point falls anywhere the design crosses the tiling rectangle, or use the Scissors tool with the Option key to add anchor points to the line segments of the design where they cross the tiling rectangle. Then select corresponding pairs of endpoints on opposite sides of the tiling rectangle and choose Average... from the Arrange menu to move corresponding points from the left and right edges along the vertical axis and to move corresponding points from the top and bottom edges along the horizontal axis.

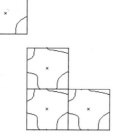

A fourth alternative is to use the Scissors tool to cut the line segments of the design where they cross the tiling rectangle and delete the segments that extend beyond the rectangle. Select the remaining design elements and the tiling rectangle by dragging the marquee over them, or choose Select All (Command-A), then use the Selection tool to Option-Shift-drag copies of the design and rectangle to form a matrix of three identical tiles, then move the endpoints of the lines that cross *two adjacent sides of the center tile* so they meet the ends of corresponding lines in the adjacent tiles. In this example, the endpoints along the top and right sides of the center tile have been dragged to meet the ends of lines in the adjoining tiles.

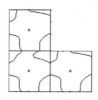

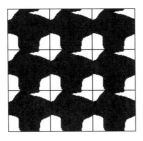

4

Regardless of which method is used in step 3, it is a good idea to check your tiles visually by selecting the whole design and the tiling rectangle, grouping the objects (Command-G), then Option-Shift-dragging copies to form a matrix of nine tiles on the screen to check the alignment of adjacent tiles and to preview the pattern. Besides verifying that the design lines up across tiles, you want to be sure that the fill patterns and strokes assigned to crossing lines match up. In this example, the Join command (Command-J) is used to connect the endpoints that cross each edge of the tile in order to create a solid shape with a fill.

5

When you have achieved the effect you want, delete all but one tile and design set, then select all the geometric shapes and the tiling rectangle by dragging the marquee over them, or choose Select All from the Edit menu (Command-A).

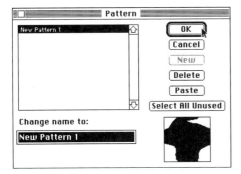

6

Choose Pattern… from the Style menu and click New to define the new pattern in the Pattern dialog box. You can use Illustrator's default pattern name (New Pattern 1), or type a name that you will recognize as describing this particular design. Click OK to close the dialog box and save the pattern.

157

7

Now that you have created the pattern, you can fill any new shape with the pattern by choosing Paint... from the Style menu (Command-I) and clicking Pattern under the Fill or Stroke option. The new pattern name should appear in the scrolling window that lists any patterns you have created in the current window or in any other artwork that is open in other windows.

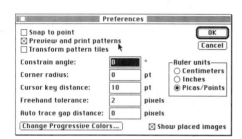

8

In order to preview the pattern, you need to be sure that the Preview and print patterns option is checked in the Preferences dialog box (Command-K).

Tip: As a general rule, you will want to work with the Preview and print patterns option on when you are creating a new pattern, but then turn it off while you work to build a complex illustration that uses the pattern.

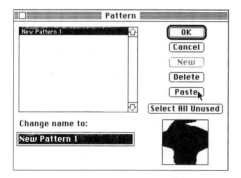

9

When you are satisfied with the pattern design, you can delete the tile artwork; the pattern will remain stored with the current file. If you want to edit the tile later, you can retrieve it by choosing Pattern from the Style menu, selecting the pattern name from the list, and clicking Paste. This creates a copy of the original tile artwork which you can edit to create a new pattern.

10

You can edit the pattern by pasting the artwork that you used originally to create the first pattern tile, changing it, then choosing Pattern... from the Style menu and selecting New, giving the revised pattern a new name. You will have to use the Paint command to apply the revised pattern to the artwork. You cannot edit a pattern and change the artwork simultaneously (as you can with custom colors).

11

You can change many aspects of your fill without redrawing a tiling element. To do so, return to the Paint dialog box from the Style menu (Command-I). Click on the Transform... button at the bottom of the Fill box. After the Transform Pattern Style dialog box appears, make any changes you would like to the pattern (such as the size of the geometrics or the angle of the pattern).

Then click in the Transform Pattern Style dialog box. When you return to the Paint dialog box you will notice a check mark next to the Transform... button, indicating the pattern has been altered. Click in the active window, and choose Preview Illustration from the View menu (Command-Y) to see the transformed pattern.

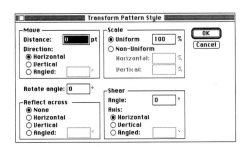

See also Patterns: Methods 1 and 2.

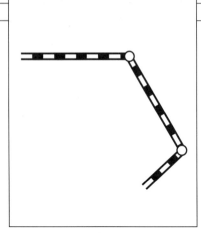

Layering

Compound Lines: Method 1

The distinguishing feature of the lines created by this technique (and the next technique) is that the lines appear to have a fill that is different from the stroke at the outer edge of the line. This makes the task of creating the effect shown in the accompanying figure a bit more complicated than using Illustrator's dashed line feature. The basic element of the compound line consists of two overlapping lines: a solid black line on the bottom layer, and a slightly thinner, dashed white line on top, as shown in the figure. This unit was created once then duplicated and pieced into routes on a map. There are really several approaches to this task. The method explained here is a "building block" approach; the method described in the next entry is a "systems" approach.

You can use these types of lines in maps to represent roads or trails or railway lines. You can also use them in line graphs, floor plans, and other schematic drawings. You can apply the same technique to the borders (strokes) of two-dimensional shapes (such as rectangles, circles, or polygons).

The building block technique is simply to create one short length of track composed of the two layered lines, and then assemble copies of it into extended routes.

1

With the Pen or Freehand tool, draw a short line—a manageable size for your basic building block. This should be close to the most common size you will need for a straight line of track in the system. Use Paint... from the Style menu (Command-I) to open the Paint dialog box, and set the attributes for this line to those you desire for the lower layer of the compound track. In this example, set Fill to None, Stroke to 100 percent Black, and Weight to 8 points, as shown in the figure. When you are done, click OK.

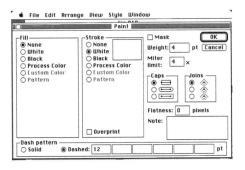

2

Select the line, if it is not already selected, copy it with Copy (Command-C), and use Paste In Front (Command-F) to add a copy of the line to the top layer. Choose Paint... (Command-I) to set the attributes for this line to those you desire for the upper layer of the compound track. The stroke weight should be lower than the bottom line.

In the example, set Fill to None, Stroke to White, and Weight to 4 points. Click on Dashed in the Dash pattern box, and type 12 in the first box to create a dashed line with 12-point dashes and 12-point spaces between dashes. Click OK when you are done.

Choose Preview Illustration from the View menu (Command-Y) to view the results. Then choose Artwork Only (Command-W) to continue working.

3

Option-drag over this basic building block to select it, and use the Selection tool and Option key to move copies into position along the path of the railway route (or whatever you are representing with the lines). Use the Rotate tool to change the angle of the line.

4

Drag over an endpoint to select one end of a straight line and stretch it or make it shorter. After you have finished editing, group the whole route using Group (Command-G). You must ungroup the lines using Ungroup (Command-U) if you later need to edit lines or to stretch copies of the basic set to different lengths.

5

Add circles for station markers at each bend in the path.

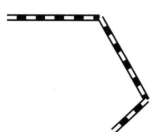

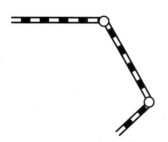

Warnings: Under this procedure you cannot globally change the attributes of the layers very easily, but it is easy to add, delete, or move part of a route.

See Compound Lines: Method 2, the next technique, for creating lines that can be globally edited.

Tips: Create and print a test sheet to determine what attribute combinations would look best in the size you will use in the final artwork. In the figure at left, the top line was created with 2-point dashes, the bottom line with 12-point dashes, and the variations between were created with the Blend tool.

See Dotted Lines, Parallel Curves, and the Osaka Railway Map.

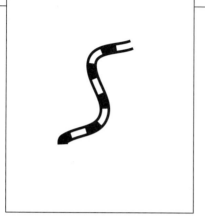

Compound Lines: Method 2

You can use the technique described here to create the same types of compound lines as described in the previous technique. However, this technique, unlike the previous, yields a system of lines that you can edit globally (that is, the paint attributes of the lines can be easily changed). In this example, you will create another roadmap route, as shown in the accompanying figure.

1

Draw the bottom layer of the whole path (such as a train line on a map) in one sweep with the Pen tool, then use the Paint command (Command-I) to set the attributes of the lower line. The bottom layer in this example has the attributes of 100 percent black stroke, no fill, and 8-point weight.

2

Choose Copy (Command-C) to copy the bottom layer, and Paste In Front from the Edit menu (Command-F). Set the second line's attributes by selecting Paint… from the Style menu (Command-I). In this example we use a 4-point weight line with a white stroke and 12-point dashes and gaps.

3

To select the two lines (if you need to move them), hold the Option key down as you use the Selection tool to drag a selection marquee across any part of the layered lines (see The Selection Tool in Part I).

Note that you can group the layered lines using Group (Command-G) but you will not be able to change the attributes of the lines globally unless you ungroup them (Command-U) and select layers one by one.

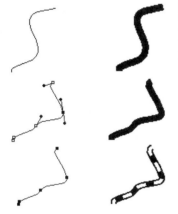

4

If you want to add, delete, or move part of a route, select the route lines and ungroup (Command-U) the two layers (if they are grouped), then Option-click on the top layer to select it and press the Backspace or Delete key to remove it. Then edit the bottom layer.

Copy the bottom layer (Command-C) to the Clipboard and use Paste In Front (Command-F). Use the Paint command (Command-I) to set the attributes to a white dashed line.

Warnings: Under this procedure, you cannot very easily add, delete, or move part of a route. This procedure is better for global editing of the stroke attributes. See the previous technique, Compound Lines: Method 1, for creating lines that can be broken up easily.

See also Compound Lines: Method 1.

Hiding Parts of Artwork

You can hide whole objects or groups of objects using Illustrator's Hide command, and you can make whole paths "invisible" in Preview and on the printout by setting the Fill and Stroke to None, but what if you want to hide *part* of a path? If the path is assigned a Fill, you can get unwanted results if you simply cut away and delete part of the path. If you use a mask, you can hide only the outer edges of the artwork. The technique described here can be used to cover up part of an object or group of objects using a method similar to painting white opaque paint over inked artwork.

This technique can be used to hide parts of an object that would otherwise be difficult to cut up (in order to delete parts), to hide work-area elements such as notes to the artist, and to hide portions of artwork that extend beyond a desired border. It can also be used to create special effects such as the wash-out in this example.

1

Create artwork composed of one or more elements. In this example the artwork is composed of a circle and a square created with the Oval tool and the Rectangle tool (respectively).

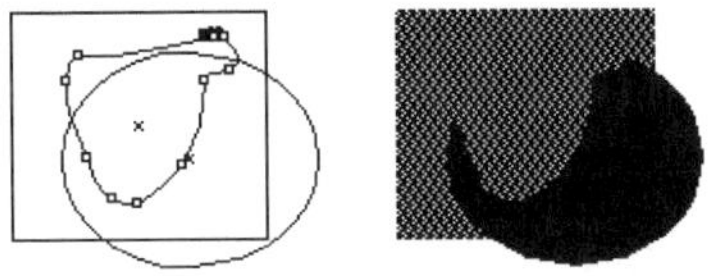

2

Use one of the drawing tools to draw an outline around the area you wish to conceal. In this example the Freehand tool is used to create an amorphous outline around part of the artwork.

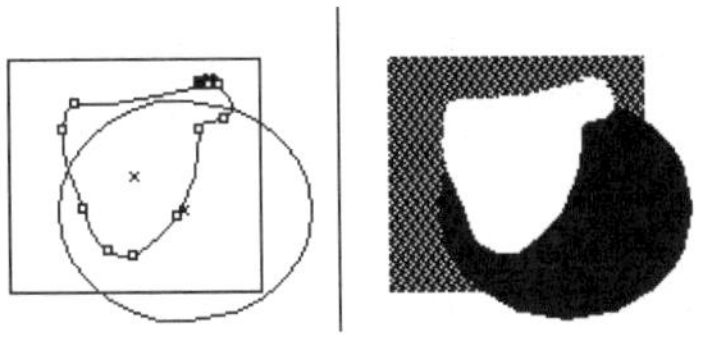

3

With the outline selected, use the Paint command (Command-I) to set the Fill and Stroke to White (or to match the overall background of the artwork).

4

Preview the illustration (Command-Y) to check your results, and then return to Artwork Only (Command-W) and make changes.

See also "Hidden Notes" and Holes in Solid Objects.

Inline Type

Inline type (as opposed to outline type) is a common decorative treatment for display type. You can use any font to create inline type with the technique described here. The accompanying figure shows an example of the inline type you will create here.

Variations of this technique can be used to create many different decorative variations of a font.

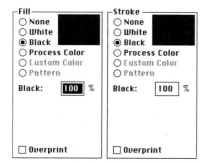

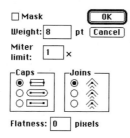

1

Create a type block with the text you wish to use. Select the Type tool and, when you click it in the active window, the Type dialog box appears with the insertion point blinking in the text box. Type the text you wish to use for the inline type, and click OK. Then choose Paint… from the Style menu (Command-I). Set Fill and Stroke to 100 percent Black, and Weight to 8 points.

The important aspect of this step is that you must set a stroke width. Variations result by choosing different weights and shades for the stroke.

If you use a wide stroke at a small point size, the type will appear compressed. Add a few points to the spacing in the Type dialog box to open up the spaces between the letters.

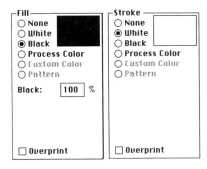

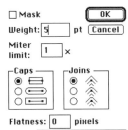

Inline Type

2

Copy the type block and paste the copy in front of the original, then paint the copy with a white fill and a five-point white stroke. To do this quickly, select the type block, then press Command-C to copy, Command-F to Paste In Front, and Command-I to open the Paint dialog box. In the Paint dialog box, set Fill to 100 percent Black, Stroke to White, and Weight to 5 points.

The important aspect of this step is that the stroke weight must be less than that used in step 1. Variations result by choosing different weights and shades for the stroke, and different Fill settings.

3

You can use Preview Illustration (Command-Y) to check your results, then choose Artwork Only (Command-W) and make changes. The Preview image of stroked type is not always accurate. Always make a test print.

Tips: Because the two text blocks that compose the inline type overlap precisely, use the following techniques to select and edit the text blocks' fill and stroke attributes. To select the top text block only, click the Selection tool on the top block's anchor point. To select both text blocks, use the Selection tool to drag a marquee over the overlapping anchor points of the text blocks (see The Selection Tool in Part I). To select the bottom text block only, select both blocks, then hold down the Shift key and click on the anchor point of the top block to deselect it.

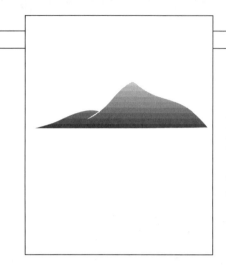

Masking

Masking is a way to crop illustrations, type, or patterns with a specific shape.

Masking can prove useful in many graphic art applications, such as packaging and logo design.

1

For this example use the Pen or Freehand tool to draw the mountain silhouette shown in the figure, which will be the masking path.

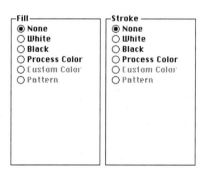

2

With the object selected, choose Paint… from the Style menu (Command-I) and select None in the Fill and Stroke boxes. Then click in the box labeled Mask. After clicking OK in the Paint dialog box, choose Lock from the Arrange menu (Command-1).

170

3

In this example, the mountain shape will mask a split fountain background. Draw a long narrow rectangle. Using the Paint dialog box, fill it with 30 percent black, ungroup it with the Ungroup command (Command-U), and—most importantly—delete the center point by selecting it and pressing the Delete or Backspace key. Position the rectangle over the highest peak of the mountain outline.

With the rectangle still selected, drag a copy of the rectangle to the bottom of the mountain outline while holding down the Shift key (constraining your movement vertically) and the Option key (to create a copy of the first rectangle). Use the Paint command (Command-I) to fill this second rectangle 100 percent black.

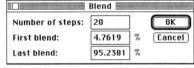

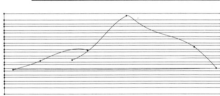

4

Shift-select all points on both rectangles, then select the Blend tool from the toolbox. Click the Blend tool on the left top corner point of each rectangle. The Blend tool dialog box appears. For this demonstration, type 20 into Number of steps and click OK. Remember, you can type in any number up to 1008 for your custom blends.

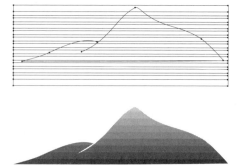

5

Now finish this first mask. If the mountain outline is not already on the lowest layer of the artwork, choose Unlock All from the Arrange menu (Command-2) and send the mountain outline to the back of the illustration using Send To Back from the Edit menu or Command-(hyphen).

Select Preview Illustration from the View menu (Command-Y).

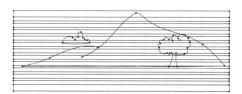

6

Add some additional drawn elements if you like. In this example we will add clouds and a tree using the Freehand tool.

If all is correct, select Artwork Only from the View menu (Command-W), Select All from the Edit menu (Command-A), and then Group from the Arrange menu (Command-G).

Warnings: Always ungroup rectangles and ovals by selecting Ungroup from the Arrange menu (Command-U) before using the Blend tool.

In order for the masking effect to work, the mask outline must be on the bottom layer. In this case the mountain was already on the bottom layer because we drew it first. If we drew the mountain after creating the blended fountain, we would have to send the mountain outline to the back (Command-hyphen).

Also, always ungroup rectangles and ovals drawn with the Rectangle and Oval tools if you intend to use them as masks. After ungrouping rectangles and ovals, be sure to delete the center points before masking. If you do not delete the center point, it will become the mask. With a single point as the mask, nothing will show when you preview the illustration.

It's a good idea to group your completed masks. The masking object masks the entire page. By grouping the masked objects along with the mask, the mask will mask only the group, not the rest of the page.

See also Masking a Mask.

Mt. Placid

Masking a Mask

Since masking is a way to crop illustrations, type, or patterns into a specific shape, you may find the need to crop or mask a mask. Here's a technique for masking a mask, to fill a shape with an image that is itself a masked view.

This technique is useful in many graphic art applications, such as packaging and logo design.

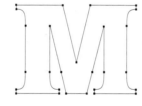

1

Create the first masked element. For this example use the artwork created in the previous technique, a blend of gray rectangles masked by a mountain outline.

2

Draw a simple block letter *M* or customize a ready-made font outline from the Adobe Collectors Edition. Select the letterform and choose Paint... from the Style menu (Command-I) to set Fill to 20 percent Black, and Stroke to None. Click the Mask box, and click OK. Position this new mask over the mountain drawing. After positioning, choose Send To Back from the Edit menu (Command-hyphen).

174

3

Preview the effect of this second mask masking your first mask by selecting Preview Illustration from the View menu (Command-Y).

4

You can make a copy of the letterform with the Copy command (Command-C) and paste it in front of everything using Paste In Front (Command-F). In the Paint dialog box, change the attributes of this new object: set Fill to None, 100 percent Black Stroke of 20 points, and most importantly, unclick the Mask box. Click OK. Preview your drawing (Command-Y), then use Select All (Command-A), then Group from the Edit menu (Command-G).

Continue to add separate elements as you wish and complete your illustration.

Tips: Always group your completed masks if you will be combining masked elements with other masks or unmasked elements in the same illustration.

Overlays: Method 1
Color Separations

The term *overlay* is used to describe any artwork that is designed to be printed or projected on top of another image. This includes the separate overlays used by the offset printer to produce multicolored images and the separate overlays used by a speaker in giving a presentation. Here is the first of three techniques for creating overlays with Adobe Illustrator.

This technique is useful for producing a separate overlay for each color to be used in offset printing the final image, or for creating a series of images that will be projected during a presentation as overlayed transparencies.

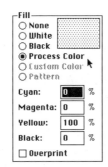

1

Draw the artwork, using the Paint command (Command-I) to assign colors to different parts of the image.

If you wish to use color to separate a series of images that will be projected during a presentation as overlayed transparencies, use the Paint command to assign only one custom color or one of the primary process colors (cyan, magenta, yellow, or black) to all of the elements on each overlay—you can print different overlays for each color using Adobe Separator.

See Overlays: Method 2 (Layers), if you want each overlay to have multiple colors and print them on a PostScript color printer.

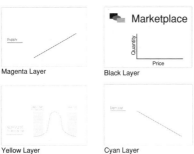

Magenta Layer

Black Layer

Yellow Layer

Cyan Layer

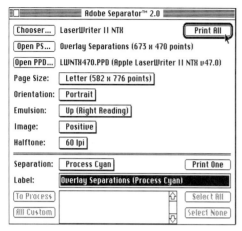

2

Print the image using Adobe Separator (see Appendix B) on a PostScript printer with the Print All option selected in the dialog box. If you are printing to a color printer, the different overlays will each be printed in a different color. Otherwise, on a black printer the overlays will be printed in black and shades of gray.

If you will be offset printing the final image in color, you can use the separated images in black and white to create plates for each color to be used in the printing process.

Tips: The full color image can, of course, be printed in color on a single sheet through a PostScript color printer when separate overlays are not required.

See also Overlays: Methods 2 and 3, Grid: Method 4, and Appendix B: Printing Color Separations with Adobe Separator.

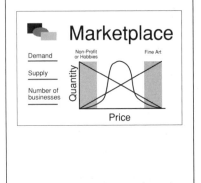

Overlays: Method 2
Layers

This second technique for creating overlays involves grouping the elements that are to appear on each layer. One advantage of this method over the first (Overlays: Method 1) is that each overlay can include more than one color.

This technique is specifically useful for creating a series of images that will be projected during a presentation as overlayed transparencies.

1

Draw the artwork that will compose the first transparency—the bottom layer when additional transparencies are overlayed during a presentation. Use the Paint command (Command-I) to set the Fill and Stroke of each element, including different colors if you wish. Then, use Select All (Command-A) to select all of the objects that compose the first transparency and use the Group command (Command-G) and the Lock command (Command-1) to group and lock them.

2

Draw the artwork that will compose the second transparency—the second layer when the two transparencies are overlayed during a presentation. Then, use Select All (Command-A) to select all of the objects that compose the second transparency and use the Group command (Command-G) to group them.

3

If a third overlay is called for, first use the Unlock command (Command-2) to unlock the first layer, then use Select All (Command-A) and Lock (Command-1) to select and lock all of the elements of the first two transparencies.

Then draw the artwork that will compose the third transparency overlay, use Select All (Command-A) to select all of the objects that compose the third transparency, and use the Group command (Command-G) to group them.

Repeat this step for each additional overlay.

4

If you need to make changes to any of the overlays, be sure that only one overlay at a time is unlocked and ungrouped while you are working. Before making edits to the elements on a different overlay, select all of the elements that are part of the current overlay and group them (Command-G). Then unlock

179

all the other layers (Command-2), choose Select All (Command-A), Shift-click on the next grouped set you wish to edit (to deselect it), lock the selected layers (Command-1). Then select the unlocked overlay you wish to edit and ungroup (Command-U).

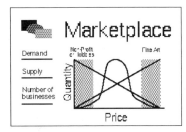

5

When the artwork is complete, preview the whole illustration (Command-Y) to proof the artwork for alignment.

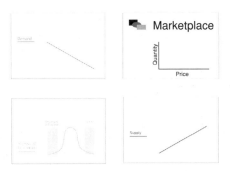

6

Print the artwork for each overlay on a separate sheet, in color or black and white. Do this by first unlocking all locked layers (Command-2), selecting all overlays (Command-A), Shift-clicking on grouped artwork for the one overlay you wish to print (to deselect it), hiding all other artwork using the Hide command (Command-3), then printing the visible overlay (Command-P).

Tips: If you will be printing the separate layers several times, or on different printers, you can save the time it would take to repeatedly select and hide overlays by saving the composite image as a document, and save as many additional documents as there are overlays (grouped layers). Then open each overlay document and delete all elements except those that compose a single overlay.

180

If any changes are required after you separate the composite artwork into different documents, make the changes in the composite document and derive the changed overlays from that document again.

See also Overlays: Methods 1 and 3 and Appendix B: Printing Color Separations with Adobe Separator.

Overlays: Method 3
Separate Documents

This third technique for creating overlays involves working with the elements that are to appear on each layer in a separate document. This can be a productivity aid when each overlay—or the final composite image—is so complicated or so large that it would tax your system's memory (and slow response rates).

1

Draw the most complicated or detailed overlay first.

2

Save it as Overlay #1, then delete some of the details, leaving only as much of the artwork as you will need for a grid or guide to create subsequent overlays. Choose Select All and use the Paint command to set Fill and Stroke to None, then save the new document as Overlay Boilerplate.

As an alternative, you can use Option-Command-C to copy a bitmap version of the artwork into the Clipboard. Then quit Illustrator and paste the Clipboard into a drawing application that supports bitmap or PICT formats and save the document as Overlay Template.

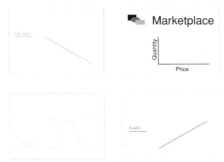

3

To create each subsequent overlay, open the Overlay Template (from step 2), or open a new document with the bitmap overlay as a template (from step 2). Add elements for the next overlay.

4

Print the overlays in color or black and white.

Tip: If all of the overlays but the first are fairly simple and non-overlapping, you can build all of the subsequent overlays in a single document and separate them using the techniques described in Overlays: Method 1 or 2.

Warning: With this method, the composite image cannot be printed as a single sheet.

See also Overlays: Methods 1 and 2, Grid: Method 4.

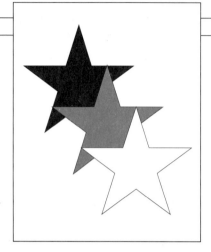

Pasting in Layers

When you want to position a selected object on the frontmost or backmost layer of an illustration, you can use the Paste In Front or Paste In Back command (Command-F or Command-B), respectively. Otherwise, when you want to move a selected object to a different layer position, use Illustrator's "smart pasting" ability, described here.

This technique is useful whenever you need to rearrange the layers of an illustration composed of three or more layers, like the three layers of star shapes shown in the accompanying figure.

1

Assuming you have a series of objects layered on top of one another, Option-click on the object you wish to move, as shown in this figure, and choose Cut from the Edit menu (Command-X). The selected object is cut to the Clipboard for pasting later.

2

Now choose the object you would like to paste behind or in front of and click on it. This selection now acts as a "reference layer" for the pasting function. The bottom star is selected in this example.

Edit

Undo Cut	⌘Z
Cut	⌘H
Copy	⌘C
Paste	⌘U
Clear	
Select All	⌘A
Paste In Front	**⌘F**
Paste In Back	**⌘B**
Bring To Front	⌘=
Send To Back	⌘–
Preferences...	⌘K

3

Then choose Paste In Front or Paste In Back from the Edit menu (Command-F or Command-B). The cut object pastes in front or in back of the object you selected as a reference layer in step 2. (If you do not choose a reference layer before pasting, Paste In Front or Paste In Back will simply paste to the frontmost or backmost layer.)

Tips: Here are some basic shortcuts to remember when layering objects:

Command- –   To move a selected object to the layer that is farthest back.

Command- =   To move a selected object to the layer that is topmost.

185

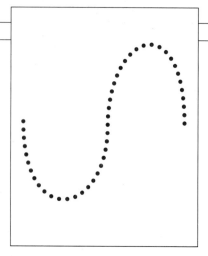

Lines

Dotted Lines

Illustrator allows you to make dashed lines of perfect dots or perfect squares, in any specific size and with any specific spacing you like. This technique will uniformly soften the feeling of your drawings while still allowing you to specify them in full black or primary colors.

This style of line is also useful for architectural and schematic drawings. It provides a great way to indicate movement or sequential steps of a process. It can also be used to add tab leaders to tabular text formats.

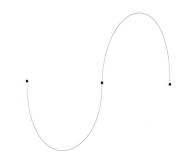

1

Draw a line or shape using one of the drawing tools (i.e., the Pen tool, the Freehand tool, or the Autotrace tool). This figure shows a curved line drawn with the Pen tool.

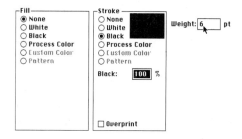

2

With the line still selected, choose Paint... from the Style menu (Command-I) to set Fill to None, Stroke to any percentage of black or a color, and Weight to a point size equal to the width measurement of the squares or dots you wish to create. In this example, use a weight of six points.

3

Click the second choice under Caps (the round ends) for a line of dots, or the third choice (the extended blunt ends) for a line of squares.

4

Click Dashed in the Dash pattern box located at the bottom of the Paint dialog box. In the first box, type the number 0, which creates either perfect circles or squares.

Typing 0 in the first Dash pattern box and clicking None in the Fill box are the only two constants you must remember to enter for this special effect to work. If you type a number of greater value in the first Dash pattern box, you will get oblong circles and rectangles instead of circles and squares.

Tab to the second box and type the number of points you want as space between dots. In this case, type 12.

Tips: Try changing the line weight and the gap measurement (the second box under Dash pattern) for different effects. For example, in step 2, you can change the size of the dot or square by specifying a thicker or thinner weight.

In step 4, changing the gap measurement will decrease or increase the distance between the dots or squares. If the gap measurement equals the line weight measurement, the dots or squares will just touch.

187

Hand-drawn Look: Method 1

You may want a line that has an uneven, hand-drawn look—one that seems to go from thick to thin, a line you might describe as calligraphic. It is easy to create this effect with Illustrator's layering features. You have complete control of the thickness of the line even after you have drawn it.

You can use this technique to create the effect of a hand-drawn or brush-stroked border around any solid shape (i.e., a closed path).

In this example, you will draw an uneven black line on a white background.

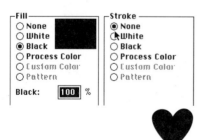

1

Using the Pen tool to draw freehand, or tracing a scanned template, draw a closed shape, such as the heart shape in this figure. The fewer points you click with the Pen tool, the smoother the line will be; the more points you click, the more uneven the line will be.

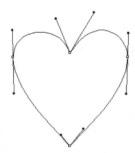

2

Use Paint… from the Style menu (Command-I) to set the Fill to the percentage of black or color that you wish for the hand-drawn line, and set Stroke to None. The figure at left shows the Paint dialog box settings for this example and the resulting heart-shaped path.

3

Using the Pen tool, draw a similar but slightly different shape that is smaller than the first. If you prefer, use the Scale tool from the toolbox and scale a copy. Then adjust the curves and anchor points to change the second shape slightly. Select the second shape and drag it on top of the first shape.

4

With the inside shape still selected, use the Paint command (Command-I) to set Fill to White (to match your paper color or background). For this effect to work, always match the fill color to the desired background color. For this demonstration, assume you are drawing on a white page.

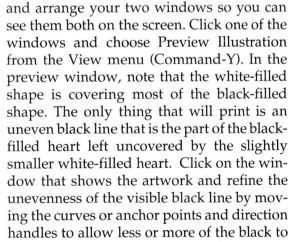

5

Select New Window from the Window menu and arrange your two windows so you can see them both on the screen. Click one of the windows and choose Preview Illustration from the View menu (Command-Y). In the preview window, note that the white-filled shape is covering most of the black-filled shape. The only thing that will print is an uneven black line that is the part of the black-filled heart left uncovered by the slightly smaller white-filled heart. Click on the window that shows the artwork and refine the unevenness of the visible black line by moving the curves or anchor points and direction handles to allow less or more of the black to show.

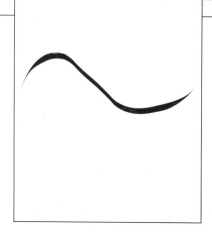

Hand-drawn Look: Method 2

In the preceding technique, you drew lines with a hand-drawn look around a solid shape. In this example, you will use a different technique to create the appearance of hand-drawn lines as open paths.

You can use this technique to add shading effects to solid figures, or to draw complete illustrations such as the Technical Illustration in Part IV.

1

Using the Pen or Freehand tool, draw or trace the line you wish to represent as an open path. The fewer points you click with the Pen tool, the smoother the line will be; the more points you click, the more uneven the line will be. This figure shows a hand-drawn curved line drawn with the Freehand tool.

2

Option-click on the line to select the whole path, then choose Copy (Command-C) and Paste In Front (Command-F) to make a duplicate of the line, layered on top of the first.

3

Click away from the pasted line to deselect it, then drag each anchor point, except the two endpoints, a slight distance away from the first position.

4

In turn, select each of the pairs of anchor points at the ends of the shape and choose Join... from the Arrange menu (Command-J). You can choose either Corner point or Smooth point in the Join dialog box, which is displayed whenever you join two points that overlap precisely. You now have a solid shape, a closed path.

5

With the shape or some part of it still selected, use the Paint command (Command-I) to set the Fill to the percentage of black or color you wish the line to be. When you have set the attributes, click OK.

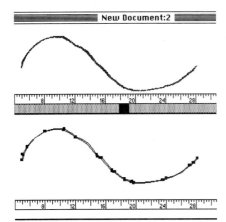

6

Select New Window from the Window menu and size and arrange your two windows so you can see them both, as shown in the figure at left. Click one of the windows and choose Preview Illustration from the View menu (Command-Y).

Click on the window that shows the artwork to make it active and begin to refine the unevenness of the hand-drawn line. Using the Selection tool, move the curves or anchor points and direction handles (see The Pen Tool in Part I) to create a thicker or thinner line. Use the Scissors tool while you press down the Option key to add anchor points, if you need them to refine the curves.

191

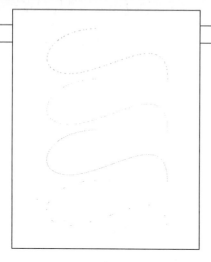

Hand-drawn Look: Method 3

With the Paint dialog box it is easy to specify perfectly black, inked lines of any weight. But sometimes you may want a softer, more irregular, effect, such as a stipple effect or a sketched or brushed ink look.

Here are some tips to help you create these effects in your drawings. There are countless variations on the suggestions listed here. You are encouraged to experiment with them.

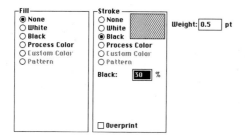

1

Draw a line using one of the drawing tools (i.e., the Pen tool, Freehand tool, or Autotrace tool). The figure at left shows a curved line drawn with the Pen tool.

2

With the line selected, choose Paint... from the Style menu (Command-I) and set Fill to None. Set Stroke to a percentage of black less than 50 percent (or choose a muted color). Set the weight fairly thin. For this example, enter 30 percent Black and type in .5 points Weight.

3

Choose Preview Illustration (Command-Y) to see the results, then return to Artwork Only (Command-W) and experiment with other paint settings. Option-drag multiple copies away and set Stroke to different percentages of black (still less than 50 percent), change the line weights, and try out different end caps. Type in random values for the dash pattern and gaps. Dash values of 2 points or more will create short strokes. A dash value of 0 will create single dots. Try entering irregular repeats, such as 1, 5, 0, 5, 2, 0. Layer two paths with different paint settings over one another.

Tips: Using different percentages of black (or muted color) and different random dash patterns can create lines in your final output resembling the etching effect created with a traditional tool called a roulette wheel.

You will find that thinner lines generally create subtler effects. Subtle line effects are difficult to preview on-screen. You probably will want to print a proof on a LaserWriter, or even a Linotronic, to fine-tune the effect. In either case, you can shorten the cycle of experimentation by setting up a variety of lines on one page and printing them all at once. Then decide which one you will use or modify for use in the final artwork.

See also Dotted Lines.

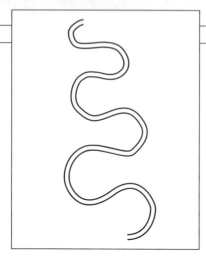

Parallel Curves

Often you will need two parallel lines separated by a specific distance. If there are no curves in the line, you can draw one line and then drag away a copy. Trying to create curved parallel lines using this method poses a problem; the original line and the copy will not run parallel at the curves. The second figure at left shows the results when a curved line is simply duplicated and moved. Moreover, it is very difficult to place a small, precise distance between each line. This technique provides the solution—and you can make the lines as curved as you like!

Curving parallel lines are often used as the indication of a highway on a map.

1

Use the Pen or Freehand tool to draw the path you wish. The figure at left shows a long, curved path, created for this example.

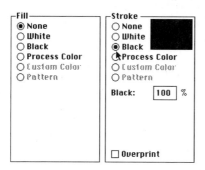

2

Option-click on the path with the Selection tool to select the entire path (the anchor points turn into filled-in black squares) and use Paint… from the Style menu (Command-I) to set Fill to None and Stroke to any percentage of black or a color to define the stroke as you like. Do not click OK yet.

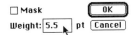

☐ Mask   ⬭ OK ⬭

Weight: ⬚5.5⬚ pt (Cancel)

3

To set the line weight for the parallel lines, you use a formula, as follows. Decide which line weight you want for each parallel line and how many points of space you want between the parallel lines. Double your desired line weight and add in the number of points you want between the parallel lines. For example:

2	pts	Line weight for each line
x 2	pts	Times 2
4	pts	Line weight doubled
+ 1.5	pts	Space between lines
5.5	pts	Total entered as line weight

Type the total into the Weight box—5.5 points in this case—and click OK.

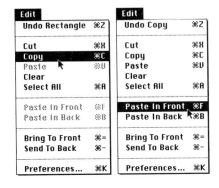

4

Choose the Copy command from the Edit menu (Command-C) to copy the line, then use Paste In Front from the Edit menu (Command-F). A copy of the line is pasted directly on top of your original, so you won't be able to see it immediately.

195

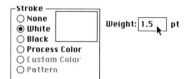

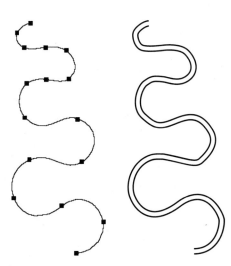

5

With the new copy of the line still selected, choose Paint… from the Style menu (Command-I) and set Stroke to White and Weight to the number of points you decided in step 3 would separate the parallel lines—1.5 points in this case.

6

Preview your parallel lines by selecting Preview Illustration from the View menu (Command-Y), then return to Artwork Only (Command-W) and make adjustments to the stroke weights if necessary to get the look you want.

Because the two paths that compose the curving parallel lines overlap precisely, use the following techniques to select and edit lines:

To select both lines, hold down the Option key and use the Selection tool to drag a marquee over any part of the overlapping lines.

To select the bottom line only, use the technique just described to select both paths, then hold down both the Option and Shift keys and click on the top line to deselect it.

To select the top line only, hold down the Option key and click the Selection tool on the top line.

7

When you have achieved the results you wish, use the Selection tool to drag a selection marquee over the curved parallel line path and choose Group from the Arrange menu (Command-G). (See The Selection Tool in Part I.)

See also Compound Lines: Methods 1 and 2.

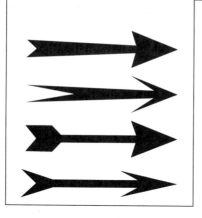

Shapes

Arrows

Arrows are common symbols used in many types of illustrations. The accompanying figure shows a variety of arrow shapes. You can use existing arrows from symbol fonts such as Zapf Dingbats, or you can create your own arrows using the technique described here.

This technique can be used to create any symmetrical object.

1

Create the top half of the arrow. The figure at left shows the top half of this arrow created with the Pen tool.

2

With the drawn elements selected, choose the Reflect tool, then hold down the Option key and click on one of the two endpoints.

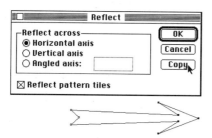

3

When you Option-click with the Reflect tool, the Reflect dialog box opens. Select Horizontal axis reflection and close the dialog box by clicking Copy. This creates a horizontal mirror image—in this case, the bottom half of the arrow.

If the arrow you create in this step is not to your liking, delete one-half and rework the other half of it, then go back to step 2.

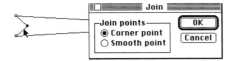

4

With the Selection tool, drag a selection marquee to select one pair of the common points where the two paths join—in this case, the back end of the arrow. (See The Selection Tool in Part I.) Type Command-J to join the pair. The Join box dialog appears. Click Corner point and click OK to complete the join. Repeat this process with the other pair of common points.

5

To make the arrow longer or shorter, select the point at one end. Press down on the Shift key after starting to drag the point horizontally. The point selected for adjusting in this example is the front tip of the arrow.

Tip: Be sure to select all of the points that compose the tip of the arrow or the base of the arrow when stretching it longer or shorter. Otherwise, you will distort the shape of the arrow.

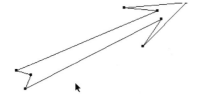

6

To rotate the arrow: Option-click the Selection tool anywhere along the path to select it; choose the Rotate tool; put the origin at the tip of the arrow; and, when the pointer becomes an arrowhead, move the pointer in the direction you wish to rotate the arrow.

199

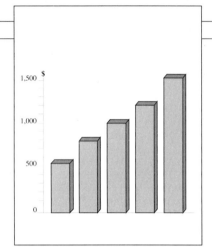

Charts: Method 1
Bar Charts

Bar charts, like the one shown in the accompanying figure, are probably the single most common form of business graphics. Here is a technique for quickly producing a series of bars, scaled to accurate dimensions.

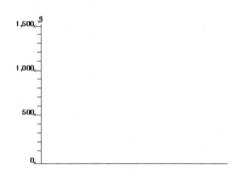

1

Use the Pen tool with the Shift key to draw two straight lines that will serve as the chart's two axes. Set tick marks to represent the increments you wish to show (see Dividing Equally). Add text to label each tick mark. This figure shows increments of $100 along the vertical (y) axis, labeled in $500 increments.

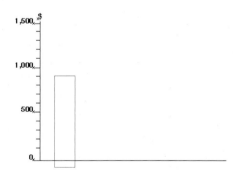

2

Decide how wide you want to make your bars. Using the Rectangle tool, draw a rectangle the width of one bar and the height of one unit on the vertical scale, or a decimal multiple of one unit (that is, ten units, one hundred units, one thousand units, etc.). For this example, make the height of the basic bar (the bar you will scale) equivalent to $1,000. You can draw this rectangle visually on the screen, or simply click the Rectangle tool once on the screen and specify precise dimensions in the Rectangle dialog box.

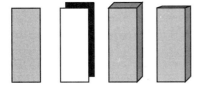

It doesn't matter exactly what size your basic unit is in points or inches, so long as you know it represents 1, 10, 100, or 1,000 chart units and it matches the scale you have set up on the axes.

If you want groups of bars or three-dimensional bars, align the first group, or add dimension and shading to the first bar, *before* you go on to step 3.

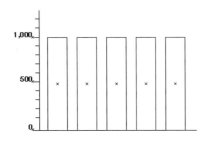

3

Make as many copies of this basic unit as you need bars by Option-clicking and dragging one copy with the Option and Shift keys held down so it is aligned along the horizontal axis. Use Transform Again to create additional copies.

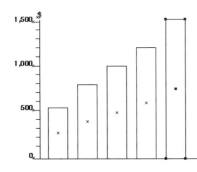

4

Choose the Scale tool and, one by one, select each bar and Option-click the Scale tool on the bottom edge of the bar. When the Scale dialog box appears, click Non-uniform scale and enter the appropriate percentage in the Vertical box. The following table shows the values to use in scaling for this example.

BAR #	DESIRED VALUE	VERTICAL SCALE
1	$550	55%
2	$800	80%
3	$1,000	100%
4	$1,200	120%
5	$1,500	150%

Finish the chart by adding a title and caption, if appropriate.

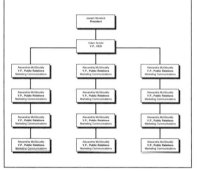

Charts: Method 2
Organization Charts

Organization charts, such as the one shown in the accompanying figure, are a very common form of business graphics. Here is a technique for quickly producing an organization chart.

Alexandria McGilcuddy
V.P., Public Relations
Marketing Communications

1

Use the Type tool to type the text of the longest name and title or department that will appear in the organization chart. These can be typed in one text block if all entries in the chart will have the same type specifications, or they can be typed as separate blocks if each element will have different type specifications. Click on the icon for centered alignment in the Type dialog box.

These text elements need not reflect reality—the person's name you type need not hold that title or be in that department—but they do need to have as many characters as the longest entries you will make in the chart.

Alexandria McGilcuddy
V.P., Public Relations
Marketing Communications

2

Use the Rectangle tool to draw a rectangle around the text, and use the Paint command (Command-I) to set the Fill to White and the Stroke to the shade and thickness you like. Use the Send To Back command (Command-hyphen) to send the rectangle to the bottom layer. This rectangle and the text will be the basic element used throughout the chart.

Alexandria McGilcuddy
V.P., Public Relations
Marketing Communications

Tips: If you want to add a drop shadow or a three-dimensional effect to the rectangle, do so *before* you go on to step 3.

The fill of the rectangle can be white or any percentage of black or a color, but it cannot be set to None or the lines drawn in step 7 will be visible behind the text.

Alexandria McGilcuddy
V.P., Public Relations
Marketing Communications

3

When you have completed the basic unit, use the Selection tool to select all of the elements, then use the Group command (Command-G) to group all of these basic elements, including the text.

4

Working in Fit In Window view (Command-M), make as many copies of this basic unit as you need for the organization chart by selecting the rectangle and all of the text elements and dragging this basic "building block" with the Option key held down (to make a copy) and the Shift key held down (if you want to align copies horizontally or vertically).

If you are making several columns of entries, it is a good idea to create one column by dragging a copy of the first box into the second position and then using the Transform Again command (Command-D) to create additional copies spaced equally apart.

Then use the Selection tool to select the whole column and hold down the Option key as you drag copies of the whole column into other positions; hold the Shift key as well if you want to align columns horizontally.

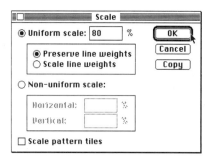

5

If the final layout is too large to fit on one page, you can use Select All (Command-A) and use the Scale tool with the Option key to reduce the size of the chart (including the size of the type).

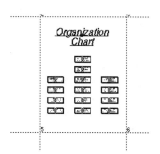

6

Once you have the overall chart arranged on the page, use the Type tool to add a chart title and caption (if appropriate).

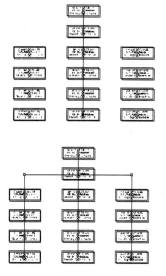

7

Use Select All (Command-A) and Lock (Command-1) to select all of the elements and lock them; then use the Pen tool with the Shift key to draw straight lines from the center of each rectangle to the center of adjacent rectangles or to adjoining lines that indicate the structure of the organization.

You can start by drawing a long path from the top box down through the longest column, and then add other paths to connect the other columns, but remember to click on the Pen tool again each time you want to start with a new endpoint.

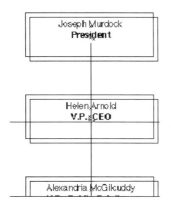

8

After drawing all lines, use Unlock (Command-2) to unlock and automatically select all of the boxed elements, then use Bring To Front (Command-+) to bring the boxed elements to the top layer, above the lines you drew in step 7.

9

Finally, use Select All (Command-A) and Ungroup (Command-U) to select all of the elements and ungroup them, and use the Zoom tool to change to a magnified view of the top of the chart. One by one, select each text element and use the Type command (Command-T) to change the boilerplate text to the appropriate name, title, and department in each box on the chart.

See also Aligning Objects: Methods 1 and 2, Grid: Methods 1 and 4, Cubes: Methods 1 and 2.

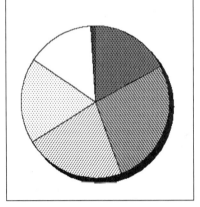

Charts: Method 3
Pie Charts

Pie charts, such as the one shown in the accompanying figure, are a common form of business graphics. Here is a technique you can use to divide a pie quickly, with wedges scaled to accurate dimensions.

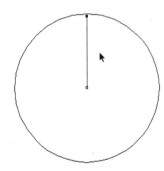

1

Use the Oval tool with the Shift key to draw a perfect circle. Click the Pen tool once on the center of the circle, then with the Shift key held down, click on the top anchor point of the circle, which forces a straight line. This draws a radius at twelve o'clock. Your drawing should look like the one in the figure at left.

2

Determine the number of degrees of the circle for each slice of the pie you wish to divide based on the following formula:

Degrees = (value of slice/total value of pie) x 360
or
Degrees = Percent share of slice x 360

In this example, you derive degree values for each slice based on the desired dollar amount, shown in the following table:

SLICE #	DESIRED VALUE	RELATIVE %	DEGREES
1	$550	1.00%	3.60
2	$800	14.54%	52.36
3	$1,000	18.18%	65.45
4	$1,200	21.82%	78.54
5	$1,500	27.27%	98.18
Totals	$5,500	100.00%	360.00

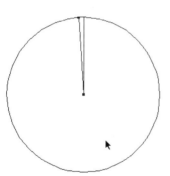

3

With the radius selected, choose the Rotate tool and Option-click on the anchor point at the center of the circle. This opens the Rotate dialog box. Type the number of degrees assigned to the first pie slice in the Angle box—3.6 in this case.

Entering a positive number will position the slice counterclockwise from the radius; a negative number will position the slice clockwise from the radius. Click Copy to close the Rotate dialog box and rotate a copy of the radius the indicated number of degrees. The figure at left shows the result of the 3.6° angle rotation.

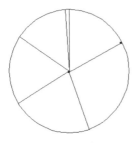

4

Continue adding each slice of the pie. With the most recently rotated radius selected, Option-click the Rotate tool on the center point and enter the appropriate number of degrees for each new slice. After you have created all of the slices, your pie chart will look like the one in the figure at left.

If you want to shade each slice differently, go on with the next steps. Otherwise, if you want all slices shaded the same, use Select All (Command-A) and the Paint command (Command-I) to set the stroke and fill desired.

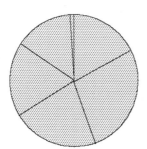

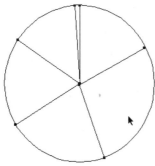

5

In the next steps you are going to make each slice of pie a closed path, composed of two radii and an arc, in order to be able to assign each slice a different fill. First hold down the Option key and drag the selection marquee around the center point to select all the radii and the circle. (See The Selection Tool in Part I.) Then Shift-click on the outer edge of the circle to deselect it, and use Copy (Command-C) and Paste In Front (Command-F) to make duplicates of all the radii.

6

Select the circle and use Ungroup (Command-U), then choose the Scissors tool and cut the circumference at each point where a radius hits it. The figure at left shows an exploded view so you can see where the circumference is cut.

7

This next step may seem complicated because of the difficulties of selecting only the anchor points where four anchor points overlap. In order to join two radii and an arc to make each slice of pie a closed path, you will temporarily move one element in order to select elements below it.

To select the first slice, Shift-Option-click on the three sides (two radii and an arc) of any pie wedge. Holding the Shift key causes multiple selection, and holding the Option key selects whole paths (that is, all anchor points).

Then Option-click on the Selection tool in the toolbox to get the Move dialog box, and type any number as a small distance for a horizontal move, such as 10 points. This moves the selected parts—the pie wedge— away from the rest of the pie.

One at a time, use the Selection tool to drag a selection marquee around each of three locations: the place where the two radii meet, and the places where each radius meets the arc, and choose the Join command (Command-J) to join each pair of points.

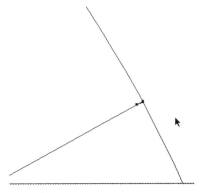

8

After joining anchor points at each of the three locations, use the Selection tool to Option-click anywhere on the slice to select the whole slice, then Option-click on the Selection tool in the toolbox to get the Move dialog box, and type the same number you used above for a horizontal move, but this time preceded by minus (a hyphen)—in this example -10. This moves the slice back into place with the rest of the pie.

Next, choose Send To Back (Command-hyphen) and (optionally) Group (Command-G). Repeat steps 7 and 8 for each slice of the pie.

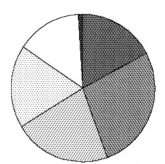

9

Finally, use Paint... from the Style menu (Command-I) to set the fill and stroke of your choice for each slice. The figure at left shows the example pie chart with different fill and stroke settings for each slice.

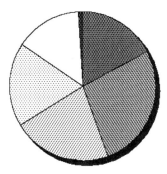

Tips: If you want a three-dimensional pie, use the Selection tool to Option-drag a copy of the circle before you cut it with the Scissors tool in step 6, and position the copy a short diagonal distance from the pie. Use the Paint command (Command-I) to give the copy a stroke and fill, and then choose Send To Back (Command-hyphen) to put the new circle behind the pie chart.

See also the techniques that describe three-dimensional effects to learn how to achieve this more realistically, or if you want each slice exploded with a three-dimensional effect.

You can also use any of the transformation tools (Scale, Rotate, Reflect, and Shear) to make the pie more interesting.

See also Aligning Objects: Methods 1 and 2, Cubes: Method 1 and 2, and Dividing Equally.

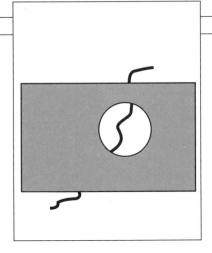

Holes in Solid Objects

You can always make a solid shape appear to have a hole in it by drawing the hole and giving it a fill of white. But what if you want the hole to be transparent to objects below it? Here is one technique that does not involve masking.

You can use the techniques described here to combine any two paths, but the most common application is cutting holes inside closed letters of the alphabet.

1

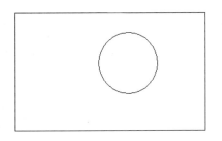

Create the whole image as two paths: the outer edge and the shape of the hole. In this example, the outer edge is a rectangle created with the Rectangle tool. The circle just right of center is the shape of the hole, created with the Oval tool and the Shift key.

2

Use the Scissors tool to cut each shape; this creates two new endpoints on each copied shape. Move one of the points from each cut to a position away from the shape.

To accomplish the temporary moving of endpoints in step 2, use this shortcut: With the Scissors tool still selected, hold down the Command key to get the selection pointer, then hold down the Shift key and click on the selected overlapping endpoints. This deselects the endpoint on top. Then use the cursor key(s) to move the still-selected endpoint temporarily.

212

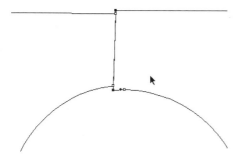

3

Select one of the new endpoints on each path, and use Join... from the Arrange menu (Command-J) to join them. Repeat the process for the other pair of new endpoints. For this example, select the top endpoint on the rectangle and the bottom endpoint on the circle.

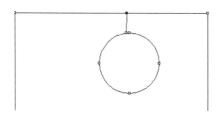

4

Use the Selection tool to move each of the displaced points back to its original position, then use Paint... from the Style menu (Command-I) to assign the fill you intend for the final artwork.

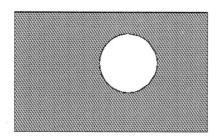

5

If you want to stroke and fill the object, you will need to cover up the join. To do so, select the object, then copy it with the Copy command (Command-C), and use Paste In Front (Command-F). With the object still selected, choose Paint... (Command-I) to bring up the Paint dialog box. Paint the object with the same fill as the original, but with no stroke. Select and group (Command-G) both objects as a unit.

See also Masking.

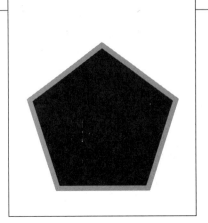

Polygons

You can use the technique described here to draw any polygon shape with equal-length sides all around—equilateral triangles, pentagons, hexagons, or polygons with seven or more sides. (You can use the Rectangle tool instead of this technique to draw perfect squares.) A five-sided polygon (pentagon) is created in this example.

1

Use the Pen tool with the Shift key to draw a straight vertical line like the one shown in the figure at left.

2

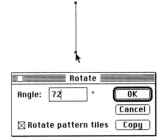

Select the entire line, then select the Rotate tool and Option-click the Rotate tool at the bottom point of the line. This opens the Rotate dialog box.

Enter a number of degrees yielded by the following formula:

360 ÷ (number of sides to the polygon)

for example, 72 degrees for a five-sided polygon, 60 degrees for a six-sided polygon, and so on.

For a five-sided polygon, type 72 (for 72°) into the Angle field of the Rotate dialog box and click Copy to rotate a copy of the line 72°.

3

With the rotated copy selected, use Trans-form Again (Command-D) three times. You now have five lines radiating from a common center.

4

Using the Selection tool, drag a marquee over the common center points, then press De-lete or Backspace. (See The Selection Tool in Part I.)

You now have five endpoints remaining to use as guides. Each one will be a corner of the polygon.

5

Use the Selection tool to select any adjacent pair of points, then choose Join… from the Arrange menu (Command-J) to draw a line connecting them.

Repeat this step until all sides of the poly-gon are drawn.

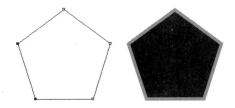

6

Use the Paint command (Command-I), paint the polygon with your desired stroke and fill settings, select the entire object, and group it (Command-G). In this example, the polygon has a 100 percent Black Fill and a 50 percent Black Stroke with a Weight of 5 points.

215

Radial Symmetry: Method 1

Radial symmetry describes any object composed of a single shape that is repeated in a pattern around a central point. An example of radial symmetry is a flower, such as the one shown in the accompanying figure. In this technique the Rotate tool is used to create simple patterns in which the shapes do not need to meet precisely at the edges—that is, they can overlap, or there can be gaps between them.

You can use this technique to create any radially symmetrical design that allows some gap or overlap between the units of the design.

1

Create an object that will become the basic unit of the radial design, using whatever tool is appropriate. In this example, use the Pen or Freehand tool to create a petal-shaped object, as in the figure at left.

2

Select the Rotate tool and Option-click the point you want to use as the center of the design—in this case, the base of the petal. In the Rotate dialog box, enter the number of degrees yielded by the following formula:

Degrees = 360°/(number of repeated units)

In this example, you will want ten units; so you will type 36 as the number of degrees (360 divided by 10). Some other common values are shown in the following table.

NUMBER OF REPEATED UNITS IN CIRCLE	DEGREES
2	180
3	120
4	90
5	72
6	60
7	51.43
8	45
9	40
10	36

Click Copy to close the Rotate dialog box and make a rotated copy of the first object, then use Transform Again (Command-D) until the circle is complete—eight more copies in this example.

3

Use Select All (Command-A) and Group (Command-G) to group the objects that make up your shape.

Tips: Once you create a design, you can create many variations by scaling, overlaying, and/or shearing the object. The figure at the left shows three copies of the flower petals scaled progressively smaller, with variations in the fill and stroke for each group of petals in the object.

Radial Symmetry: Method 2

This second technique for creating radially symmetrical designs is more controlled than the first, creating shapes that meet precisely at the edges, such as the one shown in the accompanying figure.

This technique can be used to create any radially symmetrical design.

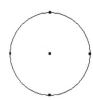

1

Use the Oval tool with the Shift key to draw a circle (as shown in the figure at left) whose center will be the center of the radial design and whose circumference will cross through the points you want the radial elements to touch or cross.

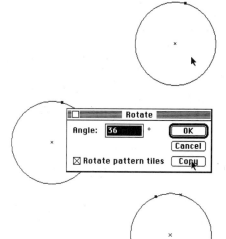

2

Use the Pen tool to set an anchor point anywhere on the circumference of the circle. In this example, the anchor point is just to the right of the top of the circle.

Select the Rotate tool, and hold the Option key as you click on the center of the circle. The Rotate dialog box appears.

In the Angle field of the Rotate dialog box, type the number of degrees yielded by the following formula:

Degrees = 360°/(number of repeated units)

See the table in Radial Symmetry: Method 1.

Click Copy to close the box and make a rotated copy of the anchor point.

3

Create an object that will become the basic unit of the radial design, using the two anchor points as guides for the edges of the shape. In this example, use the Pen or Freehand tool to draw an irregular polygon.

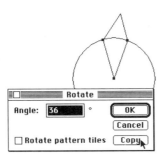

4

With the basic radial element selected, select the Rotate tool and Option-click the center of the circle, which happens to be the base of the polygon in this example. In the Angle field of the Rotate dialog box, type the number of degrees you used in step 2 (36°), and click Copy to close the box and make a rotated copy of the object. Use Transform Again (Command-D) as many times as needed to complete the design.

5

Select and delete the original circle and the two anchor points you used as guides. Then select the remaining objects and use Group (Command-G).

Tips: If your design does not touch the center of the circle, you can use Ungroup (Command-U) on the circle and delete only the circumference, leaving the center point and grouping it with the rest of the design.

The figure at left shows the correct positioning of the basic radial unit with respect to the circle and anchor points for various other designs that can be created using this technique.

219

Shared Borders

Separate shapes that share common irregular edges—that must fit together like jigsaw puzzle pieces—are a common drawing situation. Individual countries, states, or counties on a map are a typical example. This simple technique shows the most efficient way for you to handle this drawing situation.

Perfect for map work, this technique also proves useful for illustration styles that simulate dimension by using shapes of various gray fills.

1

Using one of the drawing tools, draw a shape with an irregular path similar to the figure at left. You are going to draw another irregular shape to the right of the first. It will share a common border with the first shape.

2

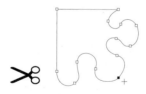

Select the Scissors tool and click at two points on the irregular path. The line length between these two cuts will become the new common border. The figure at left shows one point being selected for cutting. The other point to cut is the top point along the curved path.

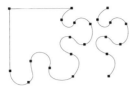

3

Using the Selection tool, Option-click on the line segment between the two cut points, selecting that section. Continue to hold the Option key and drag away an exact copy of the selected line segment.

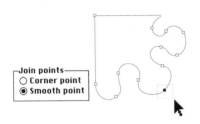

4

Rejoin the cut points on the original path using the Selection marquee and Join… from the Arrange menu (Command-J). Select the appropriate join from the Join dialog box. Click on Smooth point for this example. Your original path is now closed.

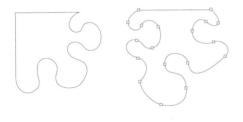

5

Choose the appropriate tool and finish drawing the adjoining shape, beginning with the exact copy of the shared border line segment. When you finish drawing, the two shapes will have identical common borders and will fit together perfectly.

    See also The Scissors Tool and The Pen Tool.

Stars: Method 1

You can use the technique described here to draw any star shape—three-pointed, four-pointed, or more.

1

Use the Pen tool with the Shift key to draw a straight vertical line like the one shown in the figure at left.

2

Select the entire line, then select the Rotate tool and Option-click at the bottom point of the line. This opens the Rotate dialog box.

Enter a number of degrees yielded by the following formula:

$$360/(number\ of\ points\ on\ the\ star)$$

This yields 72° for a five-pointed star, 60° for a six-pointed star, and so on.

Type 72 (for 72°) into the Angle field of the Rotate dialog box and click Copy to rotate a copy of the line 72°.

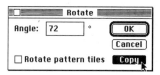

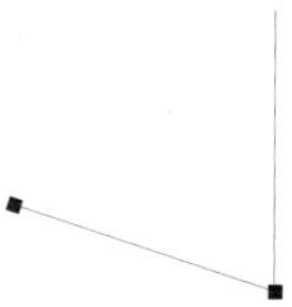

Transform Again ⌘D

3

With the rotated copy selected, use Transform Again (Command-D) three times. You now have five lines radiating from a common center.

4

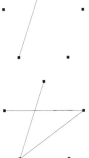

Using the Selection tool, drag a marquee over the common center points, then press Delete or Backspace. (See Selection Tool in Part I.)

You now have five endpoints remaining to use as guides. Each one will be a tip of one of the star points.

5

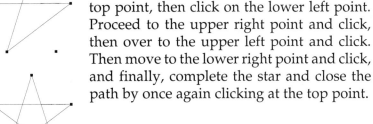

Select the Pen tool and carefully click on every other point to produce a staight line connecting them. Be sure to click and release the mouse button on each point without dragging.

For a five-pointed star, start by clicking the top point, then click on the lower left point. Proceed to the upper right point and click, then over to the upper left point and click. Then move to the lower right point and click, and finally, complete the star and close the path by once again clicking at the top point.

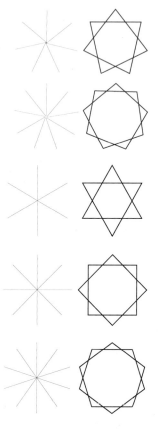

For stars with an odd number of points, clicking every other point will always result in one closed path, such as the seven- and nine-pointed stars shown in the figure at left.

For stars with an even number of points, clicking every other point will yield two paths. For a six-pointed star, click on every other point to draw two triangles. For an eight-pointed star, click on every other point to draw two squares. These and other variations are shown in the figure at left.

6

If you want a solid shaded star with no stroke (or stroke the same as the fill), you are finished. Use Paint (Command-I) to paint the star with your desired stroke and fill settings, select the entire object, and use Group (Command-G). If you would like to be able to stroke a different color around the outside edge of the star, do *not* group the elements, and go on to step 7.

Scissor cuts

Delete segments

Join endpoints

7

In a magnified view, use the Scissors tool to cut lines that cross inside the shape, then use Cut (Command-X), or press Delete or Backspace to delete the inside line segments. Use the Join command (Command-J) to join corresponding inside points.

8

You can now use Paint… from the Style menu (Command-I) to set a different stroke and fill for the star shape. In this example, the star has a 100 percent Black Fill and a 50 percent Black Stroke with a Weight of 5 points.

When you finish, select the entire object and group it using Group (Command-G).

Stars: Method 2

You can use the technique described here to draw any star shape, but here you have more control over the length of the points than with the previous technique.

1

Use the Pen tool with the Shift key to draw a straight vertical line.

2

Select the entire line, then select the Rotate tool and Option-click at the bottom point of the line. The Rotate dialog box appears.

Enter a number of degrees yielded by the following formula:

$$360/(\text{number of points on the star})$$

This yields 72° for a five-pointed star, 60° for a six-pointed star, and so on.

Type 72 (for 72°) into the Angle field of the Rotate dialog box and click Copy to rotate a copy of the line 72°.

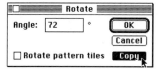

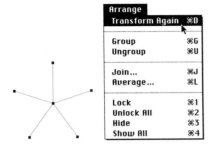

3

Select Transform Again from the Arrange menu (Command-D) three times (or more if you are creating star shapes with more than five points). You now have five lines radiating from a common center.

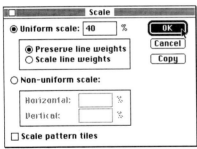

4

Select the entire object, then select the Rotate tool and Option-click on the common center points. Type *half* the number of degrees you typed in step 2—36 for a five-pointed star—in the Rotate dialog box. Click Copy to close the box and rotate a copy of the lines. This yields ten lines radiating from a common center.

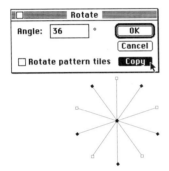

5

With the copied lines still selected, select the Scale tool and Option-click on the common center points.

With the Uniform scale option selected, type 40 into the percentage box of the Scale dialog box.

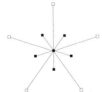

227

6

Using the Selection tool, drag a marquee over the common center points, then press Delete, Backspace, or use Cut (Command-X) to delete them. (See The Selection Tool in Part I.)

Be sure that only the center points are selected before you remove them.

You now have ten endpoints remaining to use as guides. Five will be tips of the star points, and five will correspond to the inner angle point of your star's arms.

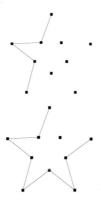

7

Select the Pen tool and connect these points sequentially with careful clicks of the mouse in a clockwise or counterclockwise sequence. Be sure to click and release the mouse button on each point without dragging. Complete the star by clicking at the point where you started.

8

Use Paint... from the Style menu (Command-I) to set the fill and stroke of the star as you wish.

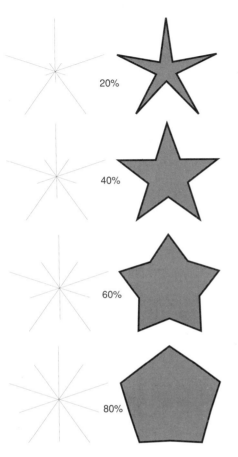

20%

40%

60%

80%

Tip: The percentage reduction you enter in step 5 determines the sharpness of the points. The greater the percentage reduction, the sharper the points. The figures here show the results of different reduction settings.

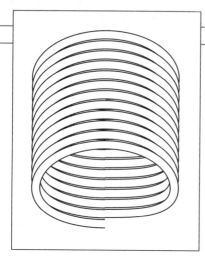

Three-Dimensional Effects

Coils and Springs

Coils and springs are common parts of mechanical devices and appear in many technical drawings, but they can be difficult to create unless you know the right techniques. Using the technique described here, you will draw a coil like the one pictured at left.

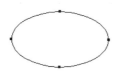

1

Use the Oval tool to draw an ellipse. Ungroup the object using the Ungroup command (Command-U). Select and delete the center point using the Delete or Backspace key.

2

Use the Scissors tool to cut the ellipse at its lowest anchor point.

3

With the Selection tool, select one of the two anchor points created by the cut, and drag it slightly up or down, holding the Shift key as you release the mouse button to constrain the movement to precisely vertical.

You can refine the shape by dragging the next anchor point (along the line from the lower of the two severed points) down about half the distance of the first movement.

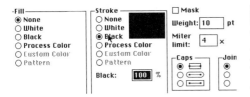

4

Use Paint… from the Style menu (Command-I) to set the Stroke of the ellipse to 100 percent Black with a Weight of 10 points (or any thickness you desire) for the coil. In this example, Fill is set to None.

Choose Preview Illustration from the View menu (Command-Y) to check the thickness of the stroke you just set.

5

With the figure selected, use Copy (Command-C) and Paste In Front (Command-F). With the copy selected, use Paint… from the Style menu (Command-I) to change the copy to a Stroke of White with a Weight of 8 points (or two points less than the weight selected in step 4).

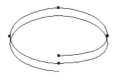

6

Select the composite figure, then use Group (Command-G). With the Selection tool, Shift-Option-drag a copy of the figure up (if you want the viewing perspective to be from the top of the coil) or down (if you want the viewing perspective to be from the bottom) to meet the first coil. Be sure to hold down the Shift key and the Option key as you release the mouse button. Select Transform Again from the Arrange menu (Command-D) to create as many additional loops of the coil as you wish.

Select Preview Illustration from the View menu (Command-Y) to see what your coil looks like.

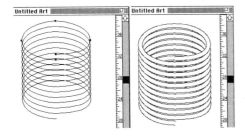

231

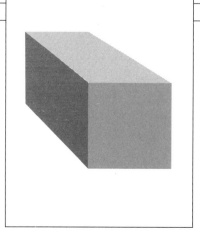

Cubes: Method 1

You can use the simple, visual approach shown here to build a six-sided wire-frame cube.

You can also use this approach to create three-dimensional objects with rectangular sides, like the drawing in the accompanying figure.

1

Use the Rectangle tool with the Shift key to draw a square like the one in the figure at left. (Recall that holding down the Shift key with the Rectangle tool forces a perfect square.) Select the square and use Ungroup (Command-U). Then select and delete the center point with the Delete or Backspace key.

2

Option-click with the Selection tool to select the square, and Shift-drag a copy of it away from the original. Position the copy against the first square so they share a border.

In this step, you can simply use the Selection tool with the Shift and Option keys to drag a copy of the first square into the new position, or you can use the Rotate tool with the pivot point set as the lower left corner of the first square and the rotation set at 90°.

Then select the two leftmost anchor points on the left square and move them up slightly at a diagonal, holding down the Shift key or using the Arrow key if you want to maintain isometric dimensions.

3

Select the object you just changed into a parallelogram. Holding the Option key to select the entire path and to make a copy, drag the copy into position to meet the opposite edge of the first square.

4

Select the first square. Holding the Option key to select the entire path and to make a copy, drag the copy into position as the fourth side (the rear).

5

To create true perspective, select the two anchor points at the upper, backmost edges of the cube and hold down the Shift key as you drag them down slightly. Then select the two leftmost anchor points of the cube and drag them right slightly.

6

To add to the sense of depth, you will need to use the Pen tool to draw a polygon that matches the top side of the cube, then you can shade each of the three "visible" sides (since only three sides would be visible if the object were solid) with a different percentage of black.

When the cube is complete, use the marquee and Option key to select the entire object, and use the Group command from the Arrange menu to make it a single object.

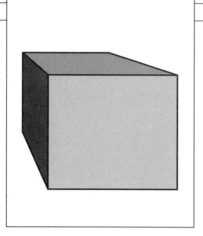

Cubes: Method 2

You can use this technique to create three-dimensional objects with irregular sides.

1

Use the Rectangle tool to draw a rectangle. Use Ungroup (Command-U) on the rectangle, and select and delete the center point using the Delete or Backspace key.

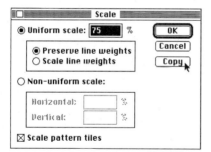

2

To make one smaller copy of the rectangle, Option-click the Selection tool on the rectangle to select the whole path, then select the Scale tool. Option-click on the rectangle to open the Scale dialog box. Click on Uniform scale and enter 75 percent. Click Copy when you are done.

With the copy selected, position it so it overlaps the first rectangle.

The positioning of the smaller rectangle will determine the apparent length of the box as well as the viewer's perspective. For example, if you position the smaller rectangle above the larger one, the cube will appear deep and will be viewed from an overhead perspective; if you position the smaller rectangle to overlap the larger rectangle, as in this example, the perspective will be nearly head-on.

 3

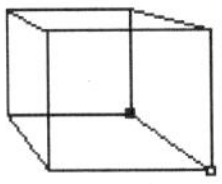

Select the Pen tool and draw polygons that match the two new "visible" sides of the cube (since the front of the cube is already a closed path, you need not recreate it).

 4

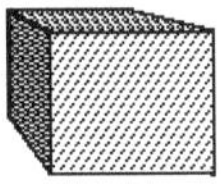

To add to the sense of depth, you can use the Paint command (Command-I) to set a gray fill (that is, some percentage of black) to shade each side.

5

When the cube is complete, use the marquee and Option key to select the entire object, and use the Group command from the Arrange menu (Command-G) to make it a single object.

See also Cubes: Method 1, Highlights, and Grid: Method 2 (Perspective).

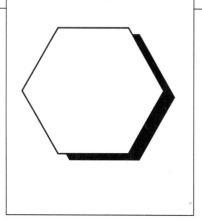

Drop Shadows: Method 1

The simplest method of creating a three-dimensional effect is to create a "shadow" of a shape. That is, a copy of the shape is placed behind the shape, offset slightly, and given a dark fill. This effect is commonly referred to as a drop shadow in graphic design.

This technique is frequently used to add dimension or visual interest to conceptual illustrations such as bar charts and organization charts. You can add special effects to any illustration by using this three-dimensional technique on text, borders, and other two-dimensional objects.

1

Create an object using whatever tool is appropriate. In this example, use the Pen tool to draw a polygon.

2

Use the Selection tool to select the object, holding down the Option key to select all points, then drag the object diagonally a short distance, still holding the Option key to create a copy of it.

3

With the copy still selected, choose Send To Back from the Edit menu (Command-hyphen).

236

4

Use Paint… from the Style menu (Command-I) to add shading to the shadow.

See also Pasting in Layers, Charts: Methods 1 and 2 (Bar Charts, Organizational Charts), Cubes: Methods 1 and 2, and Drop Shadows: Method 2.

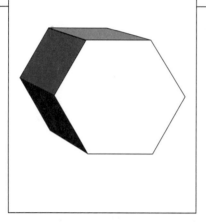

Drop Shadows: Method 2

The three-dimensional objects you can create with Adobe Illustrator are not truly three-dimensional; you cannot rotate a drawing of a house to see a front view and a back view. But you can create a third dimension visually using the technique described here.

Besides adding dimensions to create representation of solid objects such as boxes, buildings, and books, you can add special effects to any illustration by using this three-dimensional technique on text, borders, and other two-dimensional objects.

1

Create an object using whatever tool is appropriate. In this example, use the Pen tool to draw a polygon.

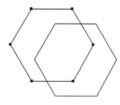

2

Use the Selection tool to select the object, Holding down the Option key, drag the object diagonally a short distance, to create a copy of it.

3

With the copied object still selected, choose Send To Back (Command-hyphen).

4

With the copied object still selected, select the Scale tool from the tool box and scale the object slightly smaller than the original object (see of The Scale Tool in Part I).

5

Using the Pen tool, draw lines between each set of corresponding anchor points to connect the two objects at the edges as shown.

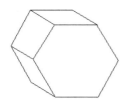

6

Working in a magnified view (using the Zoom tool), use the Scissors tool to cut anchor points where the lines drawn in step 2 meet the back face of the three-dimensional object.

Using the Delete or Backspace key, delete the "invisible" lines.

7

If you want to add shading to each face, use the Pen tool to trace the three polygons that form the sides in this example, and use Paint... from the Style menu (Command-I) to add shading to the three-dimensional faces of the object.

In this figure, use a fill of 100 percent black for the bottom face, 70 percent black for the middle face, and 40 percent black for the top face.

See also Cubes: Methods 1 and 2 and Grid: Method 2 (Perspective).

Flower Petals

Flowers are certainly among the most common objects rendered as artwork. Here is a simple technique for creating flowers like the one pictured in the accompanying figure.

You can use variations on this technique to draw other types of flowers, including roses, chrysanthemums, and other more complicated varieties.

1

Draw one petal that you will use as the basic unit. Option-click on the petal with the Selection tool to select all points, then select the Rotate tool and Option-click the base of the petal. In the Rotate dialog box, enter the number of degrees yielded by the following formula:

Degrees = 360° / (number of petals)

In this example, you will want thirty-six units; so you will type 10 as the number of degrees (360 divided by 36). (See also Radial Symmetry: Methods 1 and 2.)

Click Copy to close the Rotate dialog box and make a rotated copy of the first object, then use Transform Again (Command-D) until the flower is complete.

2

Scale the flower nonproportionally. Choose Select All (Command-A) or drag a selection marquee around all the petals to select the flower. Then select the Scale tool and click near the bottom left edge of the petals. Move the pointer to the opposite corner and drag diagonally to achieve an effect similar to the one shown in the preceding figure.

3

With the Selection tool, select and move the points at the outside tip of each petal, one by one, up or down on random petals to create a more natural, organic look.

4

You can create more complex arrangements of petals by scaling the first set to smaller sizes and overlaying several additional sets. To do this, select the whole flower with the Selection tool. Then select the Scale tool, click the center of the flower as the first point, position the pointer outside of the flower, and drag toward the center until the smaller set of petals is the size you wish. Hold down the Option key as you release the mouse button to create a copy.

For a more realistic effect, use Group (Command-G) and the Rotate tool to rotate each set slightly.

See also Radial Symmetry: Methods 1 and 2.

Highlights

You can make highlights more easily, faster, and more accurately with Illustrator 88 than with earlier versions. Remember that the Blend tool blends not only different paint attributes (as defined in the Paint dialog box from the Style menu) but different shapes as well. This allows you to blend and highlight gradations between two shapes as diverse as an ellipse and a rectangle, or two colors as different as black and white.

Highlights are usually not the same shape as the object being highlighted. With Illustrator 88 it is possible to blend smoothly disparate shapes to create more realistic three-dimensional shading effects.

1

The object to be shaded is a perfect circle, shown in the figure at left. To create your circle, choose the Oval tool from the toolbox. In the active window, the pointer becomes a cross. Hold down the Shift key as you draw the object to be highlighted. Recall that using the Oval tool with the Shift key constrains the object to a perfect circle. With the object selected, choose Ungroup from the Arrange menu (Command U).

2

Now you will draw the shape of the highlight that would appear if the object were truly three-dimensional and lighted from a single source. Choose the Pen or Freehand tool to draw a crescent shape, which is the natural highlight for a sphere. Position it inside the circle, off center.

3

With the Selection tool, click on the circle and choose Paint... from the Style menu (Command-I). Paint the circle a deep color or a deep gray and click OK. Now, with the Selection tool, select the crescent shape inside the circle, choose Paint... again (Command-I), and this time set the black fill to a lighter shade of the same color, such as 20 percent. This paints the crescent a lighter color or lighter gray. Click OK.

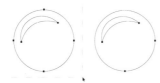

4

Use the Selection tool to drag a selection marquee over the circle and the crescent, and notice where the anchor points are located along the path of each object. (See The Selection Tool in Part I.) Click on an anchor point of the sphere, then Shift-click on a corresponding point of the highlight. These act as reference points for the blend. Continue Shift-clicking alternate points for blending reference. The more paired reference points, the more predictable the blend. (See The Blend Tool in Part I for a detailed explanation of how to determine corresponding points.)

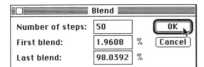

5

Now you are ready to blend. Choose the Blend tool from the toolbox and click once on each object, clicking the larger object (the object to appear on the lowest layer) first. Be sure that the circle is ungrouped, as directed in step 1.

You must select a point on the larger object first in order to identify this as the lowest layer in the blend sequence. Otherwise, if you select a point on the highlight first, the highlight and all intermediate transformations will fall into layer *behind* the larger shape and will not appear in Preview or print out.

After you click the second object, the Blend dialog box appears. Type in the number of blend steps you would like the transformation to use. The more steps you request—up to 1008—the smoother the visual illusion. After selecting the number of blend steps, click OK.

The more blend steps you use, the larger and slower the file will be. Usually no more than thirty blends are needed to yield a smooth transition on a laser printer, and fewer blends are needed when the objects are small.

6

Choose Preview Illustration from the View menu (Command-Y) to see the results of the blend on the screen.

You may need to try a couple of different blends to create the most effective visual illusion and highlight. Experiment by choosing different points to blend. Do not forget that blending is affected by the pairs of reference points you choose initially. Successful illusion blending happens when you choose two points that have a smooth and direct transition path.

See also The Blend Tool.

The artist derived the design for this kimono from several traditional kimono designs found in historical reference books. He composed the kimono using a repeated, rotated, and scaled flower motif on a purple background with blended shading. The trim patterns on the sleeves and edges were created using masking and pattern fills.

David Smith • Sausalito, CA • Courtesy of Apple Computer Japan

The artist created the primary feature of this illustration—the wedges of the fan—using two techniques: he filled some with custom patterns, and he used masks over large designs for others.

David Smith • Sausalito, CA • Courtesy of Adobe Systems Incorporated. All rights reserved.

The artist combined maps with four variations of bar charts to produce this visual representation of economic trends in Asia. He made the illustration easier to understand by using different shapes (cubes, cylinders, and bars) for the different types of data.

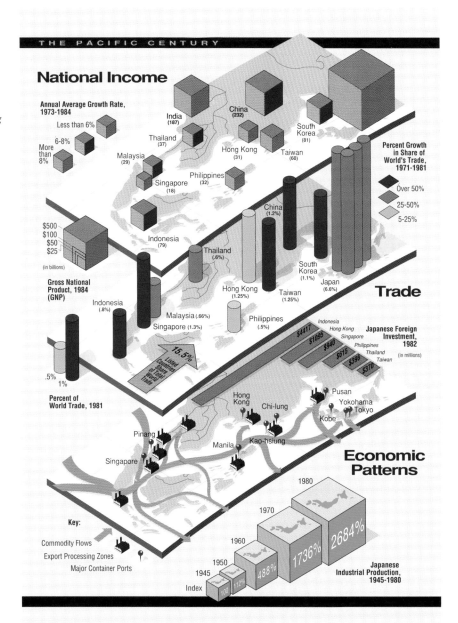

D.L. Fuller • Courtesy of EarthSurface Graphics

This map is composed of over five hundred separate elements. The artist grouped them into thirteen basic parts that each shared the same attributes: route lines (nine groups), stations (two groups), station names, and line names.

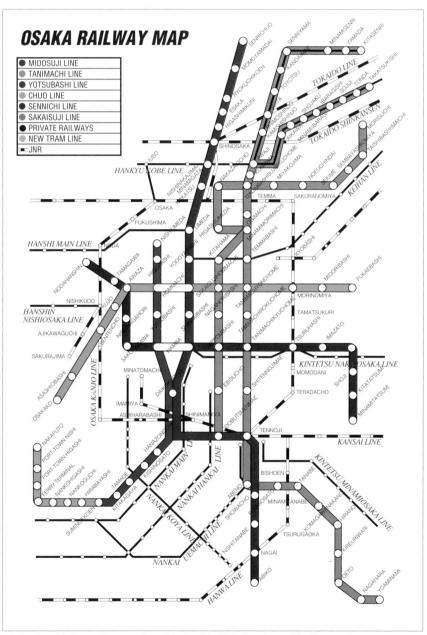

OSAKA RAILWAY MAP

- ● MIDOSUJI LINE
- ● TANIMACHI LINE
- ● YOTSUBASHI LINE
- ● CHUO LINE
- ● SENNICHI LINE
- ● SAKAISUJI LINE
- ● PRIVATE RAILWAYS
- ● NEW TRAM LINE
- ■◦■ JNR

S. Venit • TechArt, San Francisco • based on original work by White Sheet for *The Tokyo Transit Book*
Courtesy of Apple Computer Japan

Part IV:
Applications

Introduction to Applications

This part of the book presents nine finished works that were created by professional artists using Adobe Illustrator. The descriptions of each of these works include procedures and tips that can be applied to a wide range of applications. They refer to techniques that have already been described in Part III. You can adapt many of the steps described here in creating your own artwork.

The examples in this section are divided into two categories:

CATEGORY	DESCRIPTION
Charts, Maps, and Diagrams	Five examples in this section include bar charts, maps, floor plans, and railway route lines.
Illustrations	Four examples in this section include two illustrations that make use of masks and patterns, a portrait that uses complex shading, and a technical illustration that uses lines with a hand-drawn look.

Within each of these categories, you will find the examples listed alphabetically. A representation of each example is shown at the top outside corner of each page for easy reference, and you can use the Quick Reference Guide at the back of the book to look up a specific example by name.

Charts, Maps, and Diagrams

Archdiocese of Detroit Map

Overview   The artist took only two hours to produce this map of the Detroit area—a task that would have required many hours using conventional techniques (technical pens, Zip-A-Tone screens, and camera-distorted typeset text). He did this map for a magazine, and since it was reproduced by gravure on a glossy stock, rather than the usual offset newsprint, it required finer line quality and cleaner treatment than would have been required for newsprint.

The challenge of this graphic was that there was no action needed to be indicated graphically. The only information to convey was the location of these counties. So the artist decided to use a three-dimensional approach to make the map more interesting visually—to "punch it up."

Procedure   The artist traced an available map of the Detroit area using pencil and tracing paper, and scanned the traced outlines using an AST TurboScanner. He used the scanned image as the template in Illustrator for a simple tracing—no curves, all straight lines, even for the right side of the map.

The Counties   Since the news agency wanted to be able to use this artwork at other times, the artist made each county a separate object. Where the borders met, he copied individual line segments and Option-dragged them into place, using the Snap to point feature (set in the Preferences dialog box) to align borders frequently. All except the Monroe/Wayne border were straight lines that he created using the Pen tool. He set the counties with 100 percent Black Stroke, 10 percent Black Fill, and the outline of Detroit with Stroke of None and 30 percent Black Fill. Then he traced the lakes and Canada border, and added the box surrounding the map.

After completing the outlines from the template, the artist used Select All (Command-A), and then the Rotate tool to rotate the image

The archdiocese of Detroit

The archdiocese is made up of the six counties shown.

LAPEER

ST. CLAIR

OAKLAND

MACOMB

Detroit

WAYNE

Lake St. Clair

MONROE

CANADA

Lake Erie

Number of Catholics: 1.5 million

Clergy: 821 active priests, 2,200 nuns

Number of parishes: 331

Number of schools: 147 elementary, 27 secondary

Number of hospitals: 10

Other Catholic-supported facilities include: Three child-care facilities, 15 facilities for care of the aged, 11 retreat facilities, six social service facilities, four children's camps.

SOURCE: Archdiocese of Detroit

JOHN VAN PELT

Archdiocese of Detroit, created by John Van Pelt, Detroit Free Press

approximately 10°. Then he rescaled with the Scale tool—vertically only, to flatten the artwork slightly. During these steps he made a note on paper of the degrees of rotation he had entered earlier in the Rotate dialog box and the percentage scaling he had set in the Scale dialog box so that he could use the same numbers later to rotate and scale the text (county names).

The Three-Dimensional Effect   To create the three-dimensional effect, the artist selected the outlines of all six counties using the Selection tool and Shift-Option-dragged upward ten points from the bottom layer.

The next, and most painstaking, part of the work was completing the series of four-sided polygons that make up the side of the map. The artist connected them using the Pen tool to create straight lines between anchor points on each border, using Snap to point to align the corners of the polygons with the anchor points on the border. (This avoided having to zoom in close to the artwork, since Snap to point has a two-pixel grab.)

Then he filled the shapes with three different screens. He filled each one as he went along, rather than after drawing all the segments. When he knew the next shape would be, for example, 40 percent Black, he clicked on an object previously filled with 40 percent Black to select it, and pressed Command-I (to open the Paint dialog box) then Return to select the default Fill and Stroke in the Paint dialog box. Thus, the next drawn shape would have the 40 percent Black screen. If one segment needed to be behind another, he cut it (using Command-X) and pasted it in back (using Command-B).

The figure on the left, below, shows the illustration up to this point in Artwork Only view. When the artist changed to Preview mode (Command-Y), the three-dimensional effect became more obvious.

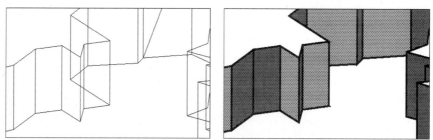

Close-up of three-dimensional border: Artwork Only and Preview

Text Labels   First, using the Type tool, the artist typed one county name, Monroe, with center alignment, in the font specified. Then he rotated it with the Rotate tool and scaled it with the Scale tool using the same numbers he used in rotating and scaling the county outlines. With the text block selected, he Option-dragged to position copies inside each county. Then he went back, selected each text block, and typed in the new county name using the Type dialog box.

The blocks of text below the map were more complicated, since Illustrator does not allow combinations of font styles within the same Type dialog box. Here, the artist made all of the bold text one block of Bold Helvetica, 17 point on 24 point leading. Next he typed the first line of book text in Helvetica, 17 point on 24 leading, with an extra carriage return at the end of the text. This produced a non-printing dot on the screen which showed the leading, as the figure below demonstrates. He created separate text blocks by Option-Shift-dragging the first block and aligning the anchor point of the copy on the dot left on screen by the extra carriage return, then he used Transform Again (Command-D) to create a total of six blocks.

.1.5 million	.1.5 million	.1.5 million
.	.1.5 million	.1.5 million
	.	.1.5 million
		.1.5 million
		.1.5 million
		.1.5 million
		.

Three steps in aligning separate text blocks: (1) type the first with an extra carriage return; (2) align a copy with the anchor point on the carriage return marker; (3) use Transform Again to create multiple blocks

Next the artist selected all of the non-bold text blocks, using the Selection tool, and dragged the whole set of ungrouped, aligned blocks so the left anchor point of the first block was aligned directly over the left anchor point of the bold type. Then he dragged all the blocks of normal Helvetica text to the right approximately one-quarter inch (the distance of the indentation used under *Number of Schools* and *Other...*), holding the Shift key to constrain the movement along the horizontal. Then he dragged the first, second, third, fourth, and sixth blocks of normal Helvetica text individually, further to the right, holding the Shift key to constrain the movement along the horizontal. Finally, he typed the appropriate text for each block. Note that the seventh block created by Transform Again served as a spacing device only and was deleted in these final steps.

The figure below shows a magnified view of the text blocks at the bottom of the illustration in Artwork Only view, and shows the same part of the illustration in Preview mode (Command-Y).

Number of Catholics: 1.5 million

Clergy: 821 active priests, 2,200 nuns

Number of parishes: 331

Number of schools: 147 elementary, 27 secondary

Number of hospitals: 10

Other Catholic-supported facilities include: Three child-care facilities, 15 facilities for care of the aged, 11 retreat facilities, six social service facilities, four children's camps.

SOURCE: Archdiocese of Detroit

Number of Catholics: 1.5 million

Clergy: 821 active priests, 2,200 nuns

Number of parishes: 331

Number of schools: 147 elementary, 27 secondary

Number of hospitals: 10

Other Catholic-supported facilities include: Three child-care facilities, 15 facilities for care of the aged, 11 retreat facilities, six social service facilities, four children's camps.

SOURCE: Archdiocese of Detroit

Close-up of bottom part of the drawing: Artwork Only and Preview

Finishing Touches The artist chopped off the corner of the map on the right by doing the following: he used the Scissors tool to add a new point, then used the new point to bring the side down to the bottom point to close the corner.

He added the title and subtitle to the top of the map and drew a white line with no fill under the subtitle of the chart to eliminate the border of the rectangle that framed the counties.

Tips

Although the artist waited until the last step before adding the text, he could have added it before rotating and scaling the counties. A trade-off is involved: by waiting, he could tell exactly what size the text had to be to fit. If, on the other hand, he had added the text before rotating and scaling the counties, he would not have had to note the rotating and scaling percentages, since he would have rotated and scaled the text along with the county outlines. He might, however, have had to adjust some of the text blocks as a finishing touch.

Because 17 point is not a screen font in the system, screen display is somewhat inaccurate. In addition, the drag to the right (in positioning the blocks of normal Helvetica text alongside the bold at the bottom of the artwork) looks farther away on screen from the bold than it appears when printed. Always print test pages to check positioning of adjacent book blocks of text.

See also Aligning Text: Methods 1 and 2, Hiding Parts of Artwork, Shared Borders, and Drop Shadows: Method 2 in Part III.

Osaka Railway Map

Overview   This map of the Osaka (Japan) Railway system was 52 by 8 inches in its original size, requiring that the font size for the station names be only 4 points in order to fit in the space allotted. The artist printed full-color versions and a color key of the Illustrator document on a QMS ColorScript 100 color PostScript printer, and she printed color separations on a Linotronic 300.

She used the following layering sequence: on the bottom layer, the artist composed the map of over five hundred separate elements, but she associated them into thirteen basic groups that shared the same attributes: route lines (nine groups), stations (two groups), station names, and line names.

You can apply the techniques employed to build this map to any illustration that is composed of several groups of similar or identical objects, including maps, floor plans, and diagrams, and to any color illustration.

Procedure   The artist scanned the map (originally produced using traditional techniques) and used Illustrator to reproduce the original as faithfully as possible, including the original four-color printing (see color plate). She drew one complete layer at a time, and grouped the objects (using Command-G) before starting to build the next layer.

She used the following layering sequence: on the bottom layer, the artist drew the single private line. In front of that, she drew the national line. In the next layer, she drew the seven city lines. Above these, in four subsequent layers, she placed the small station markers, the large station markers, the line names, and the station names, respectively.

The figure on page 258 shows the components of each layer.

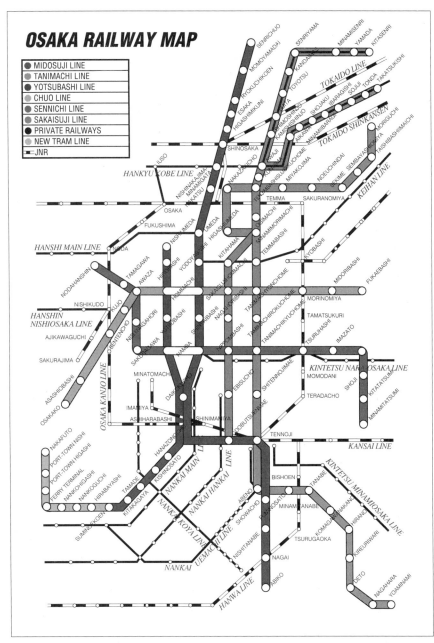

Osaka Railway Map, created by S. Venit, TechArt San Francisco, based on original work by White Sheet for The Tokyo Transit Book

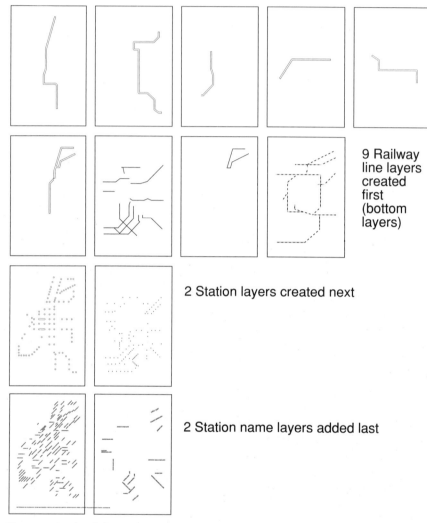

9 Railway line layers created first (bottom layers)

2 Station layers created next

2 Station name layers added last

Components of each layer

258

Working with Layers   While she was working, the artist never used the Ungroup command (Command-U) on more than one layer at a time, and she never ungrouped a set without locking (Command-1) everything else first. When she needed to add, move, or change an element that was part of a grouped layer, she followed this strict sequence of steps:

1. Selected all (Command-A).

2. Deselected the one group she wanted to change (by Shift-clicking with the Selection tool).

3. Locked all remaining selected objects (Command-1).

4. Selected the group she wanted to change (using the Selection tool).

5. Ungrouped it (Command-U).

6. Made changes to elements, or added or deleted elements of this group.

7. Selected all (that is, all parts of the current, unlocked layer) using Command-A.

8. Grouped all (Command-G).

9. Unlocked all (Command-2).

The artist drew the artwork in this illustration on page 5 of the Illustrator document, and used page 4 (the left edge of the Illustrator window) as a "control panel" for the groups, as shown in the next figure. By doing this, she was able to select the whole rail line in the artwork whenever she clicked on the object located to the left of each rail line name in the control panel area. When she clicked on the text shown for station names in the control area, she selected all the station names in the artwork.

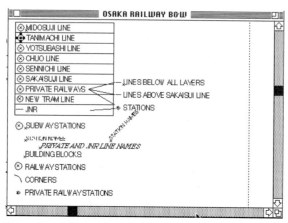

Control panel in working area

Route Lines For the railroad route lines the artist created compound lines composed of white-dashed lines on top of black lines (see Compound Lines: Methods 1 and 2 in Part III). For the subway lines she drew polygons with Black Stroke and color fills. For the station markers she drew two different sizes of circles with Black Stroke and White Fill.

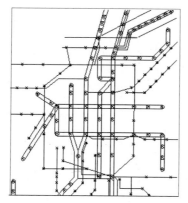

Rail tracks and subway lines

260

She copied dummy text from the control panel to create new station names and line names, then used the Type command (Command-T) to edit the copied text and to set different alignments (left, right, centered), depending on the position of the text relative to the station marker. In a few cases, she kerned (set the spacing value in the Type dialog box) or scaled (with the Scale tool) the station name narrower to fit the space allowed.

Warnings

This sort of project requires a considerable degree of meticulousness in aligning objects. This particular example required more than twelve hours to develop. It also took more than five minutes to print in black and white on a LaserWriter Plus.

Tips

Determine the sequence of layers before you start. You do not have to let good rules of thumb hamper your own creative urges, but unless you have good reasons *not* to, you should start with the bottom layer and follow the seqence of the layers in developing the illustration.

By having a representative from each group in the control area, you can easily click between groups and change grouped attributes without scrolling around on the screen to find the next group you want to change. This technique is especially useful in documents like this one, where the complexity of the illustration makes it slow to scroll and to redraw different views.

See also "Hidden" Notes, Paint Palettes, Compound Lines: Methods 1 and 2, Parallel Curves, and Overlays: Method 2 (Layers) in Part III.

The Pacific Century Chart-Map

Overview   The artist combined maps with four variations of bar charts to produce this visual representation of economic trends in Asia. He made the illustration easier to understand by using different kinds of charts (cubes, cylinders, and bars) for the different types of data.

You can apply the techniques used here to any bar charts. Adding a three-dimensional look can help to enliven a chart and create more visual interest, drawing your audience in and adding meaning to your charts.

Procedure   The artist began with a pencil sketch of the visual concept and researched the statistical data that appear in the charts. In other words, he developed a clear idea of his goal before starting Illustrator.

The Maps   He used a scanned map as a template to trace one outline, then selected the outline and set it to 40 percent Black Fill with No Stroke, using the Paint command. He added borders between countries as open paths (curves with two endpoints that are not joined). These borders were set No Fill and Black Stroke with a Weight of 1 point, using the Paint command. The artist framed the map area in a rectangular shape with curved sides that matched the curve of longitude, using Paint... from the Style menu (Command-I) with a White Fill and No Stroke, and added dashed lines over the map with a 50 percent Black Stroke to indicate latitude and longitude.

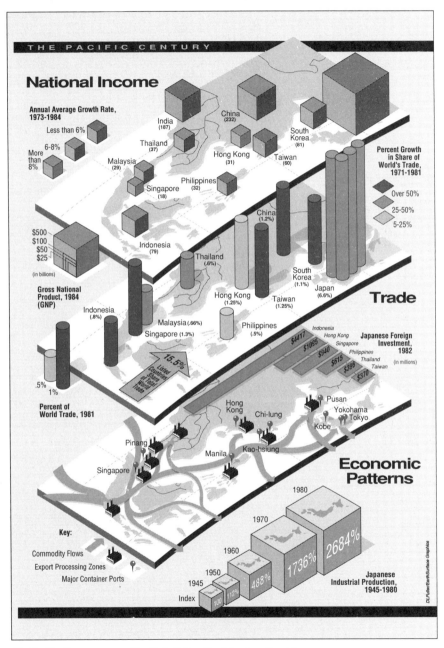

The Pacific Century, created by D. L. Fuller, EarthSurface Graphics

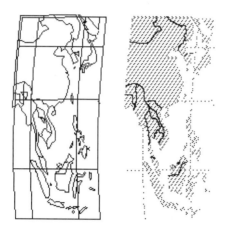

The map was traced from a scanned image, shown here in Artwork Only and Preview

He skewed the whole map visually using the Shear tool. Then, to make a mental note of the angle of the shear for later use with other elements, he held down the Option key and clicked the Shear tool to open the Shear dialog box, which showed the angle of the shear and the axis along which the angle is sheared. Finally, he added the drop shadow to the entire illustration by drawing two polygons along two edges, and used the Paint command to assign the longer edge a 100 percent Black Fill and the shorter edge an 80 percent Black Fill. He then grouped the entire illustration using the Group command from the Arrange menu (Command-G). The figure below shows the results of these steps.

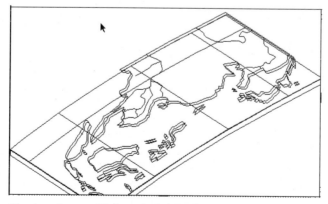

The skewed map with drop shadow border

264

Next the artist made two copies of the map and arranged them in three layers. To make the first copy, he selected the entire map and rectangle, then dragged the selection upward while holding down the Shift key (to ensure precise vertical movement) and the Option key (to make a copy) as he released the mouse button. He used the Transform Again command (Command-D) to create the next copy. He added different country or city names to each layer using the Type tool. He typed the first name and set the type specifications to 12 point Helvetica Condensed, then Option-dragged copies into position on the three maps and edited the copies to produce the different city names with the same type specifications, as the figure below shows.

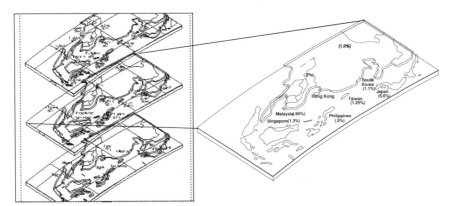

Three maps with cities or countries labeled

Bar Charts The artist then created the three different bar-type objects: cubes for the top map, cylinders for the middle map, and flat bars for the bottom map. In a new untitled window, the artist created one cube and one cylinder and then made scaled duplicates to create a total of three cubes and three cylinders, each with different fill attributes on the faces.

He created the left face of the cube by using the Rectangle tool and the Shift key to draw a square. Then he used the Shear tool while pressing the Option key to open the Shear dialog box. In the Angle space of the dialog box, he entered the same value he used to skew the map.

265

He created the right face using the Reflect tool with the left face selected to mirror a copy of the left face, and the top face by reflecting a copy of one of the other faces. He gave each face a different percentage Black Fill, using the Paint command (Command-I). Then he grouped the entire object with the Group command (Command-G).

To compose the cylinders, the artist drew an ellipse with the Oval tool, then ungrouped it using the Ungroup command from the Arrange menu (Command-U). He copied the ellipse (by Option-Shift-dragging), and moved the copy vertically so it was directly below the original. (See The Selection Tool in Part I for a description of two methods available for this step, Option-Shift-dragging or using the Move dialog box.)

Next he selected and deleted the top anchor point of the copy, leaving the bottom half of the ellipse. Then he used the Pen tool to draw two straight lines up from the bottom ellipse to the top ellipse. He selected the anchor points at each bottom corner of the cylinder and joined them using the Join command (Command-J). Then he brought the top ellipse to the front using the Bring To Front command in the Edit menu (Command-=). He used the Paint command (Command-I) to set the Fill of the top ellipse to 70 percent Black and the Fill of the length of the cylinder to 80 percent Black. He then selected the entire cylinder and Option-dragged to make two copies. He used the Paint command again to set one cylinder's Fill to 50 percent Black (ellipse) and 60 percent Black (length) and the other to 30 percent Black (ellipse) and 40 percent Black (length). He finally grouped each cylinder individually using the Group command from the Arrange menu (Command-G).

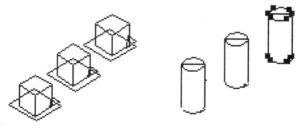

Copied sets of cubes and cylinders, all the same size

To produce scaled copies of the original cubes and cylinders to match various data values, the artist used the Scale tool and Option key to open the Scale dialog box. He numerically scaled each cube, using Uniform scale. Then he numerically scaled each cylinder along the vertical axis only using Non-uniform scale, and clicked the Copy button for each. See Charts: Method 1 (Bar Charts) in Part III for a description of scaling objects to proportionally match data values.

The figure below shows the resulting scaled cubes and cylinders.

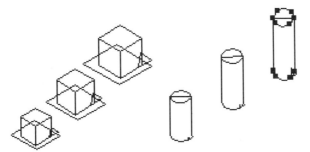

Sets of cubes and cylinders scaled to represent different data values

For the flat bars in the third map, the artist drew one bar with the Rectangle tool and duplicated it five times so there were six flat bars, arranged as shown in the figure below.

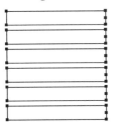

Copied set of bars

He numerically scaled each bar to match various data values by using the Scale tool and the Option key to open the Scale dialog box. In the dialog box, he selected Horizontal scale at a percentage proportional to the data and clicked OK when he was finished with each one. Then he skewed the whole set of bars with the Shear tool and Option key. The next figure shows the flat bars skewed at the appropriate angle.

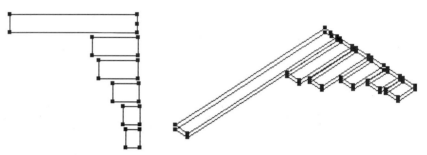

Scaled and skewed set of bars

Finishing Touches With the two documents (the maps and the bar objects) open in different windows on the screen, the artist copied (using Command-C to copy to the Clipboard) the cubes, cylinders, and bars from one document, and pasted (using Command-V) and positioned them on the map in the other document.

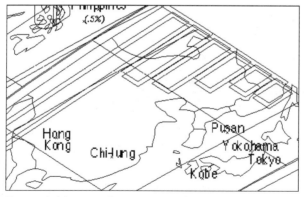

Bars copied from one document onto the maps

The artist repositioned country and city names as necessary to make room for the cubes, cylinders, and bars. He then added text labels, icons, and commodity flow arrows. He traced the outline of Japan that appears on the cubes at the bottom of the illustration, then skewed and positioned the outline on one cube, which he then scaled to five sizes.

Warnings   This complex drawing is a large document in its finished form, and a Macintosh II is recommended for maximum efficiency in working. The final artwork requires nearly 200K of disk space and is very slow in changing views.

Tips   In drawing maps, lay out the lines for latitude and longitude first as precise guides in tracing the map and labeling cities.

Type one example of a text label and set it to the appropriate type specifications, then copy that label to create additional labels.

The drop shadows were colored in the final version (see color plate). In Illustrator 1.1, a special screen was required where the color touched the land. But in Illustrator 88, you can use the Over-print option in the Paint dialog box to create a trap for the color.

See also Charts: Method 1 (Bar Charts), Cubes: Methods 1 and 2, Drop Shadows: Methods 1 and 2 in Part III.

Pontiac Silverdome Chart

Overview   This example shows the floor plan of the Pontiac Silverdome set up for the pope's mass in 1987. Although the artist worked from a scanned template in this drawing, he used it as the basis for a grid, rather than as the basis for the drawing itself. He drew most of the shapes freehand, using the grid, rather than the template, as a guide.

You can apply the techniques used here to any aerial view.

Procedure   The artist began with detailed research of blueprints, sketches, and some photographs of an architect's three-dimensional model of the Pontiac Silverdome, then developed a fairly careful drawing in pencil.

Using a scanned image of the pencil drawing as a template, the artist started with the outer edge of the processional track that surrounds the floor plan. Then the artist proceeded from the bottom layer of the drawing upward to the top layers, which is a typical technique in most three-dimensional aerial view drawings. The artist left text blocks and captions for last.

He used the Oval tool to draw a grid of ellipses (with Fill and Stroke of None) to match the edges of the concentric rings of seats, rather than precisely tracing the template. The template was necessarily a bit rough, so the ellipses in the sketch were not smooth, and the Oval tool helped make the final drawing more accurate.

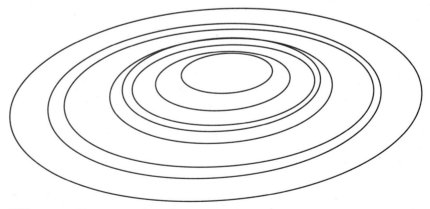

Ellipses traced from scanned template were used as grid

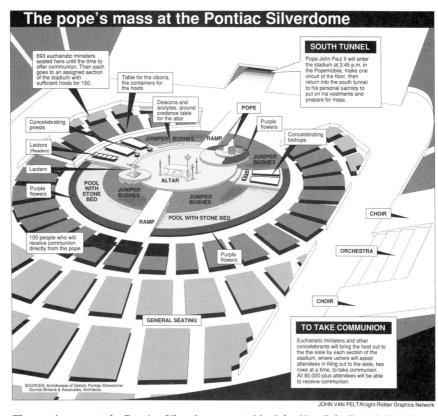

The pope's mass at the Pontiac Silverdome

693 eucharistic ministers seated here until the time to offer communion. Then each goes to an assigned section of the stadium with sufficient hosts for 150.

Table for the ciboria, the containers for the hosts

SOUTH TUNNEL

Pope John Paul II will enter the stadium at 3:45 p.m. in the Popemobile, make one circuit of the floor, then return into the south tunnel to his personal sacristy to put on his vestments and prepare for mass.

Deacons and acolytes, around credence table for the altar

Concelebrating priests

POPE

Purple flowers

Concelebrating bishops

Lectors (Readers)

JUNIPER BUSHES

RAMP

JUNIPER BUSHES

Lectern

ALTAR

Purple flowers

POOL WITH STONE BED

JUNIPER BUSHES

JUNIPER BUSHES

RAMP

POOL WITH STONE BED

CHOIR

100 people who will receive communion directly from the pope

ORCHESTRA

Purple flowers

CHOIR

GENERAL SEATING

TO TAKE COMMUNION

Eucharistic ministers and other concelebrants will bring the host out to the aisle by each section of the stadium, where ushers will assist attendees in filing out to the aisle, two rows at a time, to take communion. All 90,000-plus attendees will be able to receive communion.

SOURCES: Archdiocese of Detroit; Pontiac Silverdome; Gunnar Birkerts & Associates, Architects.

JOHN VAN PELT/Knight-Ridder Graphics Network

The pope's mass at the Pontiac Silverdome, created by John Van Pelt, Detroit Free Press,
© 1987 Knight-Ridder Graphics Network

With the Pen tool, the artist drew four-sided polygons for each seating block, making the edges of each block, which radiated from the center, follow the scanned template. The edges conformed to the Illustrator grid of ellipses in the background. All edges of the seating blocks are straight lines.

Then the artist used Select All (Command-A) and Shift-Option-dragged down to form a copy directly below the original. He copied the copy to the Clipboard (Command-C), selected the originals, then pasted the Clipboard contents behind the originals using the Paste In Back command from the Edit menu (Command-B). Using Paint... from the Style menu (Command-I), he painted the copies with the 100 percent Black Fill to create the drop shadow effect.

271

He drew the ramps as three-sided open paths, filled the same as the main floor, thus blending the open edge with the floor.

Within the altar area, he ungrouped (Command-U) and copied (Command-C) ellipses. Then he pasted them in front (Command-F) and clipped them with the Scissors tool so that parts of the path could be deleted to form matching segments where needed. These steps allowed him to construct the step levels up to the concelebrating priests, down to the concelebrating bishops, up to the papal chair, and up to the lectern. In each case, he used the copied segment to form the beginning of a new path, with the vertical drops constrained by use of the Shift key.

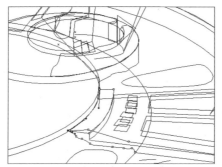 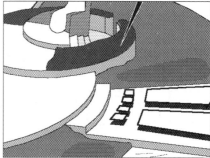

Steps formed by adding vertical lines to copied, clipped ellipses

The artist gave the areas of juniper bushes (surrounding the altar) a darker tone, using the Freehand tool to sketch an amorphous shape and then designating a Stroke of intermediate percentage to give the plants dimension.

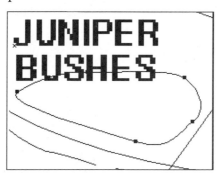 

Juniper bushes drawn as shaded areas, shown here as Artwork Only and in Preview

Finishing Touches The artist added many details, such as the altar and lectern. The first figure below shows a close-up of the altar area, with surrounding juniper bushes and ramps in the Artwork Only view, selected from the View menu (Command-W). The second figure also shows the same area of the illustration in Preview Illustration mode, selected from the View menu (Command-Y). Here you can see the results of the Fill and Stroke settings.

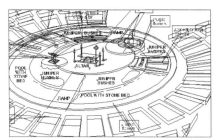 

Close-up of center part of the drawing: Artwork Only and Preview

The artist typed the text blocks in the illustration using the Type tool and positioned them on the drawing, adjusting the length of the text lines as necessary to form rectangular blocks of text with even line lengths. Lastly, he added the rectangular frames around, and arrows from, the text. Using the Paint command (Command-I), he painted the pointers with a Black Fill, White Stroke, and 0.1 Weight, so they would show up against both light and dark areas.

Tips You should spend the greatest amount of time in producing pieces like this in the initial research and planning—this project required about ten hours over several days—and in rendering some of the detailed objects such as the papal chair, lectern, and so on. The basic form of the concentric seating areas in the stadium, the landscaped podium, and the ramps are fairly quick and simple to create.

When the drawing is complete, it is a good idea to delete the grid of ellipses to minimize the size of the saved document. Do this even though the grid will not print (since it has a Fill and Stroke of None).

See also Grid: Methods 2–4 (Perspective, Page Layout, Grid Templates), Pasting in Layers, and Drop Shadows: Methods 1 and 2 in Part III.

Washington, D.C., Street Map

Overview   The artist designed this street map to show the geographical rela-
tionship between four buildings in Washington, D.C., and simpli-
fied it by eliminating superfluous street labels and other geographical markers that are part of the area covered by the map.

  You can apply the techniques used here in creating any map.

Procedure   The artist first drew the map in perspective with paper and pencil,
sketching streets in simple and rough single-line style. Next he
determined the rectangular frame needed to incorporate the major
points of the illustration, working with the newspaper's layout
editor to determine final size and dimensions. He scanned the
sketched drawing, using the scanner's features to set the final size,
and saved it in MacPaint format, then used it as the template for the
Illustrator image.

Water   With Illustrator's rulers showing (Command-R) as a guide,
the artist used the Rectangle tool to draw a rectangle over the
scanned image, capturing the desired area in the size and dimensions determined for the final artwork. He used the Pen tool to trace
the boundaries between the land and water, tracing the water as a
closed path and using Paint... from the Style menu (Command-I) to
set the Fill to 30 percent Black, the Stroke to 100 percent Black, and
the Weight to 1 point.

  (This illustration was created using Adobe Illustrator 1.1. With
Illustrator 88, the Freehand tool could have been used to trace the
water's edges.)

Streets   The artist traced streets with the Pen tool, extending
oblique roads past the edge of the rectangular frame (to be masked
later). He used the Paint command (Command-I) to set Fill to None,
Stroke to 100 percent Black, and Weight to 5 points. This step created
wide black street lines, as the first figure on page 276 shows.

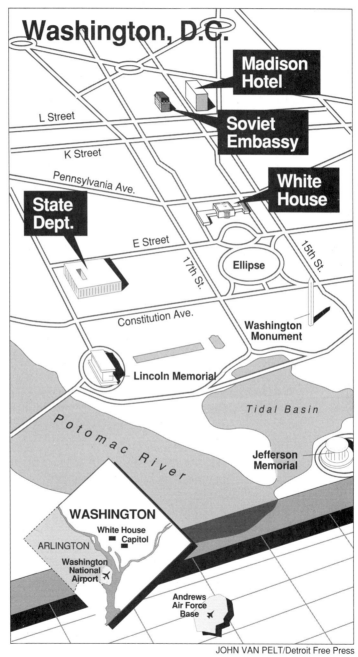

Washington, D.C., created by John Van Pelt, Detroit Free Press

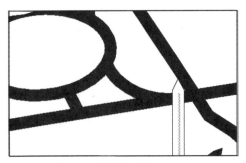

Streets drawn as wide black lines

To yield the final effect of white streets with black edges, the artist selected (with the Selection tool), grouped (using Command-G), and copied (using Command-C) all of the street lines, then pasted them in front (using Command-F) of the wide black street lines. With the Paint command (Command-I), he painted the copied set of street lines with a Fill of None, a Stroke of White , and a Weight of 4 points. This step created the effect of five-point-wide streets with half-point borders. By pasting *all* the white lines in front of *all* the black lines, the artist made sure that the intersections were free of cross lines.

Next the artist held the Option key and clicked on the Selection tool in the toolbox to get the Move dialog box, and moved the white street lines down .2 (–.2 Vertical move) and right .2 (+.2 Horizontal move) to give roads a touch of dimension, as shown in the figure below. This step gave left and top sides of roads .7 thickness, bottom and right sides .3.

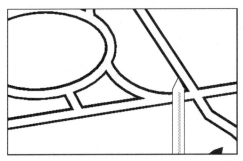

Streets composed of white lines on top of black lines, offset diagonally .2 points from each other

Finally, the artist used narrow white-filled, unstroked rectangles along each edge of the outer frame to hide the tips of streets where they fell outside the rectangular border. (This illustration was created using Adobe Illustrator 1.1. With Illustrator 88, the border rectangle could be set up as a mask—using the Paint dialog box—and the white rectangles would not be needed to hide the street extensions. See Masking in Part III.)

Land's Edge   Using the Pen tool, the artist drew two polygons (one with 50 percent Black Fill and one with 100 percent Black Fill) to add dimension to the edge of the land at the bottom of the map. He used dashed white lines with a .1-point dash and .2-point gap for the grid lines.

Buildings and Landmarks   The artist drew buildings and other landmarks without a template, often in 1600 percent magnified view, to add dimension and detail. He drew the black shadows as polygons with the Pen tool and pasted them behind (Command-B) the building structures.

Inset Map   The artist traced the inset map in a second document using a new template—scanned from a larger area map—then grouped (using Command-G) and copied (using Command-C) it from that Illustrator document and pasted it into position in the first document (using Command-V or Command-F). Then he scaled it to size using the Scale tool. He used the Carta font for airfield symbols (planes).

Finishing Touches   With the Type tool, the artist added text to label streets and landmarks. He used the Pen tool to draw black boxes with pointers to the four buildings that formed the focus of the illustration, and set the type inside each box as Helvetica Bold with White Fill, using .1 point White Stroke for an extra-bold appearance. As a final step, he copied the outer border rectangle and pasted it in front of all the other artwork for a clean outer border.

See also Compound Lines: Methods 1 and 2, Masking a Mask, and Parallel Curves in Part III.

Illustrations

Japan Fan

Overview   The artist created the primary feature of this illustration—the wedges of the fan—using two techniques: he filled some with custom patterns, and he used masks over large designs with the others. The final artwork was printed in color (see color plate).

You can apply the techniques used here to any illustration that calls for pattern fills or patterns created by masking.

Procedure   The artist first created one wedge outline with the Pen tool, and then mirrored it with the Reflect tool to create the second shape. The figure below shows how the first wedge shape is mirrored by the second. To each of these shapes, he applied a Fill of None and a Black Stroke with a Weight of 1, using Paint… from the Style menu (Command-I).

One wedge is a mirror of the other

He then arranged the wedges to form the basic fan shape. He copied the first pair using the Rotate tool, with the point of origin set at the pointed tips of the two fan wedges. He rotated the pair visually to align adjacent borders, holding the Option key as the mouse button was released to create a rotated copy of the wedges. Then the artist used Transform Again (Command-D) to produce the subsequent copies. The first figure on page 280 shows the full fan shape after all copies were made.

Japan Fan created by David Smith

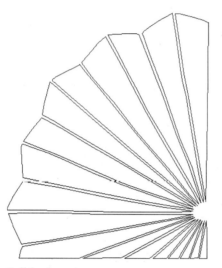

Full fan layout

Pattern Fills After designing and drawing the patterns, the artist tested each one for repeat frequency, color, and positioning within the wedge. (See Patterns: Methods 1 and 2 in Part III.) He copied (Command-C) a single wedge from the original file and pasted it (Command-V) in a new, separate file to experiment with the patterns. The figure below shows the Pattern dialog box, opened by Pattern... from the Style menu, which displays several pattern names along with a sample of the pattern whose name is highlighted. The sample appears in the lower right corner of the dialog box.

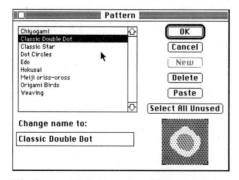

The Pattern dialog box (for adding or deleting patterns) and the pattern pallete from the Paint dialog box (for applying patterns)

Masked Wedges   Some of the fills for the wedges were actually large designs masked by the wedges. In these cases, the artist copied the wedge from the Fan file into a separate Illustrator document containing the large pattern, and masked it with the wedge. (See Masking in Part III.) He moved the wedge around over the large pattern and previewed it (using Command-Y), and in some cases rotated the large pattern using the Rotate tool, until he achieved the desired effect. Then he grouped (using Command-G) and copied (using Command-C) the masked artwork back into the Fan document.

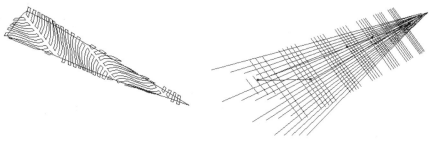

Masked wedges

Finishing Touches   The artist filled the dark background around the fan with a pattern of white dashed wavy lines. (See Patterns: Methods 1–3 in Part III.) He had to experiment with the pattern tiling to get the pattern to repeat correctly.

He drew a closed path, following the outline of the fan, about a quarter-inch away from it. Then he set the Fill to Black and sent it behind the fan wedges using the Send To Back command from the Edit menu (Command-hyphen).

Finally, he added the text at the top of the illustration with the Type tool and the Type dialog box by using the command from the menu (Command-T), placing the text behind the fan wedges.

See also Patterns: Methods 1–3, Masking, Masking a Mask, and Radial Symmetry: Method 1 in Part III.

Kimono

Overview   This kimono is 5 by 8 inches in its original size. The artist printed full-color versions of the document on a QMS ColorScript 100 color PostScript printer, and printed four-color separated negatives on a Linotronic 300 (see color plate).

He composed the kimono using a repeated, rotated, and scaled flower motif on a dark background with blended shading. He created the trim patterns on the sleeves and edges using masking and pattern fills.

You can apply the techniques employed to create the kimono to any illustration that uses a mask, a repeated motif, pattern fills, or blended shading, and to any color illustration.

Procedure   The artist derived the design for this kimono from several traditional kimono designs found in historical reference books. He scanned a halftone PMT of the original color images and used them as templates for the basic shape of the kimono and the positioning of the flowers.

He grouped and arranged the elements of the illustration in the following layers. At the back he used the outline of the kimono as a mask. Immediately in front of this he used the Blend tool to create two hundred rectangular boxes filled with blended shades of purple. He then grouped (using Command-G) and locked (using Command-1) the mask and the blended boxes.

Next the artist constructed the first flower. Then he positioned the two other flowers, which he created by scaling and rotating copies of the first flower. Finally, he pasted the kimono outline as the top object.

The rest of this section describes these basic steps in more detail.

DAVID SMITH / SAUSALITO, CA

Kimono created by David Smith

283

Kimono The artist traced the outline of the kimono from the scanned template. He traced the violet part of the cloth as a closed path and locked it (Command-1). He then created a series of two hundred grouped, narrow rectangles with the Blend tool, using one hundred steps, blending from 100 percent Pantone Violet CV at the top of the kimono to 50 percent Pantone Violet CV at the center. To complete the background, he mirrored a copy of the set of one hundred blends with the Reflect tool to shade from 30 percent at the center to 70 percent at the bottom of the kimono.

Next he grouped (Command-G) the blended boxes and positioned them over the outline. He completed the kimono background by using Command-2 to unlock the outline, Command-(hyphen) to send it to the back of the artwork, and Command-I to open the Paint dialog box, where he clicked Mask, to use the outline as a "clipping" path. (See Masking in Part III.) After clicking OK in the Paint dialog box, he selected both the outline and the blended boxes, grouped them (Command-G), and locked the group (Command-1).

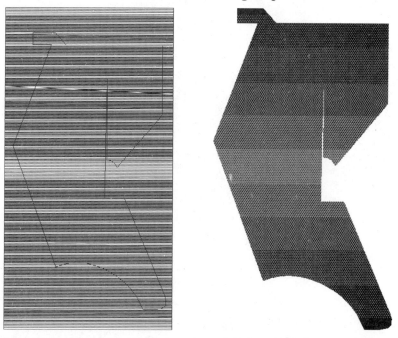

Mask over two hundred narrow boxes: Artwork Only and Preview

In subsequent work, the artist made considerable use of Command-3 and Command-4 to hide and show the background, respectively, for two reasons: first, with so many lines visible, it often became difficult to see the objects he was currently working on; and second, hiding the background made previewing and screen redrawing much faster.

The preceding figure shows the two hundred blended boxes as Artwork Only and in Preview with the kimono masked in the background.

The artist created the solid red areas (which appear black in the final art here; see color plate) that represent the inside lining of the top half of the kimono with the Pen tool, aligned precisely to the kimono outline.

He drew the patterned areas that represent the inside lining of the bottom half of the kimono as closed paths with the Pen tool, then drew a pattern of hexagons slightly larger than the area, starting with a single hexagon and using Option-drag and Transform Again (Command-D) to produce multiple copies. Once he had completed the hexagons, he masked them with the outline paths he had just drawn, then grouped the masked objects with Command-G.

Next he used the Pen tool to draw the sleeve trim and kimono edge as closed paths, filled them with a custom pattern of vertical lines in several weights and colors, and grouped them (Command-G). (See Patterns: Methods 1 and 2 in Part III.)

Flowers   First the artist drew one petal shape, then he scaled down a copy with the Scale tool. He set the larger shape with a Fill of White and a Stroke of None, using the Paint command (Command-I). He used the smaller shape to set up two reference points for blending a green color, using lighter shading at the outer edges and darker at the center of the petal. The next figure shows the blended petal shape in Artwork Only and Preview Illustration views. After blending, he drew the innermost shape of the petals with a red fill and no stroke. He then copied (Command-C), rotated with the Rotate tool, and scaled with the Scale tool the dimensional-looking petal to form a six- or seven-petal arrangement.

285

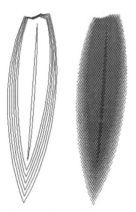

One flower petal, as Artwork Only and in Preview

Next the artist composed the central part of the flower of five radially symmetrical half-circles. Once he had drawn the first outer form, he scaled down a copy with the Scale tool. Then he set the larger shape with a white fill and no stroke, and the inner shape with a shade of red fill and no stroke. He rotated a copy of the full-size object using the Rotate tool, then scaled down a copy of the inner portion to create the center. The artist filled each of the layers with a different shade of red, then grouped them all (Command-G).

The next figure shows the center of the flower as Artwork Only and in Preview.

Center of flower, as Artwork Only and in Preview

He added the pistils by drawing one, setting it with green fill and no stroke, rotating copies around the center point using the Rotate tool, and clicking the Copy button in the Rotate dialog box. He grouped (Command-G) and overlayed the pistils on the flower center, then copied (Command-C), scaled with the Scale tool, and overlayed the set on the flower petals. The figure below shows the pistils as one grouped object prior to overlaying them on the flower petals.

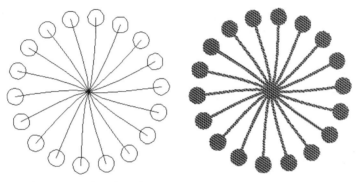

Pistils as Artwork Only and in Preview

Finally, the artist drew the fernlike leaf and the berry branches once, then used all four transformation tools—Rotate, Scale, Shear, and Reflect—to create variety, and arranged them individually for each flower. He also made individual adjustments to the stacking order using the Cut, Paste In Front, and Paste In Back commands. Finally, he used Select All (Command-A), and grouped the leaves, flower centers, pistils, ferns, and berries into a single composite object with Command-G. The figure at the top of the next page shows the finished, composite flower in Artwork & Template view; on the right is the flower in Preview mode (Command-Y).

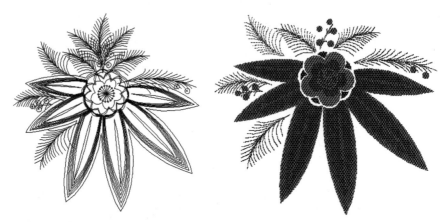

A finished flower in Artwork & Template and in Preview mode

Finishing Touches   Finishing touches included drawing ribbons over the kimono, drawing black and gray lines radiating from the bottom hem of the kimono, and pasting a copy of the kimono outline in front of all other layers (using the Paste In Front command, Command-F), giving it a Fill of None and a Black Stroke of .5 Weight. To accomplish this last step, the artist first chose Select All (Command-A), then Hide (Command-3), which left the locked kimono outline visible. Next he unlocked (Command-2) and ungrouped (Command-U) the outline and blends. Then he selected and copied (Command-C) the outline. Next he regrouped (with Command-G) and locked the outline and the blends (Command-1), chose Show All (Command-4), and, finally, used Paste In Front (Command-F) to paste the copy of the kimono outline on top.

Warnings   The grouping of objects and the stacking order of clipping paths is tricky and time-consuming. Complex work of this nature, while theoretically possible on a Mac Plus or SE, virtually requires an accelerated SE or a Mac II for reasonable performance.

Tips Determine the grouping of composite objects before you start. You can draw different elements in different files, and use Copy and Paste In Front or Paste In Back to assemble the parts into one illustration.

See also Blending Colors or Grays, Patterns: Methods 1 and 2, Masking, Masking a Mask, Pasting in Layers, Radial Symmetry: Methods 1 and 2, and Flower Petals in Part III.

Portrait

Overview   The artist traced this portrait from a scanned photograph. He created areas of different percentage fills for a realistic dimensional effect. He likened the use of progressive layers of lighter and darker tones to portrait drawing with white and black Conté crayon on gray charcoal paper.

You can apply the techniques used here in tracing any scan, but they are especially applicable to images that require shading of irregular surfaces.

Procedure   The artist scanned the original photograph, a black-and-white 2-by-3-inch passport photo, as a halftone (eight gray levels) at 300 dpi on a Microtek 300SF Flatbed scanner. He adjusted contrast and brightness to obtain a template with a full range of density (from deepest shadow to white) and with smooth gradation of density levels. He then used the scanned image as a template for the Illustrator artwork.

The artist layered the face rendering with closed, filled, and stroked paths in this logical fashion: he started with the forehead, then hair, eyes, nose, mouth, chin, and finally the neck, collar, tie, and the background and frame.

He selected a middle tone—about 40 percent Black Fill—as the "ground" or predominant tone for the face. The basic outline of the face with this midtone gray fill became the foundation for the rest of the art. He built up lighter and darker areas in layers, closely referring to the original photo. He filled each successive layer of shapes (closed paths that outline shaded areas of the face) with an intermediate value to soften the gradations. For example, he drew one of the shadows under the eyes on top of an area already at 45 percent Black Fill. He gave the new darker path a 55 percent Black Fill, but a 50 percent Stroke. Sometimes he thickened the stroke to accentuate the gradation effect. The figure on page 292 shows a close-up of this gradation effect in Artwork Only mode (Command-W) and this same close-up in Preview mode (Command-Y), which shows the gradation effects achieved.

Portrait created by John Van Pelt

Close-up of graduated shading: Artwork Only and Preview

Warning   Setting contrast and brightness for the scan required much trial and
error. The artist made about ten scans before he was satisfied with
the result.

Tips   The artist could have used the Blend tool for some of the gradations of shading, but he achieved a more realistic effect by drawing each layer of shading individually, so the transition from one shape (of shaded area) to another was adjusted by the artist to match his interpretation of the original photo, and not mathematically determined.

See also Blending Colors or Grays and Highlights in Part III.

Technical Illustration

Overview   The artist saw this assignment for a newspaper feature page as an opportunity to do something in a more creative, less rigid graphic style, even though the subject matter was technical. The illustration is a good example of the techniques described in Hand-drawn Look: Methods 1–3 in Part III. The final art was in color, using manually cut amberlith overlays.

This example demonstrates how Illustrator can be used to save time over conventional techniques. The artist comments: "This was done when I had been working with Illustrator for about a week. I debated over how to render the design, as I had in mind a rather loose brush-and-ink style. But in the tight deadline I couldn't see how I would work in the text drop-ins if I had to build the whole thing by conventional (paste-up) methods. The Macintosh was clearly the answer, and what I knew of Illustrator up to then convinced me it was capable of the flexibility I needed."

Procedure   The artist made several rough sketches with soft pencil on tracing tissue, and came up with a plan he liked. Then he scanned the rough sketch, with no further refinements. "I wanted to capture the impromptu character even though I knew I would painstakingly trace each line."

Using the scanned image as a template for the Illustrator artwork, he traced each line quickly as a closed path, with a Fill of Black and Stroke of None, working at maximum magnification. Some shapes, such as the droplets of sweat, he drew as closed paths with Black Fill with a smaller white-filled shape superimposed in White Fill. To maintain the hand-drawn look for the sweat drops, the artist drew the smaller inside shapes with the Pen tool rather than using the Scale tool to produce a copy of the outer shape.

The figures on page 296 show the magnified view of the top right part of the drawing in Artwork Only view. The artist then chose Preview Illustration from the View menu (Command-Y) to view the art.

294

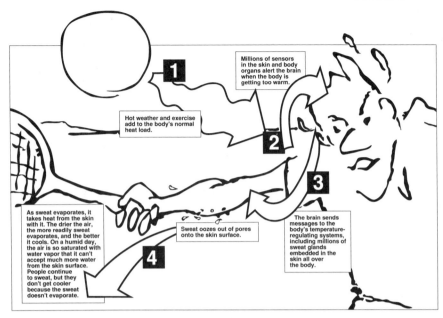

Technical Illustration created by John Van Pelt, Detroit Free Press

The artist drew the sun in the drawing, which juts over the bounding rectangle, as a closed path representing the outline only; the inside area of the sun was not part of the path. To eliminate the part of the rectangular border that crossed the sun, the artist ungrouped the rectangle (using Command-U) and clipped it with the Scissors tool.

For a cleaner look, the artist made the arrows single paths, with a thick 2.5-point Black Stroke and a White Fill. Finally, he added the text blocks using the Type tool and the Type dialog box, and the black blocks with white-filled numerals.

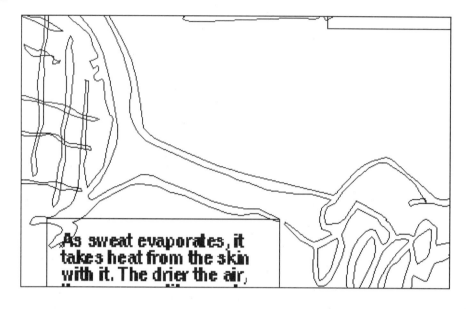

As sweat evaporates, it takes heat from the skin with it. The drier the air,

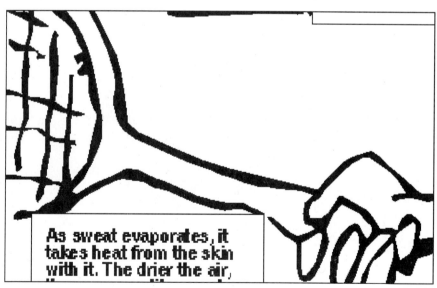

As sweat evaporates, it takes heat from the skin with it. The drier the air,

Close-up of part of the drawing: Artwork Only and Preview

Tips   In this case the artist chose to cut amberlith overlays for the color separations rather than use Illustrator's separation feature. In the final version, the amberlith was deliberately cut roughly to yield imprecise registration, adding to the sketchy look of the hand-drawn lines.

See also Aligning Text: Methods 1 and 2 and Hand-drawn Look: Methods 1 and 2 in Part III.

Appendices

Appendix A: Converting PICT Files with DrawOver

Overview   You can convert drawings that have been created or saved in PICT format into PostScript documents that can be edited in Illustrator using DrawOver™, an application that Adobe packages with Adobe Illustrator 88™. As of the writing of this book, DrawOver™ specifically handles drawings created by MacDraw 1.9 or 1.9.5, and converts straight lines, rectangles, ovals, line weights, and fill patterns that are shades of gray. Lines drawn with MacDraw's Freehand tool are converted into vectors with many anchor points along the path. Converted drawings can be edited using any of the features offered by Adobe Illustrator 88™ or version 1.1.

Procedure   First create a drawing in PICT format using an application that can be saved in PICT format. Then, from the Macintosh desktop, double-click on the DrawOver™ application icon to start it.

DrawOver™ 1.0

In the dialog box that appears next, find and double-click the name of the document you wish to convert.

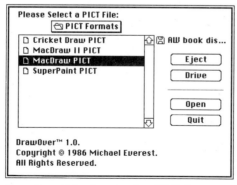

DrawOver dialog box showing PICT documents

When a window displaying a Preview image of the PICT document opens, click OK (or press Return) if this is the document you wish to convert, or click Cancel if you want to end the DrawOver process or choose a different document name.

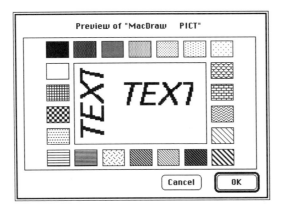

DrawOver displays a Preview of the document you wish to convert

When you click Cancel, the original DrawOver dialog box appears. When you click OK, a new dialog box appears, in which you choose the location for the converted document and type a name for the new document (or accept DrawOver's naming convention of adding .ART to the PICT file name).

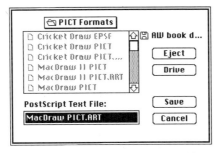

Dialog box for entry of name of new file and location

301

After you enter a name and click Save, DrawOver displays a message giving the status of the conversion as it goes through two passes.

```
Pict To PostScript Conversion

Input:    "MacDraw PICT"

Output: "MacDraw PICT.ART"

Pass 1 Total KiloBytes:    0

Pass 2 Total KiloBytes:
```

Message shows status of conversion

When the conversion process is complete, the original DrawOver dialog box reappears, and you can convert another document or quit the DrawOver application. Converted documents can be opened and edited using Illustrator 88 or version 1.1.

Warnings　　Not all elements of the original PICT drawing will be converted into PostScript. For example, text is not always converted, and many of the fill patterns that are available in MacDraw and similar applications will not be converted. Colors applied in MacDraw II are converted to black, and text from MacDraw II is not converted into PostScript. The fountain effects created in Cricket Draw are preserved, but text and fill patterns are lost. The bitmapped layer in SuperPaint is not converted.

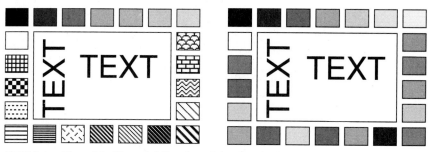

PICT format from MacDraw 1.9.5 and resulting PostScript artwork. All fill patterns are converted as shades of gray

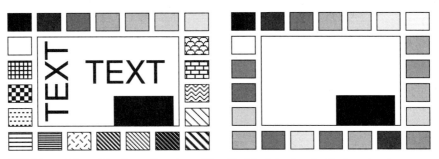

PICT format from MacDraw II and resulting PostScript artwork. Black rectangle was color in MacDraw II file

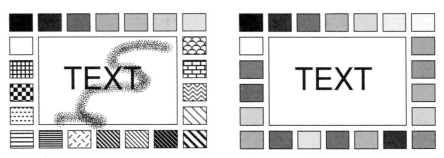

PICT format from SuperPaint and resulting PostScript artwork. Bitmapped layer is not converted

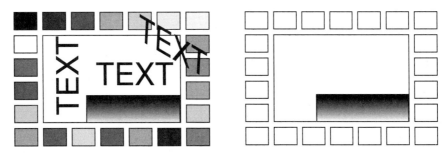

PICT format from CricketDraw and resulting PostScript artwork. Text and fill patterns are lost but fountains are preserved

Appendix B: Printing Color Separations with Adobe Separator

Overview   You can print four-color process separations or custom (spot) color separations using Adobe Separator™, an application that Adobe packages with Adobe Illustrator 88™. This appendix describes how to use Adobe Separator to print color separations. For a description of how to create colors and assign them to artwork, see the Paint command (for assigning colors) and the Preferences command (for adjusting the color display on the monitor with the Change Progressive Colors option) in Part II, and see Blending Colors or Grays and Overlays: Methods 1 and 2 in Part III.

Procedure   First use Adobe Illustrator 88™ to create an illustration and apply one or more colors (other than black and white). Then, from the Macintosh desktop, double-click on the Adobe Separator™ application icon to start it.

Adobe Separator™ 2.0

In the dialog box that appears next, find and double-click the name of the document you wish to print.

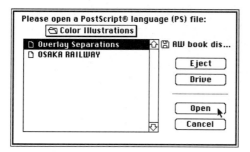

Dialog box for selecting a document to print

After you select a file, Adobe Separator displays the dimensions of the bounding box, indicating the outside dimensions of the illustration. The values initially displayed in this dialog box are calculated automatically, and represent the smallest rectangle that could be drawn around the illustration. Trim marks and registration marks will be printed outside the bounding box dimensions. You can change the size of the bounding box in order to change the location of the trim marks and registration marks. Changing the size of the bounding box does not change the size of the dimensions of the illustration itself.

Bounding Box:			OK
Left:	67	points	Cancel
Bottom:	59	points	
Right:	692	points	
Top:	481	points	

Dimensions of the bounding box

The bounding box dimensions are given in points and are measured from the bottom left corner of the page. The next figure shows the position of the bounding box that would result from the settings shown in the bounding box above.

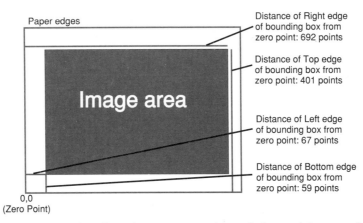

How bounding box dimensions are measured from the bottom left corner of a page

305

The next dialog box displayed by Adobe Separator asks you to specify the PostScript Printer Description (PPD) file for the printer you are using. These files are provided as part of the Adobe Illustrator 88™ Utilities Disk, and are stored in the PPD Folder. This file contains information about the printer's dot resolution, the available page sizes, whether the printer supports color output, and the acceptable screen settings. The PPD file that you select here will affect the options listed in the Adobe Separator dialog box, explained later in this section.

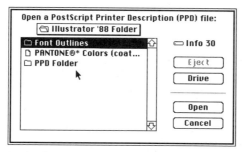

Dialog box asking for a printer description file

Find the PPD Folder and double-click on that name in the dialog box. When the PPD Folder is open, a list of the PPD files is displayed. The name of the printer file is a cryptic abbreviation of the full name and model number of the printer.

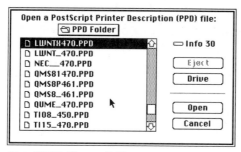

List of PPD files available

After you choose the PPD file that matches the printer you are using, the Adobe Separator dialog box appears. You can accept the default settings to print all four process color separations, or you can choose different options as described on the following pages. The text boxes that show a subtle drop shadow at the right and bottom edges are actually pop-up menus: position the mouse pointer over the text box and hold down the mouse button to view options; drag and release the mouse to choose an option.

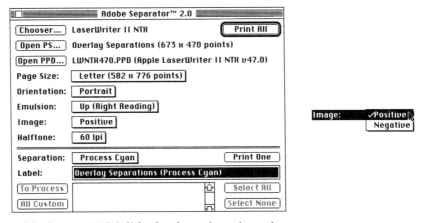

Adobe Separator™ 2.0 dialog box for setting print options

The following options are available in the Adobe Separator dialog box:

Chooser Displays the Chooser dialog box and allows you to change the printer selection. This is an alternative to selecting the Chooser command from the Apple menu. (See Chooser in Part II.)

Open PS… Displays the dialog box that lets you choose a PostScript file to be separated, described earlier.

Open PPD… Displays the dialog box that lets you choose a PostScript Printer Description file, described earlier.

Page Size Hold down the mouse button on the text box to display and choose from the list of page sizes available for the printer (as identified in the PPD file) you have chosen. The dimensions of the

307

printable area are shown next to each page size on the menu, and these dimensions include the limits for the registration marks, color labels, and crop marks that are printed.

Page Size:	
	A4 (564 x 822 points)
	A4Small (540 x 780 points)
	B5 (479 x 705 points)
	Legal (582 x 992 points)
	√Letter (582 x 776 points)
	LetterSmall (552 x 730 points)

Page Size options are displayed in a pop-up menu

If your printer allows variable page sizes, a custom page size option will be displayed on the page size menu as Other . . . , and you will be able to enter custom dimensions and offset. You will also be able to print the page transversely (rotated 90 degrees). You can use these last two options to avoid wasting film on phototypesetters.

Orientation   Hold down the mouse button on the text box to display and choose from the list of orientations available. In Portrait mode, the top of the image is printed parallel to the short edge of the paper. In Landscape mode, the top of the image is printed parallel to the long edge of the paper.

Orientation options are displayed in a pop-up menu

Note that orientation affects the position of the image on the page (as defined in the Illustrator document by the Page tool), whereas the Transverse available on some printers through the Page Size option affects the orientation of that page (as defined in the Illustrator document) on the printout paper (as defined through the Page Size option).

Emulsion   Hold down the mouse button on the text box to display and choose from the list of emulsion settings available. Emulsion Up (Right Reading) means that any text in the image is readable when the printed paper is facing you. Emulsion Down (Right Reading) means that the text is readable when the paper is facing away from you.

Emulsion options are displayed in a pop-up menu

Normally you would print with Emulsion Down (Right Reading) only when printing to a transparent film. When printing to clear film, the emulsion side is dull; the shiny side is the base.

Image   Hold down the mouse button on the text box to display and choose from the list of image options available: Positive or Negative. Positive images print exactly as shown in Preview on the screen. Negative images reverse dark and light areas. You can save a step in offset printing by printing negative separations directly to film.

Image options are displayed in a pop-up menu

Halftone   This option shows the screen ruling of the halftone pattern used to print the separations, in halftone dots per inch, stated as lines per inch (lpi). The available choices vary depending on the PPD file you have opened. If you are printing to a high-resolution device, the screen angles for the four process colors and the custom color are listed in parentheses on the pop-up menu in the following order: cyan, magenta, yellow, black, and custom color.

Note that as the screen ruling increase, the halftone dots are less noticeable, but there is a trade-off between screen ruling and the available number of gray shades, and the number of gray shades per screen ruling is determined by the resolution of your printer.

Separation   This option lets you choose the type of separations to be printed. If you choose Print All (the button in the top right corner of the dialog box), Adobe Separator prints one separation for each of the four process colors used in the illustration, and one for each custom color used. When you choose Print One (the button in the bottom right area of the dialog box), what you print is determined by your selection under this Separation option.

To select individual separations, hold down the mouse button on the Separation text box to display the list of separations in the pop-up menu. If you choose a process color, you can print one separation with the elements that use that process color.

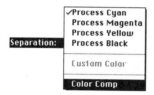

Separation options are displayed in a pop-up menu

If custom colors were used in the illustration, you can convert them to four-color process colors by clicking on the name of the custom color in the list at the bottom of the dialog box, then choosing To Process (a button to the left of the custom color list). The name of the custom color will disappear from the list. You can restore all custom colors to the list by clicking All Custom (the second button to the left of the custom color list).

If you choose Custom Color, then you must choose the custom color to be printed from the list of custom colors displayed at the bottom of the dialog box. You can choose more than one custom color at a time by holding down the Command key while selecting additional colors, and the separation will contain all of the colors selected.

Custom Color options are displayed in a scrolling window

310

If you choose Color Comp, you will get a single printed page with all colors combined. This has the same effect as printing directly from Adobe Illustrator's Print command.

Label   The text of the Label shown in this text box will be printed on the current separation when Print One is selected. The Label is created automatically when you make selections described for the Separations option, or you can type your own custom label for each separation.

Each separation is printed with registration marks, color bars, crop marks, a star target, a graduated screen, and a label, as shown in the next illustration. This information is used by the offset print shop in aligning and checking the negatives.

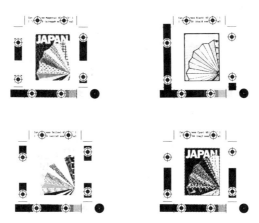

Printed separation

Tips

If you hold down the Option key, the Print One button changes to read Save One, and you can save individual separations onto a disk as PostScript language files.

You can force the crop marks to frame a full page layout (including margins) by framing the artwork with a rectangle the size of the cropped page and setting Fill and Stroke to None. This is a simple and visual alternative to setting the size manually in the hounding box.

311

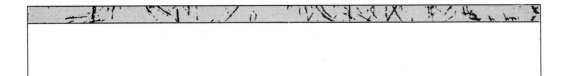

Glossary

actual size A view of a page on the screen, scaled to approximately the same size it will print, depending on the characteristics of your screen display.

additive primary colors Red, green, and blue. The three colors used to create all other colors when direct, or transmitted, light is used (television, for instance).

alignment How type lines up. Illustrator gives you three choices: align left (flush left, ragged right); align center (ragged left, ragged right); and align right (ragged left, flush right). The alignment of a block of type is indicated by the position of its alignment point.

alignment point The point used to align a block of type. The alignment point is also used to select and move the type. Each block of type has one alignment point. The point appears as a solid square when the block of type is selected, and otherwise appears as an *x*.

anchor point The point on a segment that determines where the segment starts or ends. Anchor points are invisible unless any segment of the path they form is selected. Anchor points that end curve segments have direction lines and points associated with them. A single anchor point, with no segments connected to it, appears as an *x* when not selected.

artwork The paths and type created with Illustrator that constitute a single image. Stroke and fill attributes are not visible in an Artwork Only image. Artwork is saved as a PostScript program. Compare with *preview image* and *template*.

autotrace To trace around the shapes or lines in a template automatically.

average To find the average location of selected anchor points and move the selected points to that location. When you average points, the points remain distinct points. Compare with *join*.

baseline A horizontal line that coincides with the bottom of each character in a font, excluding descenders (tails on letters like *p*). In Adobe Illustrator, the baselines of a block of type are visible when the type is selected. You click on a baseline to select type, and drag it to move type.

benday   An old printing term for screen tints. Taken from the name of a company that used to produce screens for the printing industry.

bevel join   A squared-off corner, created when the notch formed by two perpendicular lines is filled with a triangle. Compare *miter join* and *round join*.

Bezier curve   A curve, named after Pierre Bezier, that is defined mathematically by four control points. These control points are the four direction points at the ends of the two direction lines that are tangent to each curve. All curves in Adobe Illustrator are Bezier curves. See *curve*.

bitmap   An electronically displayed graphic image made up of a matrix of dots. Templates and Preview images are bitmap images.

blend   To create a series of successive shapes or shadings between two selected paths.

blueline   A prepress proofing material, used to proof black-and-white art before printing.

boilerplate   A document set up with text and graphic elements that will be included routinely in a series of documents based on the boilerplate without the need to recreate the repeated elements each time. See also *template*.

butt cap   A square line cap that is perpendicular to the end of a line. It is called a butt cap because the cap butts up against the end of the line. Compare *round cap* and *projecting cap*.

cap   See *line cap*

Chromalin   An integral proofing system produced by DuPont. See *integral proof*.

click   To press and then immediately release the mouse button.

clip art   Off-the-shelf art for the Macintosh. Clip art pieces are stored as MacPaint documents.

clipping path   A mask as defined in Illustrator's Paint dialog box.

closed path   A path with no endpoints; a loop. Compare with *open path*.

coated stock   Paper that has a light clay or plastic coating. A glossy or slick paper is coated. The same color of ink will appear different when printed on different types of stock. Compare with *uncoated stock*.

coincident   Occupying the same position. In a straight line, an anchor point and its two direction points are coincident.

collinear   Occurring along the same straight line. The anchor point and two direction points of a smooth point are collinear.

color keys   A color overlay proofing system produced by 3M Company. See *overlay proofs*.

color separations   In offset printing, separate plates used to lay different colors of ink on a page printed in multiple colors, to reproduce the proportional amount of cyan, magenta, yellow, and black in the original. Adobe Separator™ prints color separations of documents created in Illustrator 88™.

comp   A graphic arts term for comprehensive drafts. In Adobe Illustrator, a paper proof printed on a color printer before you print the final negatives is the equivalent of a comp.

condensed type   A narrow typeface having proportionally less character width than a normal face of the same size. Although you can achieve this effect by graphically scaling characters from the normal font, usually condensed characters are individually designed as a separate font. Condensed typefaces are used where large amounts of copy must fit into a relatively small space (tabular composition being the most common area of usage). See also *kerning*.

constrain   To restrict drawing, moving, or transforming to an angle that is a multiple of 45 degrees, relative to the angle of constraint you specified in the Preferences dialog box.

continuous tone image   A photographic image that contains gradient tones from black to white. When you scan an image, it is converted from a continuous tone image to a halftone.

corner point   An anchor point that is not on a straight line with its two direction points. Corner points are used to join two segments traveling in different directions. Compare with *smooth point*.

corner radius   The radius of the circle used to form rounded corners in a rectangle.

crop marks   Lines printed on a page to indicate where the page will be trimmed when the final document is printed and bound. Adobe Separator™ prints these marks if the bounding box is smaller than the paper size.

current attributes   The fill, stroke, and type attributes that are in effect when you create a path or specify type. The current attributes appear in the Paint dialog box when no objects are selected.

cursor key distance   The distance that selected objects move each time that you press a cursor (arrow) key. The distance is set in the Preferences dialog box.

curve   A smooth path defined by two anchor points and two direction points. The anchor points define where the curve starts and ends. The direction points determine the shape of the curve.

custom color   An ink color that you assign to objects in your drawing. With custom color, you can use Adobe Separator™ to produce one negative for each color used in the artwork. Compare with *process color*.

cyan   The subtractive primary color that appears blue-green and absorbs red light. Used as one ink in four-color printing. Also known as process blue.

CYMK   Shorthand notation for cyan, yellow, magenta, and black.

dash pattern   The pattern of lines and gaps between lines that make up a dashed line. You create a dash pattern by specifying the length, in points, of each dash and of each gap between dashes.

default   The initial setting of a value or option. Used to describe the value(s) or mode that Illustrator will use in processing information when no other value or mode is specified. A preset response to a question or prompt. Default settings can be changed.

define (pattern)   To draw or place artwork inside a rectangle and then give it a name in the Pattern dialog box.

dialog box   A window or full-screen display in response to a command that calls for setting options.

digitizer   See *scanner*.

direction line   The straight line connecting an anchor point and its direction point. A curve is tangent to the direction line at the anchor point.

direction point   A point that defines the direction from which a curve enters the curve's anchor points. The position of a curve's two direction points determines the curve's shape.

dots   See *halftone dots* and *pixel*.

drag   To hold down the mouse button while you move the pointer.

DrawOver   An application that converts MacDraw files to Adobe Illustrator documents.

Dylux   A brand name for blueline proofing material.

emulsion   The photosensitive layer on a piece of film or paper.

Encapsulated PostScript (EPS) format   A file format that describes a document written in the PostScript language and that contains all the code necessary to print the file.

endpoint   An anchor point at the beginning or end of an open path. Illustrator displays endpoints as *x*'s.

fill   To paint an area enclosed by a path with black, a gray shade, a color, or a pattern.

film   Photosensitive material, generally on a transparent base, which receives character images, and may be chemically processed to expose those images. In phototypesetting, any photosensitive material, transparent or not, may be called film.

flatness   The maximum distance, in device pixels, of any point on a rendered curve from the corresponding point on the true curve.

folio   Page number.

font   One complete set of characters in the same face, style, and size, including all of the letters of the alphabet, punctuation, and symbols. For example, 12-point Times Roman is a different font from 12-point Times Italic, 14-point Times Roman, or 12-point Helvetica. Screen fonts (bitmapped fonts used to display text accurately on the screen) can differ slightly from the printer fonts (outline fonts used to describe fonts to the laser printer) because of the difference in resolution between screens and printers.

freehand tolerance   A value that controls how sensitive the Freehand tool is to variations in your hand movement.

ghosting   The shift in ink density that occurs when large, solid areas interfere with one another. Also, a procedure in which two images are combined together electronically. The images are given specific weight in relation to each other to create the effect.

grid   The underlying design plan for a page. In Illustrator, the grid can be composed of a series of nonprinting horizontal and vertical lines that intersect to form a "grid."

gripper   The top part of a page where the printing press grabs the paper. Nothing can be printed in this area.

group   To combine two or more objects so that they act as a single object. You can manipulate groups just as you do individual objects.

hairline   The thinnest rule possible—generally 0.25 point.

halftone   An image composed of dots of different sizes. Using a scanner, you can convert continuous tone images, such as photographs, into halftones.

halftone dots   Dots as they appear on the printed page. The size of the halftone dots depends on the screen ruling used.

hide   To remove a path or block of type from the artwork temporarily. Objects that are hidden do not preview or print.

insertion point   A blinking vertical line that indicates where characters you type will appear.

integral proof   A color proofing system that bonds all four process colors to a single sheet.

interpreter Code built into PostScript-compatible printers and typesetters that converts PostScript commands into a form the printer can use to draw an image, or software that converts Post-Script commands before sending them to a printer.

join (noun) See *line join*.

join (verb) To connect the endpoints of an open path. When you join the endpoints of one path, Illustrator closes the path with a straight-line segment. When you join the endpoints of two open paths, Illustrator combines them into one longer path. Compare *average*.

kerning The amount of space, in points, that is added or taken away from between pairs of characters in a type block. Kerning affects the amount of white space displayed in a type block.

knockout A generic term for a positive or overlay that "knocks out" part of an image from another image. The most obvious example of this is white type on a black background. The white type is knocked out of the background.

landscape A horizontal printing orientation in which the top of the artwork is along the larger side of the page. Compare *portrait*.

layer To place objects in layers. See also *painting order*.

leading The amount of vertical spacing, in points, between lines of type in a type block.

line The straight line between two anchor points. In a line, each anchor point and its corresponding direction point occupy the same location.

line cap A cap placed at the end of a solid line or segments of a dashed line. Illustrator provides three kinds of line caps: butt, round, and projecting.

line join The style of connector used when Illustrator strokes a path. The choice of joins becomes important when stroking paths that contain corners. Illustrator provides three kinds of joins: miter, round, and bevel.

line weight The weight or thickness of a line, expressed in points.

Line weight is a characteristic of the Stroke, set in the Paint dialog box.

lines per inch (lpi)   See *screen ruling.*

magenta   The subtractive primary color that appears blue-red and absorbs green light. Used as one ink in four-color printing. Also known as process red.

marquee   A dashed rectangular region created when dragging the Selection tool to select objects.

mechanicals   Traditionally, the final pages or boards with pasted-up galleys of type and line art, sometimes with acetate or tissue overlays for color separations and notes to the offset printer.

mechanical separations   Color separations, usually black-and-white art, that are used to print different colors of ink on offset printing color pages.

memory   A hardware component of a computer system that can store information for later retrieval. The area inside the computer where information is stored temporarily while you are working (also called RAM or random access memory). The amount of memory a computer has directly affects its speed and the size of the documents you can create.

menu   A list of choices presented in either a drop-down or pop-up window, from which you can select an action.

miter join   A corner created by extending the edges of two converging lines until they meet. Compare *bevel join* and *round join.*

miter limit   The ratio that determines the angle at which Illustrator switches from a mitered (pointed) line join to a beveled (squared-off) line join. The miter limit is equal to the maximum ratio of the diagonal line through a line to the width of the lines producing the join. The smaller the miter limit, the less sharp the angle at which Illustrator switches from a mitered to a beveled line join.

moiré pattern   A grid pattern (usually undesirable) that can result when two or more screen tints are overlaid incorrectly. See also *rosette.*

negative   A reverse image of a page, produced photographically on a clear sheet of film as an intermediate step in preparing plates from camera-ready mechanicals for offset printing.

object   An anchor point, segment, path, or type block, or a group of anchor points, segments, paths, and type blocks.

offset   To move the image away from the right edge of the film or paper on which it is printing.

offset printing   A type of printing that uses an intermediate step to transfer a printed image from the plate to the paper. The type of printing done using a printing press to reproduce many copies of the original that is printed out on a laser printer. The press lays ink on a page based on the raised image on a plate that is created by photographing the camera-ready masters.

open path   A path with two endpoints; that is, a path that has a beginning and an end. Compare with *closed path.*

orientation   The page position: portrait or landscape.

overlay   A transparent acetate or tissue covering over a printed page, where color indications and other instructions to the offset printer are written. Also, an overhead transparency that is intended to be projected on top of another projection.

overlay proofs   A color proofing system that uses a transparent overlay for each of the four process colors.

overprint   To specify that a colored object show through another colored object that overlaps it. Normally the object underneath is hidden by the object in front, and the inks are not overprinted.

paint   To fill a region defined by a path with black, a percentage gray shade, or color, or to stroke a line.

painting order   The sequence in which the objects in a document are painted. Objects are painted from back to front, meaning that in a series of layered objects, the frontmost object will obscure all or part of the objects that lie behind it.

Pantone Matching System   A popular system for choosing colors, based on ink mixes.

path   One or more connected segments. You can fill a path, or you can stroke a line that is centered on the path.

pattern   One or more objects that has been bounded by a rectangle and defined as a pattern. Once defined, patterns can be used to paint paths.

phototypesetter   A device that sets type photographically, using a photochemical process and special film as output.

pica   A unit of measure equal to 12 points, or approximately one-sixth of an inch.

PICT format   A format used to store MacDraw documents. Before Illustrator can read a MacDraw document, it must be saved in PICT format.

pixel   Short for picture element. A point on the graphics screen; the visual representation of a bit on the screen (white if the bit is 0, black if it's 1). A single dot on the Macintosh display. A template is a collection of pixels. Also, the dot a printer uses to create a halftone dot.

place   To import a scanned image or an EPS format file into an Adobe Illustrator document.

point   Unit of measure, used in Illustrator for specifying type and line attributes. There are approximately 72 points in an inch.

point of origin   A fixed spot that you specify in your artwork, from which a transformation begins.

portrait   A vertical printing orientation in which the top of the artwork is along the short side of the page.

PostScript   A computer language invented by Adobe Systems that is used to define the appearance of type and images on the printed page. When you save an Illustrator document, you are actually saving a PostScript language program.

PPD file   PostScript Printer Description file. The document used by the Adobe Separator program to set the default information for the type of printer you are using.

preset attributes   The paint, stroke, and type attributes that are in effect if you have not specified any other attributes. Default attributes.

preview image   The view of your Illustrator artwork that is displayed on your screen as a bitmap and that approximates the printed output. You can specify whether paint and pattern attributes appear in the preview image. A version of the preview image is saved along with the PostScript language code for the artwork document when you specify one of the preview options before saving your artwork. Compare *artwork*.

primary colors   The elemental colors of either pigments or light. Red, green, and blue are additive primaries. White light is produced when red, green, and blue lights are added together. Cyan, magenta, and yellow are subtractive primaries. The inks used to print three-color process or four-color process with black.

process color   One of the four colors—cyan, magenta, yellow, and black—blended to produce colors in the four-color process. With process color you produce a maximum of four negatives, regardless of the number of colors used in your artwork. Compare with *custom color*.

process separations   Four-color separations made from color artwork.

progressive color bar   A bar displaying all the possible combinations of cyan, magenta, and yellow. Progressive color bars are printed on each sheet of a process color printing job to ensure proper ink coverage and color. The bar is usually trimmed off before the job is shipped. Sometimes the progressive color bar will also include black and screen tints of the combinations.

progressive colors   The four process colors plus white and the various combinations of cyan, magenta, and yellow. The Change Progressive Colors... option in the Preferences dialog box allows you to adjust the appearance of the progressive colors on your computer display.

projecting cap   A square line cap placed at the end of a solid or dashed line. The cap is perpendicular to the end of the line and extends one-half line width beyond the line's endpoint. Compare *butt cap* and *line cap*.

QuickDraw   A graphics language built into the read-only memory (ROM) of the Macintosh.

reflect   To create a mirror image of an object.

reflected light   See *subtractive primary colors*.

registration   The accuracy with which images are combined or positioned, particularly in reference to multicolored printing where each color must be precisely aligned for the accurate reproduction of the original.

registration mark   One of a number of small reference patterns placed on separations printed by Adobe Seoparator™ to aid in the registration process.

resolution   The number of dots per inch displayed on a screen or printer. The Macintosh screen has a resolution of 72 dots per inch. The Apple LaserWriter has a resolution of 300 dots per inch. The resolution of PostScript language image-setting devices (Laser-Writer Plus, Linotronic 300, and so on) is measured in pixels per inch. See *pixel*.

RGB   Shorthand notation for red, green, and blue. See *additive primary colors*.

rosette   The circular dot pattern that occurs when screen tints are overlaid correctly.

rotate   To pivot an object about a given point.

round cap   A semicircular line cap placed at the end of a solid or dashed line. The diameter of the cap is equal to the width of the line. Compare *butt cap* and *line cap*.

round join   A corner created when two lines are connected with a circular arc whose diameter is equal to the width of the line. Compare *bevel join* and *miter join*.

scale   To change the size of an object either vertically, horizontally, or both.

scanned image   The image that results when a photograph, illustration, or other flat art is converted into a bitmap. On the Macintosh, scanned images are stored as MacPaint documents.

scanner   An electronic device that converts a photo, illustration, or other flat art into a bitmap. A video camera is a scanner that converts three-dimensional objects into bitmaps.

screen ruling   The number of lines per inch in a screen tint or halftone.

screen tint   A screened percentage of a solid color.

segment   A line curve that is defined by an anchor point and its direction point.

select   To define an object to be acted upon by the next command or mouse operation. You must select an object before you can change or edit it in any way. You generally select an object by clicking on it with the Selection tool or by dragging the selection marquee around it.

selection marquee   A dashed rectangular region created when dragging the Selection tool to select objects.

selection pointer   An arrow-shaped pointer used for selecting and moving objects.

shear   To slant an object vertically, horizontally, or along an arbitrary line.

shrink   A positive image that has been reduced in width to create trap. See *trap*.

smooth point   An anchor point connecting two segments in which the anchor point and its two direction points are located on the same straight line.

spacing   The amount of space, in points, that is added or removed between pairs of characters in a type block. Spacing affects the amount of white space in a type block.

spec sheet   A copy of the drawing showing the various color values.

spot color   See *custom color*.

spread   A negative image that has been automatically expanded by Illustrator to create trap. See *trap*.

stripper   The person who "strips" negatives in the proper position so that they will run correctly on the press. The stripper is also usually the person who cuts the color-separation masks when mechanical separations are made.

stroke   To draw a line that is centered on its path.

subtractive primary colors   Cyan, yellow, and magenta. The three colors used to create all other colors when reflected light is used (for instance, in printed material).

tangent   Touching a line or curve at only one point. The direction line is tangent to the curve at the anchor point.

tangent line   See *direction line*.

template   The scanned image or the image in MacPaint or MacDraw PICT format that you use as the basis for Illustrator artwork. A bitmap. The template appears on the screen as a gray image behind the artwork; it is not part of the final printed document. Compare with *artwork* and *preview image*.

tile (page)   To divide Adobe Illustrator's drawing area into pages for the page size currently specified in the Page Setup dialog box.

tile (pattern)   To repeat a pattern in columns and rows across the layer of the document in which that pattern paints a path.

tint   A percentage of one of the process or custom colors.

toggle   A command that lets you switch between two settings. The Show/Hide Rulers command is an example of a toggle.

toolbox   The set of tools displayed (as icons) to the left of the drawing area when a document is open.

transmitted light   See *additive primary colors*.

transverse   Rotation of the page on the film or paper on which it is printing. Currently, this option is applicable only to Linotronic typesetting machines.

trap Overlap needed to ensure that a slight misalignment or movement of the separations will not affect the final appearance of the job.

uncoated stock Paper that is not coated. Uncoated stock is usually less smooth and absorbs ink more readily than coated stock. Compare with *coated stock*.

ungroup To separate groups into individual objects or into subgroups.

x axis The horizontal reference line to which objects are constrained.

y axis The vertical reference line to which objects are constrained.

yellow The subtractive primary color that appears yellow and absorbs blue light. Used as one ink in four-color printing.

zoom To magnify or reduce your view of the current document.

Quick
Reference
Guide

Adobe Illustrator 88

Quick Reference Guide

Tools

Tool	Plus Shift Key	Plus Option Key
Selection	When clicking or before starting to drag — Extends or reduces the selection	When clicking or before starting to drag — Selects top object when top object is clicked; Selects all objects under marquee; Displays Move dialog box when selection tool is clicked in toolbox
Selection	After starting to drag — Constrains motion to horizontal, vertical, or 45° increments	After starting to drag — Duplicates selection when selection is dragged
Hand	No effect	No effect
Zoom	No effect	Displays zoom-out pointer
Type	No effect	No effect
Freehand	No effect	Creates corner point
Auto trace	No effect	No effect
Pen	No effect	Creates corner point
Rectangle	Constrains rectangle to a square	Constructs rectangle from center to corner as opposed to corner to corner
Oval	Constrains oval to a circle	Constructs oval from center to edge to edge as opposed to edge to edge
Blend	No effect	No effect
Scale	Constrains scale along x, y, or both axes	While clicking origin, displays transformation dialog box
Rotate	Constrains rotation to 45° increments	While dragging to create transformation (after origin has been specified), creates transformed duplicate; leaves original in place
Reflect	Constrains reflection to horizontal, vertical, or 45° increments	
Shear	Constrains shear to horizontal, vertical, or 45° increments	
Scissors	No effect	Creates new anchor point
Measure	Constrains measurement to horizontal, vertical, or 45° increments	No effect
Page	No effect	No effect

Menu Command Shortcuts

To Choose	Press	To Choose	Press
File		**Arrange**	
New	⌘ N	Transform Again	⌘ D
Open ...	⌘ O	Group	⌘ G
Open ...w/template dialog	⌘ U	Ungroup	⌘ U
Option & ⌘ O		Join	⌘ J
Save	⌘ S	Average	⌘ L
Print	⌘ P	Lock	⌘ 1
Quit	⌘ Q	Unlock All	⌘ 2
		Hide	⌘ 3
		Show All	⌘ 4
Edit		**View**	
Undo/Redo	⌘ Z	Preview	⌘ Y
Cut	⌘ X	Artwork & Template	⌘ E
Copy	⌘ C	Artwork Only	⌘ W
Copy ...PICT Preview Option & ⌘ C		Actual Size	⌘ H
Paste Option & ⌘ V		Fit in Window	⌘ M
Clear Backspace		Show/Hide Rulers	⌘ R
Select All	⌘ A	**Style**	
Paste in Front	⌘ F	Paint	⌘ I
Paste in Back	⌘ B	Type	⌘ T
Bring to Front	⌘ =		
Send to Back	⌘ –		
Preferences	⌘ K		

Preferences K⌘

Choice	Setting	Default
Snap to point	On or off	On
Preview and print patterns	On or off	On
Transform pattern tiles	On or off	Off
Ruler units	Centimeters, inches, or picas/points	Picas/points
Constrain angle	Value in degrees	Zero
Corner radius	Value in cm, in, or pts.	Zero
Cursor key distance	Value in ruler unit	One
Freehand tolerance	Value in pixels	Two
Auto trace gap distance	Value in pixels	Zero
Change progressive colors	Access video color dialog boxes	Std. Apple® monitor values

Accessing Tools from the Keyboard

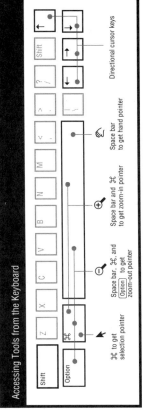

Shift

Option

⌘ to get selection pointer

Space bar, ⌘, and Option to get zoom-out pointer

Space bar and ⌘ to get zoom-in pointer

Space bar to get hand pointer

Directional cursor keys

Drawing Lines and Curves

		1	2	3	4	5	6
Freehand	Drawing and adjusting a path	Click tool	Drag	To erase, hold ⌘	Release mouse		
	Extending and closing a path	Click tool	Press on anchor point	Drag to extend line	Position pointer over end point	Release mouse	
Auto trace	Tracing a template shape	Open template	Click tool	Position pointer on edge	Click	Release mouse	
	Tracing part of a shape	Open template	Click tool	Position pointer on edge	Press on point A	Drag to point B	Release mouse
Pen	Drawing straight lines	Click tool	Click	Click	*Constraining lines to 45° increments*	Click tool	Click
							3 Press Shift and click
	Drawing curves	Click tool	Press and drag	Press and drag	Press and drag		
	Creating corners	Click tool	Click	Click	Press Option and drag	Release Option; press and drag	
	Changing from curves to lines	Click tool	Press and drag	Press and drag	Press Option and click	Release Option; click	

Drawing Rectangles and Ovals

Procedure	Constructing from edge to edge	Constructing from center	Constructing a square or a circle	Constructing a square or circle from center	Constructing with exact measurements
	Drag	Press Option; drag	Press Shift; drag	Press Shift and Option; drag	Click; type values
Drawing rectangles					Rectangle Dialog Box
Drawing ovals					Oval Dialog Box

Making Patterns

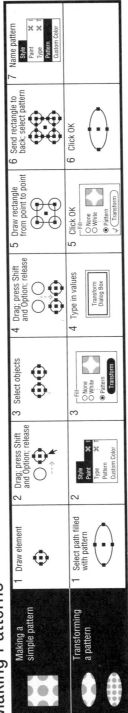

Making a simple pattern
1. Draw element
2. Drag; press Shift and Option; release — Style / Paint / Type / Pattern / Custom Color
3. Select objects
4. Drag; press Shift and Option; release
5. Draw rectangle from point to point
6. Send rectangle to back; select pattern
7. Name pattern — Style / Paint / Type / Pattern / Custom Color

Transforming a pattern
1. Select path filled with pattern
2. Style / Paint / Type / Pattern / Custom Color
3. Fill — None / White / Pattern / Transform
4. Type in values — Transform Dialog Box
5. Click OK — Fill: None / White / Pattern / Transform
6. Click OK

Masking

Creating a mask
1. Create artwork
2. Create masking path
3. Style / Paint / Type / Pattern / Custom Color
4. Select mask; paint — Paint Dialog Box / ☒ Mask
5. Send mask to back — Edit / Undo ⌘Z / Send to Front ⌘= / Send to Back ⌘–
6. Select mask and artwork
7. Arrange / Transform Again ⌘D / Group ⌘G / Ungroup ⌘U / Join ⌘J / Average ⌘L

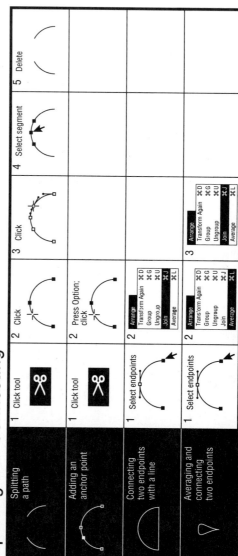

Creating Blends and Gradations

	1	2	3	4	5	6	7
Creating simple gradations	Draw rectangle; ungroup; paint	Duplicate rectangle	Paint 2nd rectangle with new fill (Style / Paint / Type)	Select all points on rectangles	Click tool	Click corresponding points (A)	Type # of steps (Blend Dialog Box)
Creating complex gradations	Draw an apple and a highlight	Paint highlight 100% white fill (Style / Paint / Type)	Select points on objects	**HINT** For best results, select the same number of points in each object	Click tool	Click corresponding points (A)	Type # of steps (Blend Dialog Box)
Blending between two shapes	Draw a square and circle; ungroup	Paint with no fill, 1 point stroke (Style / Paint / Type)	Select objects	Click tool	Click corresponding points (A)	Type # of steps (Blend Dialog Box)	

Splitting and Connecting

	1	2	3	4	5
Splitting a path	Click tool	Click	Click	Select segment	Delete
Adding an anchor point	Click tool	Press Option; click			
Connecting two endpoints with a line	Select endpoints	Arrange / Transform Again ⌘D / Group ⌘G / Ungroup ⌘U / Join ⌘J / Average ⌘L	Click		
Averaging and connecting two endpoints	Select endpoints	Arrange / Transform Again ⌘D / Group ⌘G / Ungroup ⌘U / Join ⌘J / Average ⌘L	Arrange / Transform Again ⌘D / Group ⌘G / Ungroup ⌘U / Join ⌘J / Average ⌘L		

Transforming Objects

Procedure	1 Select object(s)	2 Click tool	3 Click origin	4 Press (A) and drag	Constraining	Duplicating	Specific Transforming
					5a Press Shift 6a Continue dragging 7a Release mouse 8a Release Shift	5b Press Option 6b Continue dragging 7b Release mouse 4b Release Option	3c Press Option 4c Click origin 5c Type values 6c Click OK
Scaling							Scale Dialog Box
Rotating							Rotate Dialog Box
Reflecting							Reflect Dialog Box
Shearing							Shear Dialog Box

Moving Objects

Procedure	1 Select object(s)	2 Press (A) and drag	3 Release mouse	Constraining	Duplicating	Specific Moving
				3a Press Shift 4a Continue dragging 5a Release mouse 6a Release Shift	3b Press Option 4b Drag 5b Release mouse 6b Release Option	2c Press Option 2c Click arrow tool 4c Type move values 5c Click OK
Moving						Move Dialog Box

335

Selecting

Selecting a segment	Click	OR	Drag
Selecting an anchor point	Click on point	OR	Drag
Selecting a path	Press Option; click	OR	Press Option; drag
Selecting an additional object	Press Option and Shift; click	OR	Press Option and Shift; drag
Selecting all points in an area	Press Shift; click	OR	Drag

Adding and Editing Type

Type — Adding type	1 Click tool (T)	2 Click	3 Enter type and specify values (Type Dialog Box)
Typo — Editing type	1 Select type (Type)	2 (Style: Paint ⌘ I; Type ⌘ T; Pattern; Custom Color)	3 Edit type and values (Type Dialog Box)

Using the Page Tool

Defining the page edges	1 Click tool	2 Drag	3 Release

Layering

Move object(s) in front of or in back of all objects	1 Preview	2 Select object	3 (Edit: Undo ⌘ Z; Send to Front ⌘ =; Send to Back ⌘ –)	4 Preview		
Move object(s) in front of or in back of selected objects	1 Preview	2 Select object	3 (Edit: Undo ⌘ Z; Cut ⌘ X; Copy ⌘ C; Paste ⌘ V)	4 Select object to be pasted in front of	5 (Edit: Undo ⌘ Z; Paste in Front ⌘ F; Paste in Back ⌘ B)	6 Preview

Indexes

Sequential List of Topics

Topic Index

General Index